THE MINNESOTA
BOOK OF DAYS

The MINNESOTA Book of Days

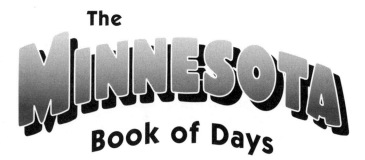

An Almanac of State History

A Chronological
Compendium
of Remarkable
and Curious
Events in the
History of the
North Star State

Compiled by Tony Greiner
Foreword by Howard Mohr

Minnesota Historical Society Press

www.mnhs.org/mhspress

Manufactured in Canada

10 9 8 7 6 5 4 3 2 1

♾ The paper used in this publication meets the minimum
requirements of the American National Standard for Information Sciences—Permanence for Printed Library materials,
ANSI Z39.48-1984

International Standard Book Number
0-87351-416-5 (paper)

Library of Congress Cataloging-in-Publication Data

The Minnesota book of days : an almanac of State history /
compiled by Tony Greiner ; foreword by Howard Mohr.
          p. cm.
"A chronological compendium of remarkable and curious
events in the history of the North Star State."
Includes bibliographical references and index.
ISBN 0-87351-416-5 (pbk : alk. paper)
          1. Minnesota—History—Miscellanea.
          2. Almanacs, American—Minnesota.
          I. Greiner, Tony.

F606.6 .M56 2001
977.6—dc21   2001037076

Unless otherwise indicated, all illustrations are from the collections of the Minnesota Historical Society.

Title pages: Calf with young owner, Minnesota State Fair, 1935;
Boreas Rex and Lord High Chancellor, St. Paul Winter Carnival,
1896; Lillian Boyer, stunt flyer, 1923

Page 1: Prize-winning produce, Minnesota State Fair, 1926

THE MINNESOTA BOOK OF DAYS

Paul Bunyan's sweetheart, Lucette Diana Kensack, Hackensack

FOREWORD

When the Minnesota Historical Society Press asked me to write the foreword to *The Minnesota Book of Days: An Almanac of State History,* they were figuring I would be the right guy for it mostly because in 1989 Penguin USA published a book of mine called *A Minnesota Book of Days (And a Few Nights).*

The books are very similar.

For instance, both are printed on paper and have 366 days full of Minnesota history. Not only that, several entries in the *Almanac* are related to accomplishments by famous Minnesotans, including inventors. In the same vein, my *Book of Days* deals with a few obscure Minnesotans whose inventions were sadly ahead of their time, as on December 2, 1958:

> On this day, Gandy Olson of Wingerton unveiled his Suntan Bed, a machine that looked like a hog roaster with purple lights and required a person to climb inside it nude in order to get an attractive brown skin. The press was merciless, calling Olson a misguided lunatic for thinking that the American public would ever go for such a ridiculous contraption. The demoralized Gandy dumped his roaster in the Mississippi, tore up the patent application, moved to a trailer park in Georgia and began his life as a pecan grader.

There are some minor differences between the books. My *Book of Days* contains all the known sightings of Minnesota Bigfoot, but the *Almanac* leaves them all out, including this one for November 17:

Minnesota Bigfoot was sighted this afternoon in 1986 using his Cash Card to get $50 from a machine in Roseville. His secret number was also sighted—9832—because he didn't shield the keyboard when he typed it in. He also left his receipt sticking out of the slot. He had a lot to learn about money management.

I suppose the *main* minor difference between our books is that the information in the *Almanac* is true, whereas most of my historical facts have been slightly adjusted and in some cases completely made up. This is the sort of thing that might upset a history purist. I don't consider it a problem, myself. My standard for historical accuracy is simply broader.

Take this entry for May 8 from the *Almanac of State History:*

1924 Ice in Duluth's harbor traps thirteen ships, confining 400 individuals aboard.

Here's my May 8:

On this day in 1976 Don Larry was captured by a bratwurst-shaped flying saucer and later dropped off at a fishing-lure factory near Owatonna, Minnesota, with small electrical burns on his earlobes, a big pimple on the end of his nose, and no elastic in his beltless trousers.

If you climbed into a time machine and whirled back to the Duluth of May 8, 1924, you would be able to join the huge crowd on shore waving at the stuck boats and making wisecracks about Minnesota winters.

But what would happen if you set the dials for Owatonna on May 8, 1976? I don't want to get too technical here, so let me just say "Einstein" and "convoluted continuum." Does Don Larry really exist? Of course he does. I happen to know (I am fascinated by coincidence) that Don's grandfather was the pilot on the *Steelhead Steamer,* one of the ships frozen in the Duluth harbor on that day in 1924. Captain Larry was carrying the ambassador from Norway and thirteen tons of goat cheese.

Here's an *Almanac* item for July 13, 1881: "Faribault begins requiring dog licenses." It's true. You can look it up.

What the *Almanac* doesn't mention is that a hundred years to the day, in 1981, an emu stampede disrupted the Miss Faribault pageant and parade.

I guess what I'm saying is that there's historical fact and then there's enhanced historical fact. I'm in the enhanced camp, along with many politicians around the world. But my aim in touching up history is not to get votes or to avoid prosecution. At the very least I want to make people smile.

Many of my entries are *based* on personal history—my own life in other words, as far as I can recall it. In my entry for December 11, 1961, John R. gets the high bid on a defunct rural K–12 school building in the city of Clayburgh and hauls it brick by brick and board by board, including the basketball court, to the building site on his farm. John's living room has a hardwood floor with the original paint on the free-throw circle and lane. The basket and the backboard are on the north end over the door to the lunchroom. Sometimes John and his wife, Paula, play one-on-one in their sock feet. I can hear your question, and the answer is No: He set the bleachers up outside facing the bus barn and teeter-totter.

Believe it or not, my uncle truly did get the high bid on an old school building and built his "new" house entirely of materials from it. John R. (not his real name) is in his early eighties now. He and I both had—separated by a few years—played basketball many a time in the original gym.

The events selected for the *Almanac of State History* range from the light-hearted to the serious and disturbing. It's no secret that human history, even in Minnesota, has not been all that pleasant at times. The *Almanac's* selections are fascinating in themselves, but they should also inspire readers to seek further information on subjects of interest to them.

Holy Smokes, this was supposed to be a foreword, not a forenovel, so let me wrap this up by saying that the *Almanac* is a gold mine of certified and fact-checked Minnesota history.

There's something for everybody in here, and quite a bit for me.

Howard Mohr

Joseph Henry Sherburne posed with bottle and cigar, 1875

PREFACE AND ACKNOWLEDGMENTS

Dates are out of style now in history. We've all heard the rants against making students memorize the date an event occurred and recite history by rote. These arguments are true enough, but the anti-chronological folks miss the point: a date gives us an opportunity to place an event in context; it is the peg from which we can hang a tale.

This book was inspired by the work of Roy Swanson, who self-published his *Minnesota Book of Days* in 1949 for Minnesota's territorial centennial. I thought Swanson's book had interesting stories and a format that allowed for a wide range of entries. When I started revising and updating it about a decade ago, I learned that Minnesota is a state blessed with a strong sense of self and history. This awareness of history means a researcher has a wealth of material from which to choose, and the sources don't always agree with each other. I have done my best to check the fourth or fifth source to confirm the details of the entries. I do not pretend that this volume is a comprehensive history of the state; in fact, I hope that this format—passing mention of an event, a place, a name—will inspire readers to delve more deeply into the history of the state. If you think that I have overlooked a significant event or person, please note that on page 321 is an invitation for submissions of additional entries.

Thanks go to a number of people: Greg Britton, director of the Minnesota Historical Society Press, who floated the idea of updating Roy Swanson's book, and

Ann Regan, managing editor, who remembered that
I had been working on this project before my move to
Oregon. Julie Levang of the Duluth Public Library helped
in tracking down a number of events and dates in their
fine Minnesota Collection. Denise Carlson, Tracey Baker,
and the staff of the MHS library also lent a hand, notably
by permitting me to scribble notes to myself whenever
I stumbled across something interesting. Tino Avaloz
was always an inspiration, especially in his determina-
tion to save Minnesota's old (and new) newspapers.

Shannon Pennefeather at the Minnesota Historical
Society Press was project editor, preparing the original
text for publication and assembling a team to confirm
facts, expand entries, and research additional events.
This team consisted of Jaffer Batica, who confirmed the
fall of the Pigman as well as assorted details for other
fascinating entries, Shana Redmond, who researched and
wrote a number of entries on African Americans, and
Deborah Swanson, who, in addition to fact-checking
numerous entries, discovered a near escape from Ramsey
County Jail in 1883.

Steve Osman at Fort Snelling checked the originals
of Lawrence Taliaferro's diaries and changed what I
thought was a mutiny to a mere meeting. Thank you,
Steve—I could have made a big one. Susan Hoehn sent
numerous newspaper clippings, and her husband
Arthur tracked down bits on Forts Ripley and Ridgely.
Susan Price and Mike Ruetten gave early encourage-
ment, and Susan Butruille gave timely advice on the
business end of the book world.

Lastly, a hug and a kiss to my wife, Mary, a sixth-
generation Minnesotan who told me tales of Earl Battey,
the Armistice Day Blizzard, and Princess Kay carved in
butter. She has always been the book's biggest fan, has
never questioned why I collect facts, and didn't complain when we lugged my files halfway across the country. She missed many a movie to the refrain of "this
thing ain't gonna write itself" and fell asleep too many
nights to the blue glow of the computer monitor. This
thanks comes with love.

THE MINNESOTA
BOOK OF DAYS

Snow scene, 1932

JANUARY 1

1840 Lawrence Taliaferro, tired of bribery attempts by crooked individuals, steps down as Indian agent at Fort Snelling, a position he had held since 1820. Indians and whites alike esteemed him for his honesty and intelligence, and his diaries of life at Fort Snelling provide a detailed record of frontier Minnesota. He died on January 22, 1871, aged eighty-one. *See* March 27

January 1, 1840

1850 At the Minnesota Historical Society's first annual meeting, the Reverend Edward D. Neill gives a lecture, the Sixth Regiment's band provides music, and a grand ball is held in St. Paul's Central House.

1869 Black residents of Minnesota hold a grand convention in St. Paul's Ingersoll Hall "to celebrate the Emancipation of 4,000,000 slaves, and to express . . . gratitude for the bestowal of the elective franchise to the colored people of this State."

1878 On an unusually balmy day, the steamer *Aunt Betsy* carries a load of passengers from St. Paul to Fort Snelling. Crowds line the Jackson Street landing, the bluffs, and the Wabasha Street Bridge to watch, and the passengers carry palm-leaf fans to stave off the heat.

1893 Workers nail the final spike in the 818 miles of track stretching from Pacific Junction, Montana, to Everett, Washington, completing the Great Northern Railroad and connecting St. Paul to the Pacific Ocean.

1969 The Coast Guard closes Split Rock Lighthouse after fifty-nine years of service. It becomes a state park the following year.

JANUARY 2

1883 Faribault chief of police David J. Shipley is fatally shot by Lewis M. Sage while attempting to arrest him after Sage threatened to shoot his own wife. Sage is later convicted of manslaughter in the fourth degree and sentenced to four years in the Minnesota State Prison at Stillwater.

1890 Hjalmar Petersen is born in Eskildstrup on the island of Fyn in Denmark. A veteran country-newspaper editor, he would serve as the state's governor for four months in 1936 and 1937 (the shortest gubernatorial term in Minnesota history), following the death in office of Floyd B. Olson. Petersen died on March 29, 1968, while vacationing in Columbus, Ohio.

1917 About 1,000 lumbermen walk away from their jobs on the second day of a strike led by the Industrial Workers of the World. The workers, employed by the Virginia and Rainy Lake Lumber Company and the International Lumber Company, demand a pay increase, a nine-hour day, and sanitary living conditions.

JANUARY 3

1848 A sewing club—the St. Paul Circle of Industry—is formed to raise money for a new school building in St. Paul. The building would be completed in August 1849.

1905 The state legislature meets for the first time in the present capitol building.

1916 Maxene Andrews is born in Minneapolis. With her sisters LaVerne (born July 6, 1911) and Patty (born February 26, 1918), she would form the Andrews Sisters singing group, known as "America's Wartime Sweethearts" and remembered for their 1941 hit "Boogie Woogie Bugle Boy."

1940 The Marlborough apartment-hotel burns in Minneapolis, leaving at least four people missing, twenty-five in hospitals, and eighteen dead. Apparently caused by a burning "cigaret" carelessly thrown into a garbage chute, the fire is described by the *Minneapolis Journal* as the worst catastrophe in the city since the explosion of the Washburn "A" mill on May 2, 1878.

January 3, 1940

JANUARY 4

1854 The Territorial Agricultural Society holds its first meeting. This group evolves into the State Agricultural Society, governing body of the State Fair. On the same day, the fifth territorial legislature convenes in an official capitol building for the first time.

1874 The Catholic Industrial School is incorporated. The school begins operations in 1877 on the shores of St. Paul's Lake Menith, since drained and now the site of the University of St. Thomas. In 1879 the school moves to Clontarf, where Franciscan teachers instruct white and Indian boys in agricultural and industrial arts. Funding for such institutions is later cut, and the school would be sold to the federal government in 1897.

1920 William E. Colby is born in St. Paul. He would serve as director of the Central Intelligence Agency from 1973 to 1976, under Presidents Richard Nixon and Gerald Ford.

JANUARY 5

1805 Joseph R. Brown is born in Harford County, Maryland. A drummer boy at Fort Snelling, he would learn the Dakota language and, later, be the first white man to explore Minnehaha Creek and to see Lake Minnetonka. A prominent pioneer, he would be a trader, a member of the Wisconsin Territorial Legislature, a participant in both the Stillwater Convention and the Minnesota Constitutional Convention, the editor of the *Minnesota Pioneer* and the *Henderson Democrat,* and an officer during the U.S.–Dakota War. He would also be the first lumberman to float logs down the St. Croix River and would stake out the first road from St. Paul to Prairie du Chien. He died on November 9, 1870. *See also* August 23 and October 6

January 5, 1805 Joseph R. Brown (standing at left) with Dakota Indian delegation to Washington, D.C., 1858

1892 Mining classes begin at the University of Minnesota, as Professor William R. Appleby instructs a class of four students.

1928 Walter "Fritz" Mondale is born in Ceylon, Minnesota. A lifelong public servant, he would represent Minnesota in the U.S. Senate, occupy the vice-presidency under Jimmy Carter, run for president against Ronald Reagan, and serve as U.S. ambassador to Japan.

JANUARY 6

1976 After presiding over the Reserve Mining lawsuit for two and a half years, Judge Miles Lord is removed from the case because he was thought to have a bias against the company.

1996 Maude Kegg, elder of the Mille Lacs Band of Ojibwe and author of books on her childhood and Ojibwe stories, dies. Born on August 26, 1904, she was raised in the traditional Ojibwe culture. In 1990 she earned a National Heritage Fellowship from the National Endowment for the Arts for her traditional beadwork.

JANUARY 7

1816 Stephen Miller is born in Carroll, Pennsylvania. After moving to Minnesota at age forty-two, he would be a general in the Civil War and serve as the state's fourth governor from 1864 to 1865. He died in Worthington on August 18, 1881.

1850 John R. Irvine obtains a license to operate a ferry across the Mississippi River at St. Paul's Upper Landing (formerly at the foot of Chestnut Street). The city's Irvine Park is named for him.

1857 The Congregational church in Faribault is dedicated, with the Reverend Lauren Armstrong serving as its first pastor.

1873 The Blizzard of 1873 strikes, with temperatures of forty-nine degrees below zero and winds of seventy-five miles per hour. Over the next two days, at least seventy people die in the western and southern parts of the state. Conditions are so blinding that in New Ulm a boy who has to cross the street to his home is found frozen eight miles away, and a rural man and his ox team freeze to death just ten feet from his house.

1917 On this Sunday, all Catholic priests in the St. Cloud diocese are required to give at least one sermon in English.

1972 After a lengthy battle with alcoholism, Pulitzer Prize–winning poet John Berryman jumps to his death from the Washington Avenue Bridge in Minneapolis.

JANUARY 8

1851 Hole-in-the-Day, an Ojibwe leader, sends a letter to the Minnesota territorial legislature inviting its members to come to a St. Paul church and hear him speak about the sufferings and needs of his people and their desire for peace. "They are like some poor animal driven into a hole, and condemned to die," he will say, inspiring some of the most influential whites in the territory to form a committee to solicit contributions for the Ojibwe.

1920 Jacob A. O. Preus, Jr., son of soon-to-be Governor Preus, Sr., (*see* August 28) is born in St. Paul. After becoming president of the Lutheran Church–Missouri Synod in 1969, he, along with other advocates of traditionalism, would be troubled by alleged liberalism in the faculty at Concordia Seminary in St. Louis and their attitude toward biblical authority. A crucial struggle about doctrinal purity would ensue, with Preus successfully being re-elected president in 1973 and thus securing the traditional ways of the synod.

1924 Six die when a car crashes through the ice on Lake Andrews, near Alexandria.

1934 During the Great Depression, the U.S. Supreme Court upholds a Minnesota mortgage moratorium law, a decision that state Attorney General Harry H. Peterson applauds as a "victory for the people of Minnesota that will enable many farmers and city dwellers to hold onto their homes until good times return." *See* May 1

1971 President Richard Nixon signs a law creating Voyageurs National Park. Supported by former governor Elmer L. Andersen and Charles A. Lindbergh, Jr., the legislation had been approved by Congress on October 5 of the previous year.

1991 Former Minnesota Twins and California Angels player Rod Carew is elected into the Baseball Hall of

Fame. "A wizard with the bat," Carew achieved a .328 lifetime batting average, hitting over .300 in fifteen consecutive seasons with both teams. *See* February 3

January 8, 1971 John Blatnik (standing), Harold LeVander, Elmer L. Andersen, Governor Wendell R. Anderson, and Karl F. Rolvag

JANUARY 9

1840 Wisconsin Territory forms St. Croix County in the area between the Mississippi and St. Croix Rivers. Dahkotah, a town platted (surveyed and mapped) by Joseph R. Brown and now part of Stillwater, is the county seat.

1977 In a fourth Super Bowl appearance in eight years, the Minnesota Vikings football team loses for the fourth time, to the Oakland Raiders, 32–14.

JANUARY 10

1925 "The Arrowhead" is selected as the official moniker for northeastern Minnesota, the result of a nationwide contest sponsored by the Northeastern Minnesota Civic and Commerce Association of Duluth.

1975 A fierce, three-day blizzard strikes, bringing one to two feet of snow (with some drifts reaching twenty feet) and winds up to eighty miles per hour, closing most Minnesota roads, stranding a train at Willmar, and killing thirty-five people and 15,000 head of livestock. The *St. Paul Pioneer Press* reports that an offshoot of an Arctic storm has blasted into the Midwest, commenting that the "Wind ain't whistlin' Dixie."

1976 During a heavy snowstorm, 325 cars are damaged in a pileup on a Minneapolis freeway.

JANUARY 11

1883 Henry Wilson, a "professional burglar," and his pal Frank Wilmar, a horse thief, are caught by an alert janitor and the sheriff as they attempt to escape from the Ramsey County jail in St. Paul. They had stolen a sledgehammer from workmen and nearly managed to pound a hole through the stone floor of a cell into the basement.

1907 The St. Paul Institute of Science and Letters is incorporated, with Charles W. Ames as its first president. The institute's museum is first located in the Auditorium, then moved to the Merriam mansion on University Avenue, and now dwells in downtown St. Paul, known as the Science Museum of Minnesota.

1909 Canada and the United States sign a treaty forming the International Joint Commission, a legislative body charged with preventing and settling disputes in the boundary waters region.

JANUARY 12

1816 Willis A. Gorman is born in Flemingsburg, Kentucky. He would be appointed second territorial governor of Minnesota in 1853 and would later serve in the legislature, command the First Minnesota Regiment in the Civil War, and be St. Paul's city attorney from 1869 until his death on May 20, 1876.

1840 Governor James D. Doty of Wisconsin Territory (which includes part of the future Minnesota) writes to the U.S. secretary of war protesting an extension of the Fort Snelling military reservation and asking how the federal government can take land "by the simple declaration that it is necessary for military purposes" and without consent of the territorial legislature. The protest is in vain, and military authorities eventually expel "squatters" living in the fort area, causing many of them to move to the site that will become St. Paul.

1876 The Minnesota Forestry Association is formed to work for the passage of conservation laws to protect the state's forests. At one time boasting 10,000 members, the association would prove so successful that state agencies and civic groups would take on its activities, and in 1948 the group would vote itself out of existence.

1888 A major blizzard strikes the state, hitting western Minnesota especially hard and causing the deaths of between 100 and 150 people, many of them children on their way home from school.

1913 Alexander T. Heine flies the first airplane over Minneapolis.

January 12, 1913

JANUARY 13

1944 The cruiser *Duluth* is launched in Newport News, Virginia, christened by Ella T. Hatch, wife of Duluth mayor Edward H. Hatch. In May 1945 the ship becomes part of the U.S. fleet in World War II.

1978 Hubert H. Humphrey dies. Humphrey was born in Wallace, South Dakota, on May 27, 1911. State campaign manager for Franklin D. Roosevelt in 1944 and a founder of the anticommunist group Americans for Democratic Action, Humphrey entered the national spotlight after delivering a rousing address on civil rights at the 1948 Democratic National Convention. He served in the Senate beginning in 1948 and was elected vice president under Lyndon B. Johnson in 1964. He lost to Richard Nixon in a close race for the presidency in 1968 and then in 1970 was reelected to the Senate, where he served until his death.

January 13, 1978 Walter F. Mondale (*see* January 5, 1928) and Hubert H. Humphrey, 1975

1982 Nature writer and environmentalist Sigurd Olson dies in Ely. Born in Chicago in 1899, Olson served as a canoe guide in the boundary waters region and was active in environmental issues beginning in the 1920s, playing a prominent role in the battle for federal protection of the Boundary Waters Canoe Area Wilderness and serving as president of the Wilderness Society.

JANUARY 14

1846 Stillwater's first post office is established, with Elam Greeley as postmaster.

1850 The Minnesota Territorial Supreme Court opens for its first term, with Judge Aaron Goodrich presiding.

1938 The Hallie Q. Brown House, named for the African American civil rights advocate and suffragist, moves into its first permanent building in St. Paul. Offering tutoring and day camps for children as well as emergency food and clothing for needy families, the community center would later relocate and combine with the Martin Luther King Center in St. Paul.

1976 Sauk Centre teachers end a week-long strike after the teachers' association and the school board ratify a contract settlement that calls for a salary increase (with an additional twenty-five minutes of supervisory time) and provides teachers with no less than 250 minutes per week of preparation time.

1993 Ann Bancroft of St. Paul reaches the South Pole by skis, becoming the first woman to travel overland to both the North and South Poles (*see* May 2). She leads the American Women's Expedition on a sixty-seven-day trek during which the four women cover 660 miles on skis. Additionally, in 2001 Ann Bancroft and Liv Arneson would become the first women to ski across Antarctica.

January 14, 1993 Map of Winnipeg to St. Paul race course (*St. Paul Pioneer Press*, 1917)

1993 The movie *Iron Will*, a fictionalized account of a 1917 dogsled race from Winnipeg to St. Paul, opens nationwide. Albert Campbell, a métis (mixed-blood) from Le Pas, Manitoba, won the real race, which was part of St. Paul's Winter Carnival. The first written account of any dogsled race detailed a trip from Winnipeg to St. Paul in the 1850s.

JANUARY 15

1829 Jacob H. Stewart is born. In 1864 Dr. Stewart would become St. Paul's first Republican mayor, and he would also serve the state as a congressman and as surgeon general. Stewart Avenue in St. Paul is named for him.

1849 Henry H. Sibley is admitted to Congress as the delegate of Wisconsin Territory. This title is remarkable, for the bulk of Wisconsin Territory had already been formed into a state, but the citizens of the remaining part, St. Croix County, had sent Sibley to Washington to represent them.

1851 James M. Goodhue, editor of the *Minnesota Pioneer,* brawls in the street with Joseph Cooper, brother of territorial judge David Cooper. Cooper is upset because Goodhue printed a libelous column about his brother, which included the phrases "He is . . . a miserable drunkard . . . and on the Bench he is an ass, stuffed with arrogance, self conceit, and a ridiculous affectation of dignity." Goodhue is stabbed and Cooper shot during the fracas, but both survive.

JANUARY 16

1874 Willmar Village is incorporated. Platted (surveyed and mapped) in 1869, the township was named for Leon Willmar, a Belgian agent for European investors in the St. Paul and Pacific Railroad Company. Willmar would become a city in 1901.

1958 The *Winona Daily News* announces that thirty-six chinchillas, along with feed, cages, and other supplies, have been donated by a student and his father to the biology department of St. Mary's College, to be used in research on improving the breed, whose fur is often made into expensive coats for women.

JANUARY 17

1934 Banker Edward G. Bremer is kidnapped at the corner of Goodrich Avenue and Lexington Parkway in St. Paul. On February 7, after his family pays a $200,000 ransom, Bremer is freed in Rochester. Bremer's remarkable memory leads investigators to the kidnappers, the Barker-Karpis gang, the members of which would all be caught or killed by 1936.

JANUARY 18

1849 Stephen A. Douglas, senator from Illinois, introduces a bill to organize Minnesota Territory.

1887 Boxing great John L. Sullivan breaks his arm in the first round of a fight with Patsey Cardiff in Minneapolis, but the bout continues for five more rounds before a tie is called.

1892 Frank Hibbing arrives in St. Louis County to test for a mine at the site that would eventually bear his name.

JANUARY 19

1836 Six students attend the opening of the Lake Harriet Mission School for the Dakota, founded by the Reverend Jedediah D. Stevens. An early example of education within the boundaries of present-day Minnesota, the school was sponsored by the Presbyterian Missions Board and taught by the founder's niece, Lucy C. Stevens, in a cabin built by Gideon H. and Samuel W. Pond (*see* May 6).

1862 Seeing battle for the first time and suffering forty-five casualties, the Second Minnesota Regiment plays a key role in the Union victory at Logan's Cross Roads, Kentucky.

1928 Dainin Katagiri Roshi is born in Osaka, Japan. A Zen Buddhist abbot and teacher, Roshi would move to Minnesota in December 1972 and found the Minnesota Zen Meditation Center, located in Minneapolis near Lake Calhoun.

1935 Nathalie "Tippi" Hedren, who would star in the movie *The Birds,* is born in New Ulm.

JANUARY 20

1896 On a theatrical tour, western character Calamity Jane (Martha Cannary Burk) appears at the Palace Museum in Minneapolis, dressed in the male attire of buckskin jacket and trousers and giving "the people of the eastern cities an opportunity of seeing the Woman Scout who was made so famous through her daring career in the West and Black Hill countries."

January 20, 1896
(*Minneapolis Journal*)

1961 A fire destroys the Crosby family home, which had been built at the foot of Montreal Street in St. Paul and is now the site of Crosby Farm Park.

1969 President Lyndon B. Johnson bestows the Medal of Freedom, the highest civilian honor awarded by the United States, on civil rights activist Roy Wilkins. Wilkins was born in Mississippi but spent most of his life in St. Paul. In 1923 he graduated from the University of Minnesota, where he was the *Minnesota Daily*'s first black reporter

January 20, 1969

and editor. He served as executive director of the NAACP from 1955 to 1977. A postage stamp honoring him was issued in 2001.

1981 L. Bruce Laingen, who grew up in Odin, is one of fifty-two hostages released from the American Embassy in Teheran after being held by Islamic militants for 444 days. Laingen was chargé d'affaires at the embassy.

JANUARY 21

1844 Jacob V. Brower is born in York, Michigan. After moving to Minnesota in 1860, he would survey the headwaters of the Mississippi River and play an instrumental role in the preservation of Lake Itasca State Park. He died in 1905.

JANUARY 22

1819 Morton S. Wilkinson is born in New York State. He would move to Stillwater in 1847, become Minnesota's first practicing attorney, and serve in Congress as a senator (1859–65) and a representative (1869–71). He died in 1894.

1857 Five Benedictine monks obtain a charter to establish St. John's Seminary in Collegeville. The seminary evolves into St. John's University, the oldest Catholic institution of higher learning in the state.

1962 An out-of-control car careens over the side of St. Paul's High Bridge, lands upside-down on a row of telephone wires, rebounds into the air, and lands on its four wheels. Amazingly, no injuries are reported in the seventy-five-foot fall.

1967 During the era of rock 'n' roll, KSJR (St. John's Radio) begins broadcasting from St. John's University in Collegeville as a station devoted to classical music and the fine arts. KSJR would develop into Minnesota Public Radio, one of the largest and most successful public radio systems in the country.

JANUARY 23

1855 A cable suspension bridge opens between Minneapolis and Nicollet Island. The first permanent span over the main channel of the Mississippi River, it could be crossed by paying a toll of three cents (one way) or five cents (round trip) per human foot-passenger, fifteen cents per horse, and two cents per head for sheep.

January 23, 1855

1865 First National Bank of Minneapolis commences business with a capital of $50,000. With beginnings in a private bank co-owned by its first president, Jacob K. Sidle, the institution would go through several name changes, celebrating seventy-five years in business in 1939 as First National Bank and Trust Company of Minneapolis and then reverting to its original name in 1943.

1929 The three-day trial of Lake Charles resident Ben Shock, charged with not having a license for his beagle, begins. Declaring a case of mistaken identity, Shock claims that his beagle had died and that the license fee collector had seen him with another beagle. Shock refuses to pay bail and is jailed for thirty days while the judge ponders the case, finally ruling that Shock had been wronged and should be set free.

1976 Milton Reynolds, an Albert Lea native who became a millionaire by his astute and early mass production and promotion of a new type of ball-point pen in the 1940s, dies in Chicago.

1986 Northwest Airlines agrees to buy Republic Airlines for $884 million, a purchase that would form a single Twin Cities–based carrier and the third-largest airline in the United States.

1986 William Rubin, former president of Flight Transportation Corporation of Eden Prairie, and Janet Karki, his chief financial officer, are found guilty by a federal jury in St. Paul of perpetrating "the largest financial fraud in Minnesota's history" by engineering a sale of about $25 million in stock for a mostly fictitious company.

JANUARY 24

1848 Citizens of St. Croix County, Wisconsin Territory, protest a plan to incorporate their county into the new state of Wisconsin. Their land would become part of Minnesota Territory in 1849.

1881 Suffering from dyspepsia, heart disease, and depression, Justus C. Ramsey, younger brother of statesman Alexander, commits suicide in St. Paul. After winning $10,000 in a lottery, Justus had arrived in Minnesota from Pennsylvania in 1849, invested heavily in real estate, and served in the territorial legislature. In early August 1862 he was one of a party that attempted to deliver an annuity payment in gold from the U.S. government to Dakota Indians. The Civil War delayed the gold's arrival from Washington and put the Dakota in a state of deprivation and near-starvation, factors leading to the U.S.–Dakota War that erupted on August 18. Ramsey and his companions reached Fort Ridgely on August 20, the day before it was attacked, and remained there during the siege. Unable to disperse the money, the party later returned with the kegs of gold to St. Paul.

JANUARY 25

1867 St. Paul's Mansion House hotel burns to the ground after a fire starts in the kitchen and there is a delay in getting enough hose for a steam fire engine. "The circumstances . . . strongly point to incendiarism as the cause," remarks the *St. Paul Pioneer,* noting that a fire set in the same place nearly destroyed the hotel in fall 1865.

1886 A six-day bicycle race begins at the Washington Avenue Rink in Minneapolis, with some of the best-known professional male bicyclists in the country competing for the prizes of a medal (sponsored by the *Minneapolis Tribune* and "emblematic of the long distance championship of America") and an "elegant suit of clothes, which will be presented by Oscar the Tailor." Held within the rink, the race is also an endurance test for each participant, who pedals his high wheel bicycle, with a big front wheel and a small rear wheel, around the track for the "largest score" of miles covered. The winner on January 30 is "dark horse" Albert Schock of Chicago with 923 miles and five laps.

1915 Clay School serves the first "penny luncheon" in Minneapolis, "a financial and dietetic experiment" by the Woman's Club of Minneapolis and the Parents and Teachers' Association. For two cents each, students purchase a meal of creamed rice (with raisins) and bread and cocoa, a "more wholesome . . . repast than many of the youngsters have been buying . . . in confectionery stores in the neighborhood." If the luncheons prove successful, the *Minneapolis Journal* notes, "the school board will be asked to authorize their establishment in a number of other public schools."

1983 The U.S. Court of Appeals for the Seventh Circuit in Chicago rules that Minnesota Ojibwe, including the Mille Lacs Band, retain the hunting, fishing, and gathering rights guaranteed by nineteenth-century treaties with the federal government. *See* March 24

JANUARY 26

1836 Lucius F. Hubbard is born in Troy, New York. Arriving in Minnesota in 1857, he would establish and edit the newspaper *Red Wing Republican* and would serve as general in the Civil War and in the Spanish-American War. He would be ninth governor of the state, from 1882 to 1887, his second term lasting three years to cover the legislature's change to biennial sessions. During his tenure the Railroad and Warehouse Commission would be established. He died February 5, 1913. Hubbard County is named in his honor.

1861 Frank O. Lowden is born near Sunrise City (now Sunrise) and later moves to Illinois, where he becomes a lawyer and marries Florence, daughter of George M. Pullman, the wealthy inventor of the railway sleeping car. After Pullman's death, Lowden would manage some of the Car King's enterprises, serve in Congress, become governor of Illinois, lose a nomination for president, and decline a vice-presidential nomination.

1924 Minneapolis policeman George Kraemer fatally shoots Peter C. Johnson with a sawed-off shotgun in a dark basement as Johnson attempts to crack open a safe he and his "assistant," William Carson, stole during a robbery.

1942 Private Milburn Henke of Hutchinson, serving with the American Expeditionary Force, is the first enlisted man deployed to the European theater.

1949 Minnesota Mining and Manufacturing Company announces the invention of a machine for the mass recording of tapes.

JANUARY 27

1871 Congressman from Kentucky James Proctor Knott delivers the speech "The Glories of Duluth" in Congress, mocking the city in an effort to defeat a bill granting land to the St. Croix and Lake Superior Railroad. Duluth's citizens appreciate the free publicity, however, and the town of Proctor is named for him.

1960 Grand Portage National Monument, established by Congress in 1958 and located within the Grand Portage Indian Reservation, is dedicated when Secretary of the Interior Fred A. Seaton accepts the site from the Grand Portage Band of the Minnesota Chippewa Tribe. The eight and one-half mile "Great Carrying Place" near the mouth of the Pigeon River was a major gateway into the interior of North America for exploration, trade, and commerce.

JANUARY 28

1890 Farmers in Clarks Grove, Freeborn County, form a dairy cooperative. This co-op is not the state's first, but its success would inspire other communities to use Clarks Grove's organizational system and its bylaws, which were written in Danish, as a model.

1891 As Ojibwe Indians assemble for a Ghost Dance, a rumor of an uprising at Lake of the Woods spreads and many white settlers flee the Roseau Valley. Upon investigation, Sheriff Oscar Younggren discovers the truth about the Indians' peaceful gathering. Fearing that the settlers might take revenge upon their return, a few Ojibwe feed and water the settlers' animals in their absence.

JANUARY 29

1900 A fire destroys much of the business section of Morristown, Rice County, burning twenty buildings, including a bank, post office, and hotel.

1906 Catholic bishop John Ireland dedicates the organ in the Church of the Immaculate Conception in Faribault.

JANUARY 30

1867 Ralph Waldo Emerson lectures in Winona at the courthouse. Sponsored by local library associations, Emerson's tour of the Midwest also includes stops in Faribault, St. Paul, and Minneapolis.

1958 The States of Minnesota and North Dakota agree that Minnesotans who work in North Dakota and North Dakotans who work in Minnesota will not be required to pay income tax in both states.

1992 Charlie Boone reaches an agreement with WCCO-AM radio regarding his impending retirement from full-time announcing duties, which will end the thirty-year Boone and (Roger) Erickson partnership, one of the station's most popular features.

JANUARY 31

1780 Explorer Jonathan Carver dies in London. Arriving at the future site of St. Paul in 1766, Carver met with Dakota leaders and witnessed ceremonies in the cave that bears his name. His descendants would later allege that the Dakota had ceded him a sizeable tract of land, but the U.S. Senate would reject this bogus claim in 1823. Carver had written a book about his adventures in which he made no mention of the land grant. *See* November 14

1883 The Minneapolis Society of Fine Arts, the founding organization of the Minneapolis Institute of Arts and the Minneapolis School of Art (now the Minneapolis College of Art and Design), is incorporated, with William W. Folwell of the University of Minnesota as its first president.

January 31, 1883

FEBRUARY

FEBRUARY 1

1840 Thomas B. Walker is born in Xenia, Ohio. After making his fortune in lumber, he would plan and develop the Walker Art Gallery, which opened in 1894. He would also play an instrumental role in the creation of the Minneapolis Public Library. He died in 1928.

1886 St. Paul's first Winter Carnival opens, hosting competitions in curling, skating, and ice polo and boasting the first ice palace in the United States. Built in Central Park, the palace is 140 feet long, 120 feet wide, and 100 feet high. The Winter Carnival suggests that those Minnesotans who do not enjoy complaining about their winter may actually enjoy the season.

February 1, 1886 St. Paul Winter Carnival ice palace by moonlight

1887 The Northwestern Publishing Company is incorporated in St. Paul as a general job order printing office, with the subsidiary enterprise of publishing the *Western Appeal* (which would become *The Appeal* in 1889), a weekly African American newspaper that had first appeared in 1885. Editor John Quincy Adams later calls it "A National Afro-American Newspaper" and intends it to be a bold and active paper printing articles that an oppressed people want to read.

1933 Wendell R. Anderson is born in St. Paul. A member of the silver medal-winning 1956 U.S. Olympic ice hockey team, a lawyer, and a former legislator (in both House and Senate), he would serve as governor from 1971 to 1976. After helping to establish a firmer control on state finances through the "Minnesota Miracle" fiscal reforms of 1971, Anderson would end his career as an elected official by appointing himself to fill Walter F. Mondale's U.S. Senate seat following Mondale's election as vice president of the United States in November 1976.

FEBRUARY 2

1842 Knute Nelson is born in Evanger in the Voss district of western Norway. He would move to Alexandria in 1871, and from 1893 to 1895 he would hold the state's highest office, serving as the first Scandinavian-born governor in U.S. history. After this stint as governor, Nelson would serve in the U.S. Senate, where he wrote the bills creating the departments of commerce and labor. He died on April 28, 1923.

1846 Stillwater replaces Dahkotah as the county seat of St. Croix County, Wisconsin Territory. Later annexed by Stillwater, Dahkotah had been the county seat for six years.

1910 In an important act of historical preservation, the Daughters of the American Revolution buy the

Henry H. Sibley House in Mendota and convert it into a museum, which they maintain for over eighty years before transferring the title to the Minnesota Historical Society.

1996 Minnesota's coldest temperature is recorded at Tower, a minimum extreme of 60 degrees below zero (Fahrenheit) that bests by one degree the previous scientifically measured low established in 1899. *See* February 9

FEBRUARY 3

1809 Congress creates the Illinois Territory, which includes all of present-day Minnesota east of the Mississippi River.

1931 Airmail service between the Twin Cities and Winnipeg begins.

1979 The Minnesota Twins baseball team trades future hall-of-famer Rod Carew to the California Angels in exchange for outfielder Ken Landreaux, right-handed pitcher Paul Hartzell, two rookies (left-handed pitcher Brad Havens and catcher–third baseman Dave Engle), and an estimated $200,000. Carew, who bats left-handed and throws right-handed, remarks, "I love the Minnesota fans and like living here. But it was no longer any fun playing . . . I feel that California has the players to win the [American League] pennant." He would post a .318 batting average in his first year with the Angels and help them reach the league playoffs. *See* January 8

FEBRUARY 4

1803 The Reverend William T. Boutwell is born in Lyndeborough, New Hampshire. In 1832 he would accompany Henry R. Schoolcraft on the trip that confirmed Lake Itasca as the source of the Mississippi River, and he would supply the Latin words from which Schoolcraft named the lake (*veritas*, true, and *caput*, head). He would also serve as missionary to the Ojibwe in various Minnesota locations until 1847, when he moved to Stillwater, where he died on October 11, 1890. *See* July 13

1893 Senator William B. Dean offers a resolution in the Minnesota Senate recommending that the "wild lady-slipper or moccasin flower, *Cypripedium calceolus*" be named the state flower; the resolution is later adopted by both Senate and House. Following the discovery that this species of lady slipper does not grow in Minnesota, a new resolution would be adopted in 1902, changing the state flower to the pink-and-white lady slipper *(Cypripedium reginae)*. *See* February 19

1952 The Citizens League is formed in Minneapolis. An independent, non-partisan organization, the league involves citizens in studying public issues and developing policy solutions at the local, metropolitan, and state levels.

FEBRUARY 5

1924 Forty-one iron-ore miners drown or are fatally buried in mud, and seven more escape by climbing a ladder, during the Milford Mine Disaster, which occurs north of Crosby on the Cuyuna Range in northern Minnesota when a nearby lake suddenly empties into an underground mining operation. A county inspector, who had visited the mine the week before the accident, would later state that every precaution had been taken and that the flooding was unavoidable.

FEBRUARY 6

1862 Redwood County is established, named for a translation of *Chanshaypai,* a Dakota name for one of the county's rivers. Previously part of Brown County, this territory would later become, in addition to Redwood, the counties of Lac qui Parle, Lincoln, Lyon, and Yellow Medicine.

1967 Duluth's Accordionaires, a group of twenty-four accordion players, give a triumphal concert in their hometown. Organized in 1950, the group had performed around the world, including stops in Japan and the Soviet Union.

FEBRUARY 7

1851 The territorial legislature votes to make St. Paul the capital and to put the prison in Stillwater.

1867 Laura Ingalls (Wilder) is born near Pepin, Wisconsin. Her family would settle in Walnut Grove, Redwood County, from 1874 to 1880 (living briefly in Iowa for the year 1876–77). She is remembered for writing the Little House on the Prairie books, which chronicle her family's experiences as pioneers. She died February 10, 1957, in Mansfield, Missouri.

1922 Ga-Be-Nah-Gwen-Wonce, an Ojibwe man also known as "Wrinkled Meat" and reputed to be 137 years of age, dies at Cass Lake.

February 7, 1922

1976 Cecil E. Newman, publisher of two African American newspapers in the Twin Cities, dies. Born in Kansas City on July 25, 1903, Newman moved to Minneapolis in 1922 and launched the *St. Paul Recorder* and the *Minneapolis Spokesman* in 1934.

FEBRUARY 8

1831 Joseph A. Wheelock is born in Bridgetown, Nova Scotia. Moving to St. Paul in 1850, he would become involved in the newspaper business, helping found the *St. Paul Daily Press* in 1861 and serving as editor of its successor, the *St. Paul Pioneer Press,* for thirty years. He would also be active in the development of St. Paul's parks and boulevards, and Wheelock Parkway is named in his honor. He died in 1906.

1905 The Minnesota Federation of Colored Women's Clubs is organized in St. Paul. Popular at the turn of the century, women's clubs were reform and social welfare organizations.

1916 Representing the state of Minnesota, a statue of pioneer, trader, and senator Henry M. Rice is unveiled in Statuary Hall in the nation's capitol, Washington, D.C. *See* November 29

February 8, 1916 Bust of Henry M. Rice, Senate Chamber, Minnesota State Capitol

1933 Two bandits rob the Shenandoah Pharmacy on Chicago Avenue: twenty-one-year-old Eddie Larson is shot by Minneapolis police officers Carl A. Johnson and C. E. Bettinger after he fires at them from behind a counter, and nineteen-year-old Fred Sammler, who was rifling the cash register, is wounded by Johnson. Larson dies shortly after arriving at General Hospital, and Sammler later admits that he and Larson had committed several holdups earlier that evening.

FEBRUARY 9

1820 Peter M. Gideon is born near Woodstock, Ohio. A self-educated horticulturist, he would develop the Wealthy apple (named for his wife) and others hardy enough to endure the Minnesota climate. Gideon

Memorial Park marks his farm on the shore of Lake Minnetonka. He died in 1899.

1895 The University of Minnesota's School of Agriculture defeats Hamline University 9 to 3 in the world's first intercollegiate basketball game, played on the Hamline campus by nine-man teams, who shot the ball into peach baskets without backboards.

1899 One of Minnesota's coldest scientifically recorded temperatures is measured at Leech Lake, a low of 59 degrees below zero (Fahrenheit). *See* February 2

FEBRUARY 10

1763 In the treaty ending the French and Indian War, France transfers to Britain the territory that would become Minnesota.

1806 Lieutenant Zebulon M. Pike, exploring the Upper Mississippi territory included in the recent Louisiana Purchase, arrives at the North West Company post on Leech Lake. Incensed that the British Union Jack still flies there, he orders it shot down and replaced with the Stars and Stripes. Pike was something of an ingrate, however, as he enjoyed the hospitality of the post both before and after the incident. British fur posts remain in the region until the end of the War of 1812.

1971 About 250 demonstrators in Minneapolis protest the Vietnam War with a march from the University of Minnesota campus to the Federal Building on Washington Avenue, where they throw a few snowballs and then disperse to distribute leaflets and "get into raps with people about the war."

FEBRUARY 11

1811 Henry Jackson is born in the state of Virginia. He would move to St. Paul in 1842 and rent a place from

Pierre "Pig's Eye" Parrant. A trader and merchant, he would serve as the city's first postmaster and its first justice of the peace.

1888 The Town and Country Club is founded in St. Paul. First located on the shores of Lake Como, in 1891 the club would move to its present location near the Marshall Avenue Bridge. A golf course, originally tomato cans sunk in a pasture, is set up in 1893, and it is now the second oldest course in the country.

1891 The Duluth, Missabe and Northern Railroad is established by the Merritt brothers to carry iron ore from the Mesabi Range to Lake Superior ports. Leonidas Merritt had discovered iron near Mountain Iron the previous November.

FEBRUARY 12

1895 Minnesota is the first state to declare Abraham Lincoln's birthday a legal holiday.

1939 More than 3,000 people (two-thirds of them children) escape death or serious injury when they rush out of the Amphitheatre in Duluth seconds before the steel-and-wood roof of the expansive sports

February 12, 1939
Duluth Amphitheatre, ca. 1930

arena collapses under the weight of snow during an intermission in the annual Duluth police department and Virginia (Minn.) fire department hockey game. The swift evacuation is credited to the fact that many spectators are in the front lobby at the time, as well as to the presence of most of the city's police officers and the calmness of organist Leland McEwen, who remains at his post playing soothing music until the last moment.

February 12, 1988 Joe Huie in front of his cafe

1988 Famed restaurateur Gim Joe Huie dies in Duluth. Born in Guangdong province, China, in 1892, Huie first came to the city in 1909 and made it his American home while returning to the land of his birth for extended stays until the Communist government established control there in the late 1940s. In 1951 he opened Joe Huie's Cafe, on Lake Avenue in Duluth, which for twenty-two years offered authentic Asian food at reasonable prices in a companionable atmosphere.

2000 Cartoonist Charles M. Schulz dies in California. That summer, in St. Paul, his childhood home, 101 individually decorated, five-foot-tall statues of Snoopy are displayed in a celebration of Schulz's life. Later in the year, two auctions of Snoopy statues (including some from the celebration and some made specially for auction) are held with the announcement that the money raised will be used as memorial funds to create a bronze sculpture of Schulz characters for downtown St. Paul, as well as to benefit the College of Visual Arts in St. Paul and provide scholarships at the Art Instruction Schools, a Minneapolis-based correspondence school where Schulz studied and taught. Snoopy statutes not placed for auction, it is also announced, will be returned to the local businesses and organizations that originally sponsored them. *See* October 2 and November 26

FEBRUARY 13

1857 Isanti County is created, named for a Dakota band that lived in the region in the seventeenth century.

1906 William Williams is hanged in a bungled execution in the Ramsey County jail for the murders of a woman and her teenaged son, with whom he was sexually involved. Williams is the twenty-fifth man and the last person of twenty-six legally executed in the state, as capital punishment would be abolished in Minnesota in 1911 following public revulsion and outcry caused by vivid newspaper accounts of his protracted sufferings, due to a too-long rope. *See* April 22

1909 President Theodore Roosevelt establishes Superior National Forest. Six weeks later Ontario's government responds in kind by creating Quetico Provincial Forest Reserve. Exploitative practices are restricted in these areas, thereby preserving the beauty of lakes and trees for future generations.

1918 Patty Berg is born in Minneapolis. A consummate golfer and member of the World Golf Hall of Fame, she would win the U.S. Women's Open in 1946 and claim victory in seven Western Open Tournaments and four Titleholders Championships.

February 13, 1918 Patty Berg golfing, ca. 1935

1933 Leeann W. Chin is born in Canton, China. She would immigrate to the United States in 1956 and open her first restaurant in Minnetonka's Bonaventure Shopping Mall in 1980. Her chain of Leeann Chin restaurants, now expanding outside the state, specializes in Sichuan and Cantonese food.

1976 More than 400 bookbinders in the Twin Cities area go on strike against the Quality Park, Minnesota, Heinrich, Mackay, and Tension envelope companies after a bargaining session fails to resolve differences about a new contract, including a disagreement about a cost-of-living clause. The striking members of the Graphic Arts International Union would settle with all their employers two months later. *See* April 12

FEBRUARY 14

1833 William Watts Folwell is born in Romulus, New York. An educator and historian, Folwell would serve as the University of Minnesota's first president, help found the Minneapolis Institute of Arts, and author a four-volume history of Minnesota. He died in 1929.

February 14, 1833 William Watts Folwell in his study, 1918

1850 The Fort Snelling post band travels to Stillwater to play for a Valentine's Day dance.

1852 Mankato, a variation of *Mahkato*, the Dakota word for the Blue Earth River, is founded.

FEBRUARY 15

1822 Henry B. Whipple is born in Adams, New York. As Minnesota's first Episcopalian bishop, Whipple would work tirelessly to promote his church in the state. Moving to Faribault in 1852, he would build the first Episcopal cathedral in the country, as well as the Shattuck School, Seabury Divinity School, and St. Mary's Hall. He would also devote himself to working with and for the Dakota and Ojibwe, who called him "Straight

Tongue." After over 300 Dakota had been sentenced to death for participating in the U.S.–Dakota War of 1862, Whipple would intercede with President Abraham Lincoln, who then commuted most of the sentences. Whipple died in Faribault on September 16, 1901.

1870 A groundbreaking ceremony for the Northern Pacific Railroad line is held at Northern Pacific Junction, later called Carlton. The line to the Pacific Ocean, completed on September 8, 1883, with the same spike used to begin construction in Minnesota, is the first single-company transcontinental line.

FEBRUARY 16

1855 Faribault is platted (surveyed and mapped). Trader Alexander Faribault had settled there in 1826.

1860 The Minnesota State Agricultural Society is incorporated, replacing the territorial society that had previously existed.

1864 The Waseca County Horse Thief Detectives are organized in Wilton. One of several such pioneer groups, it would continue to hold social meetings after 1880, and, when horse-thieving became a thing of the past, it would focus its energies on tracing stolen cars.

FEBRUARY 17

1815 The Treaty of Ghent goes into effect, formally ending the War of 1812. The treaty dictates that the British must vacate posts located on U.S. soil, including those in present-day Minnesota.

1881 Norman County is established. Although the name was believed to honor influential settler Norman W. Kittson (*see* March 5), it is now understood that Norwegian settlers selected the name in remembrance of their homeland.

1921 Sister Carmela Hanggi, principal of Cathedral School in St. Paul and a member of the Sisters of St. Joseph of Carondelet, founds the School Safety Patrol in Minnesota, which becomes an international model for parochial and public institutions. At first a school-police program for boys who serve as guards helping fellow elementary-school students cross busy streets, Sister Carmela's enterprise would inspire the organization of numerous programs that now include girl guards and bus patrols.

February 17, 1921 Children escorted by the school police, ca. 1930

1972 The U.S. Department of Justice files a pollution suit against Reserve Mining Company, which operated a taconite plant on Lake Superior and dumped tailings contaminated with asbestos-like fibers into the lake. Lasting five years, the proceedings would be the nation's longest and most expensive environmental legal battle to that date.

FEBRUARY 18

1868 The University of Minnesota is reorganized by the legislature into a central college of science, literature, and the arts plus various associated colleges. Although the university had been incorporated on February 25, 1851, no classes had been held. In 1869, the board of regents elects William W. Folwell as the institution's first president, and classes begin soon afterward.

1870 Swift County is created, named in honor of the state's third governor, Henry A. Swift. *See* March 23

1931 William R. Merriam, the state's eleventh governor, dies in Washington, D.C. Born on July 26, 1849, in New York, he served as governor from 1889 to 1893. He was also director of the U.S. Census of 1900.

1953 Governor Clyde Elmer Anderson signs a bill establishing the red pine *(Pinus resinosa)*, commonly known as the Norway pine, as the Minnesota state tree.

FEBRUARY 19

1840 Andrew R. McGill is born in Saegerstown, Pennsylvania. He would serve as the state's tenth governor from 1887 to 1889 and, later, as state senator and St. Paul's postmaster. He died in St. Paul on October 31, 1905.

1851 An act signed by Congress sets aside 48,080 acres to support a state university, and the University of Minnesota is first incorporated six days later.

1902 The pink-and-white lady slipper *(Cypripedium reginae)* is named the state flower by the legislature (following the discovery that the previously chosen variety of lady slipper is not native to Minnesota). This wild orchid has a brilliantly colored bloom and thrives in damp woods, swamps, and bogs; it would be protected by a state law passed in 1925 that forbids picking the flower. *See* February 4

FEBRUARY 20

1811 Henry H. Sibley is born in Detroit, Michigan. A major player early in the state's history, Sibley would be a fur trader, politician, businessman, military leader, and university regent. He died in St. Paul on February 18, 1891.

1855 The territorial legislature creates twelve counties, all named in honor of individuals who played a significant role in the state's history. Brown is named for pioneer Joseph R. Brown (*see* January 5); Carver for explorer Jonathan Carver (*see* January 31); Dodge for Wisconsin governor Henry Dodge and his son Augustus; Faribault for fur trader Jean Baptiste Faribault (*see* October 29); Freeborn for member of the territorial legislature William Freeborn; Mower for Stillwater lumberman John E. Mower; Olmsted for St. Paul mayor David Olmsted; Renville for fur trader Joseph Renville; Stearns for legislator Charles Thomas Stearns; Steele for pioneer Franklin Steele (*see* July 19); Todd for Fort Ripley commander John Blair Smith Todd; and Wright for New York statesman Silas Wright.

1862 More counties are created. Three are named for bodies of water—Big Stone for Big Stone Lake, Chippewa for the Chippewa River, and Traverse for Lake Traverse—and two for notable individuals—General John Pope, cartographer (*see* June 6), is honored with Pope County, and Isaac I. Stevens, railroad surveyor (*see* May 31), is remembered with Stevens County.

1992 Minnesota gets its taste of the nationwide savings and loan debacle when Hal Greenwood, Jr., former chairman and CEO of the failed Midwest Federal Savings and Loan Association, is sentenced by a federal judge in St. Paul to forty-six months in prison and ordered to forfeit $3.6 million. Following federal deregulation of the thrift industry during the 1980s, savings and loans around the country had become over-extended, and many engaged in loans without sufficient reserves to cover themselves if the loans failed. Greenwood was one of the few savings and loan officials to be sentenced.

FEBRUARY 21

1855 Henderson is incorporated. Joseph R. Brown had settled there in 1852, and he named the town for his aunt, Margaret Brown Henderson, and her son, Andrew.

FEBRUARY 22

1855 The Mississippi, Pillager, and Lake Winnibigosh-ish bands of Ojibwe sign a treaty ceding to the U.S. government a major portion of heavily wooded north-central Minnesota, in which lumbering companies had expressed a keen interest. The treaty establishes still-existing reservations at Leech and Mille Lacs Lakes.

1861 The state first celebrates George Washington's birthday as a legal holiday.

FEBRUARY 23

1854 Winona County is established, named for a Dakota woman, the cousin of the last leader named Wabasha, who played a role in the transfer of the Win-nebago (Ho-Chunk) from their Iowa reservation to one in Blue Earth County. Another Winona (the name means "first-born daughter") is remembered in the leg-end of a young woman who leapt from a rock rather than marry the man selected by her parents. Maiden Rock on Lake Pepin marks that event.

1854 Houston County is created, honoring Sam Hous-ton of Texas, a popular presidential candidate.

1856 Meeker County is created, named for Bradley B. Meeker, one of the first three judges to serve on the Minnesota Supreme Court. *See* June 11

1892 Watson's Colored Chorus, an African American musical group with 250 singers from Minneapolis and St. Paul, gives a concert featuring "Choruses, Glees, Banjo, Guitar and Vocal Solos, Jubilees and Plantation Songs" at Minneapolis's Lyceum Theater; the best reserved seats cost fifty cents apiece.

1983 Mark Pavelich becomes the first United States–born National Hockey League player to score five goals in a game when the Eveleth native and member of the gold medal–winning "Miracle on Ice" 1980 U.S. Olympic hockey team leads the New York Rangers to an 11 to 3 victory over the Hartford Whalers in New York City.

FEBRUARY 24

1858 Minnesota is nicknamed the "Gopher State." The legislature had guaranteed a $5 million loan to railroad interests, and a cartoon showing a railroad car of corrupt men being pulled by nine striped rodents with human heads, representing the people of the territory, is printed on this date. *See* March 9

February 24, 1858

1925 Minnesota loses to Canada two and a half acres of water area from the Northwest Angle (the northwestern point of the Lake of the Woods) when the United States and the Dominion of Canada sign an agreement that more accurately defines the international boundary between the two countries established by the Webster-Ashburton Treaty of 1842. *See* August 9

FEBRUARY 25

1856 Morrison and Sherburne Counties are created. Morrison is named for fur traders William and Allan Morrison. Sherburne is named for Moses Sherburne, a justice in the territorial supreme court.

1860 Watonwan County is established, named for the river. *Watonwan* means "I see" in Dakota, but the name of the river may have been a misspelling of *Watanwan,* or "fish bait."

1879 Kittson and Marshall Counties are created. Kittson honors Norman W. Kittson, a prominent territorial pioneer (*see* March 5), and Marshall honors William R. Marshall, fifth governor of the state (*see* October 17).

FEBRUARY 26

1853 Edward D. Neill obtains a charter for the Baldwin School, which would become St. Paul's Macalester College. *See* September 16

1857 Territorial delegate Henry M. Rice succeeds in lobbying Congress to pass the enabling act for the state of Minnesota. This act defines the state's boundaries and authorizes the establishment of a state government.

1857 Mount Zion Hebrew Congregation, the first Jewish organization in Minnesota, is formed in St. Paul.

1883 Hubbard County is organized, named for Lucius F. Hubbard, who served as governor from 1882 to 1886. *See* January 26

1985 Minneapolis native Prince sweeps the Grammy Awards as his soundtrack to *Purple Rain* earns an award for best soundtrack, best rock performance, and best R&B song.

FEBRUARY 27

1843 Thomas Lowry is born in Logan County, Illinois. After arriving in Minneapolis in 1868, Lowry would play an instrumental role in establishing the Twin Cities' streetcar system. He died in 1909.

1857 Waseca County is formed, named with a Dakota word meaning "rich in provisions." Also on this day, a humorous episode in Minnesota's history begins. Joseph Rolette, a fur trader representing Pembina in the territorial legislature, steals the text of a bill to move the capital from St. Paul to St. Peter. Although the bill had been passed, it had not been signed by the governor. Rolette disappears until the legislature adjourns on March 7, hiding in the Fuller House attic while the bill rests in the hotel safe.

FEBRUARY 28

1866 Beltrami County is formed, although permanent white settlement would not occur in the area until the 1880s. It honors Italian adventurer Giacomo C. Beltrami, who had explored the region in 1823. *See* August 31

1872 Minneapolis and St. Anthony are united into one city.

1891 Horsecar service ends in St. Paul.

FEBRUARY 29

1844 Al Sieber is born in Germany. Sieber would move to Minneapolis in 1856, join the First Minnesota Regiment in 1862, and after the Civil War become an army scout in the American west. Wounded twenty-nine times in combat, he would be killed during construction of the Roosevelt Dam in 1907.

1868 The first issue of the *St. Paul Daily Dispatch* is published. This newspaper would appear in various editions until 1984, when it merged with the *St. Paul Pioneer Press.*

February 27, 1857 Joseph Rolette

MARCH 1

1856 The territorial legislature incorporates the St. Peter Company, which is authorized to engage in milling and waterpower work and to develop real estate. The company's stockholders hope to move the state capital to St. Peter, but their efforts are thwarted (*see* February 27). James J. Hill would purchase the company's charter in 1901, hoping that its real estate powers would prove useful to the Great Northern Railway.

1856 Minneapolis is approved for a town government by the territorial legislature. It would become a city ten years later. The legislature also forms three counties: Lake County, named for Lake Superior; McLeod County, named for Martin McLeod, a fur trader and member of the territorial legislature (*see* August 30); and Pine County, named for the extensive pine forests of the region or perhaps for the Pine River and Pine Lakes.

1881 The first state capitol building burns. Three hundred people escape safely, but the building, including the law library, is a total loss. Luckily, most of the Minnesota Historical Society's artifacts are rescued from the basement. A second capitol is built on the same site, a square block bounded by Wabasha, Cedar, Exchange, and Tenth Streets, but is later replaced by the present capitol.

1899 *The Theory of the Leisure Class: An Economic Study of Institutions,* authored by Thorstein Veblen, is published. A graduate of Carleton College, Veblen earns recognition as a dynamic economist and social theorist, and his book remains influential today.

1921 Patrick Des Jarlait is born on the Red Lake Reservation. He would paint colorful, stylized images of Ojibwe traditional life.

1994 "Runaway Train" by the Minneapolis group Soul Asylum wins a Grammy for best rock song.

March 1, 1921 *Woman and Blueberries* by Patrick Des Jarlait, 1971

MARCH 2

1859 The *Turnverein,* a German organization that sponsored social, educational, and physical events, gives its first dramatic presentation in St. Anthony's Turnverein Hall. Turner clubs provided a strong German presence throughout the country until World War I.

1878 The city of Anoka is created. It had first been settled in 1851 and then platted (surveyed and mapped) in 1854.

1922 A party of 115 Mennonite men, women, and children from Manitoba pauses briefly in the Twin Cities on the way to settle in Mexico. Among the first of an estimated 20,000 members of this Protestant Christian denomination expected to leave Canada during the next three years, the travelers arrive by rail in passenger coaches accompanied by twenty-two stock cars full of provisions, livestock, farm equipment, and furniture. They plan to live in self-imposed isolation in order to practice their centuries-old religious beliefs and pacifistic way of life, which had caused difficulties with the Canadian government regarding compulsory school attendance and military conscription during World War I.

1949 Melrose native Captain James Gallagher of the U.S. Air Force completes the first nonstop flight around the world. With a crew of thirteen he flew *Lucky Lady II,* a B-50 bomber assigned to the 43rd Bomb Group, refueling four times while in the air and completing the 23,452-mile trip in ninety-four hours and one minute.

1974 Uncle Hugo's Science Fiction Bookstore, now the oldest of its kind in the United States, opens in South Minneapolis.

MARCH 3

1849 Minnesota Territory is signed into existence by President James K. Polk. The territory has a population of about 10,000 Indians and 5,000 white settlers and includes present-day North and South Dakota east of the Missouri River. The U.S. Postal Service would release a three-cent centennial stamp on this date in 1949.

1853 Fillmore County, honoring President Millard Fillmore, is created.

1855 St. Louis County, the state's largest (6,611 square miles), is established, named for the St. Louis River.

March 3, 1849

1855 The legislature decides to send an immigration commissioner to New York. Beginning in June, Eugene Burnand of St. Paul represents the territory in Manhattan, where he encourages immigrants to make Minnesota their new home.

1990 A team led by Will Steger of Ely completes the 3,800-mile International Trans-Antarctica Expedition, the first dog-sled traverse of the continent by its widest distance.

MARCH 4

1854 St. Paul and Stillwater are incorporated as cities.

1892 In Tower, Father Joseph F. Buh publishes issue eleven of *Amerikanski Slovenec* (American Slovene), the first national newspaper for Slovenes in the United States. The paper had started in Chicago but had ceased publication after ten issues. Buh, who served St. Martin's Catholic Church in Tower and St. Anthony parish at Ely, would supervise the paper's publication until 1899.

1911 Jerry McCarty and Peter Juhl escape from the main cell house at the Minnesota State Prison in Stillwater after McCarty somehow obtains a key that unlocks the bar running in front of the cell doors. Juhl, a trusty making his evening rounds with a torch for igniting tapers "stuck by convicts in their cell doors with which to light their pipes for a final night smoke," uses the key to release McCarty, and the two "hard cases" hastily climb over a wall. On July 15 McCarty, a burglar who had been sent to Stillwater for shooting at police officers, and Minneapolis patrolman Joseph Ollinger would kill each other in a close-range revolver battle. On August 12 Juhl, sentenced for robbing a jewelry store, would be captured on the crowded Selby Avenue–Lake Street streetcar after mortally wounding St. Paul detective Frank Fraser, who clings to Juhl until another officer fells the escapee with his police club.

1941 Elcor native Sam LoPresti, goaltender for the Chicago Blackhawks hockey team, makes an astounding eighty saves in a game against the Boston Bruins. Despite this valiant effort, three pucks get by him, and Chicago loses 3–2.

1942 Tammy Faye LeValley (Bakker) is born in International Falls. With her husband, Jim Bakker, she would help found three of the largest Christian television networks in the world, including the Praise the Lord ministry. After Jim is jailed for fraud and conspiracy (a charge for which she escaped conviction), she would divorce him and marry Roe Messner.

MARCH 5

1814 Norman W. Kittson is born in Sorel, Canada. Arriving in Minnesota in 1834, Kittson would find wealth by developing trade between St. Paul and the Red River and would also serve as a legislator and as mayor of St. Paul. Late in life, Kittson would build a mansion in St. Paul on a trail that led to town. To accommodate those accustomed to following the trail, Kittson would leave his front and back doors open for folks to pass through. The Cathedral of St. Paul now stands on the site.

1852 Farmers in Benton County form the state's first county agricultural society. Oliver H. Kelley, who would later found the National Grange (*see* September 2), is one of ten charter members. County agricultural society members share information about stock, seeds, fruit, and farming practices.

1853 Seven counties are formed by the territorial legislature: Blue Earth, named for the Blue Earth River, along which blue clay was once found; Goodhue, named for newspaper editor James M. Goodhue (*see* March 31); Le Sueur, for French explorer Pierre Charles Le Sueur (*see* October 1); Nicollet, for French geographer Joseph N. Nicollet (*see* July 24); Rice, for territorial delegate to Congress Henry M. Rice (*see* November 29); Scott, for General Winfield Scott, hero of the Mexican War; and Sibley, for Henry H. Sibley, trader and politician (*see* February 20).

1853 The legislature incorporates the St. Paul Mutual Insurance Company, forerunner of the insurance giant St. Paul Companies, the state's oldest business corporation.

MARCH 6

1852 Hennepin County is formed, named for Louis Hennepin, the Franciscan missionary who saw and named the Falls of St. Anthony in 1680.

1857 The U.S. Supreme Court renders the Dred Scott decision, in which the justices declare that Missouri slave Dred Scott, not being a citizen, has no right to bring suit. Scott had lived at Fort Snelling and in other "free" areas with his owner, Dr. John Emerson, and he claimed that residence in free states and territories made him a free man. While living at Fort Snelling from 1836 to 1838, Scott married Harriet Robinson, a slave of Indian agent Lawrence Taliaferro.

1862 Henry B. Whipple, the Episcopal bishop of Minnesota, writes a letter to President Abraham Lincoln on behalf of the Indians of the state, describing corruption among agents of the U.S. Bureau of Indian Affairs and asking for "justice for a wronged and neglected race." The tragic U.S.–Dakota War, partly caused by the dishonest and greedy acts of venal Indian agents seeking to "retire upon an ample fortune," occurs in Minnesota later this year. *See* August 17

1868 Grant, Lyon, and Wilkin Counties are formed out of Lac qui Parle County, which ceases to exist (*see* March 6, 1871). Grant and Lyon are named for Civil War Generals Ulysses S. Grant and Nathaniel Lyon. Wilkin County had previously been named for Robert Toombs, who later became a Confederate leader. The county was then named Andy Johnson, for the president, but his political attitude disturbed the county's residents, leading them to adopt the present name, which honors Civil War Colonel Alexander Wilkin (*see* July 14).

1871 The name Lac qui Parle is given to a new county. The name, French for "lake that talks," likely refers to echoes among the bluffs surrounding the lake of the same name. Yellow Medicine County is also formed, named for the root of the moonseed, used by the Dakota as a medicinal herb.

2000 Duluth becomes the first city in the nation to ban the sale of mercury thermometers (to prevent the element from polluting the environment). Minnesota had prohibited use of mercury thermometers in hospitals in 1992.

MARCH 7

1882 The Minnesota State Butter and Cheese Association is organized in Rochester. The group promotes dairy farming in the state and counts among its successes the "grand sweepstakes" award for the best butter at the 1885 World Industrial and Centennial Exposition in New Orleans.

1913 Early this morning, a plainclothes policeman is beaten and thrown out of a room at the St. Paul Hotel where members of the state legislature and their friends are said to be playing cards. The officer returns with six more plainclothes men and "exciting scenes" follow, including the flight through a window into another room by a man who had hit the first policeman with his fist. Although at least one man is told to appear later in court, the entire matter is dropped while the legislators complain of a "frameup" by the police to make trouble for members in disfavor with the city administration.

MARCH 8

1858 Douglas County is formed, honoring Stephen A. Douglas of Illinois, who advocated Minnesota's statehood. *See* January 18

1892 A snowstorm covers Duluth on this day and the next. Many people must exit their houses through second-story windows.

1920 The U.S. Supreme Court settles a boundary squabble between Minnesota and Wisconsin over control of the Duluth harbor, finding in Minnesota's favor.

MARCH 9

1848 Schoolteacher Harriet E. Bishop forms Minnesota's first temperance society. Temperance societies opposed drunkenness.

1858 The legislature approves an amendment to Minnesota's constitution that legalizes the loan of the state's credit in an issue of bonds "up to but not exceeding $5,000,000," with the idea of exchanging state bonds for railroad-company bonds and thus stimulating the building of railroads and their subsequent benefits to land sales and the state economy. The "$5 million loan" would continue to be an issue in Minnesota politics for many years, even after the railroad bonds are substantially redeemed in 1881. *See* February 24

1874 Cook County is formed, commemorating Civil War hero Major Michael Cook from Faribault.

MARCH 10

1804 The Upper Louisiana Territory, including present-day Minnesota west of the Mississippi River, is formally transferred from France to the United States in a ceremony in St. Louis.

1858 Inventor and businessman Marshall B. Lloyd is born in St. Paul. He would be involved in many ventures in Canada and the Dakotas before moving to Minneapolis in 1900. Once there, he would invent machines to weave wire into doormats and, later, the woven-wire bedspring mattress. Head of the Lloyd Manufacturing Company, he would then move to Menominee, Michigan, and invent a wicker-weaving machine that was thirty times faster than hand-weaving.

1983 Mickey's Diner in St. Paul, built in 1939, is listed on the National Register of Historic Places and becomes a protected landmark.

MARCH 11

1862 The troops of the First Minnesota Infantry Regiment occupy the town of Berryville, Virginia, where they find the print run of the local paper half completed. Members of the company print their own four-page edition, which contains humorous news about the army and the war. Copies of this paper are rare and valued Civil War memorabilia.

1863 The Mississippi, Pillager, and Lake Winnibigoshish bands of Ojibwe sign a treaty with the U.S. government that consolidates and expands the Cass Lake, Lake Winnibigoshish, and Leech Lake Reservations into the Leech Lake Indian Reservation in north-central Minnesota. The treaty, which would be renegotiated in 1864, requires numerous Ojibwe living elsewhere in the state to move to Leech Lake.

1893 Wanda Gág is born in New Ulm. An author and artist, she would write and illustrate the children's classic *Millions of Cats*.

March 11, 1893 Wanda Gág with one of the cats used as a model in *Millions of Cats*, 1928

MARCH 12

1872 Rutherford B. Hayes, between terms as governor of Ohio, spends the morning in St. Paul visiting the state capitol and "other places of note in the city." He would serve as U.S. president from 1877 to 1881.

1877 Duluth, having suffered a loss of population, reverts from a city back into a town.

MARCH 13

1858 Kanabec County is formed out of Pine County. *Kanabec* is an Ojibwe word for "snake," and the Snake River flows through the county.

MARCH 14

1841 William Dunwoody is born in Pennsylvania. After settling in Minneapolis in 1869, he would find his fortune in the grain and flour business. By the time of his death in 1914, he would contribute millions of dollars to a number of civic organizations, including the Dunwoody Industrial Institute, the Minneapolis Society of Fine Arts, and the YMCA.

1919 Max Shulman is born in St. Paul. An author and Hollywood screenwriter, he is best remembered for creating the character Dobie Gillis, who appeared in short stories, novels, and a television show.

1924 The last guest checks out of Stillwater's historic Sawyer House, which had operated as a hotel for sixty-seven years. The Lowell Inn stands on the site today.

MARCH 15

1927 The Arrowhead Bridge across the St. Louis River opens, linking West Duluth to Superior, Wisconsin.

1941 Thirty-one people, mostly unsuspecting motorists caught on the roads, die in a blizzard, the second killer snowstorm of the season. *See* November 11

MARCH 16

1876 The St. Paul Society for Improving the Condition of the Poor (later the Society for the Relief of the Poor) is organized to give aid to people who need food, fuel, and work. Early officers include Henry M. Rice, Alexander Ramsey, Henry H. Sibley, and William R. Marshall.

1882 Noted aesthete Oscar Wilde lectures at the Opera House in St. Paul. He had spoken the day before at the Academy of Music in Minneapolis.

1912 Clyde Elmer Anderson is born in Brainerd. A champion of social and humanitarian causes, he would serve a record eleven years as the state's lieutenant governor beginning in 1939 and then as the state's twenty-eighth governor from 1951 to 1955. He died in 1998.

MARCH 17

1851 St. Paul hosts the state's first St. Patrick's Day parade. Although Irish immigration to St. Paul would not peak until 1890, many Irish had already settled in town, working both as household servants and as laborers on the docks of the Upper Landing.

MARCH 18

1858 Otter Tail, Becker, and Breckenridge Counties are formed. The first is named for the lake and river and is a translation from the Ojibwe name, probably for an otter-tail-shaped sandbar in the lake. Becker County honors George L. Becker, one of three representatives the new state of Minnesota had planned to send to Congress. When it was discovered that the state was permitted only two representatives, lots were drawn and Becker lost. Breckenridge County honors Vice President John C. Breckenridge, but when he later became a Confederate in the Civil War the residents of the county would vote to change the name to Clay County, honoring Unionist Henry Clay instead.

1858 In St. Peter, Methodist minister Edward Eggleston marries Lizzie Snider. Eggleston is best remembered for his novel *The Hoosier School-Master,* set in Indiana, but a less popular novel, *The Mystery of Metropolisville,* deals with land speculation in Minnesota in the 1850s.

1891 Margaret Culkin (Banning) is born in Buffalo. She would live in Duluth for many years, authoring more than thirty books, including *Mesabi* and *Country Club People.*

MARCH 19

1849 Aaron Goodrich is appointed chief justice of Minnesota Territory. *See* November 28

1867 A treaty signed in Washington, D.C., establishes the White Earth Reservation for Ojibwe tribes, and the transfer of the Mississippi Ojibwe to the site begins June 14. Chief Hole-in-the-Day, wanting no mixed bloods on the reservation, tries to block their settlement. Bad relations result from this policy, and Hole-in-the-Day is assassinated on June 27, 1868, near his home in Crow Wing.

March 19, 1867 Chief Hole-in-the-Day

1880 The first bridge connecting Fort Snelling to Mendota is completed.

1992 Rebecca Rand, Minnesota's best-known brothel operator, pleads guilty in Ramsey County District Court to three prostitution-related felonies and agrees to turn her buildings over to authorities, as well as pay $200,000 to settle a civil-forfeiture suit. She observes, "I went through so many years without a pimp or anyone taking my money. . . . Now the government decided to do that."

MARCH 20

1858 Kandiyohi County is established, at first comprising only the southern half of its present area. In 1870, the county would absorb its northern neighbor, Monongalia County. *Kandiyohi,* a Dakota name for some lakes in the county, means "where the buffalo fish come."

1920 Black leader W. E. B. DuBois gives a lecture in St. Paul, sponsored by the local chapter of the NAACP.

1992 Surviving crew members of the U.S. Army Air Corps bombing raid led by Lieutenant Colonel Jimmy Doolittle on Tokyo during World War II gather in Red Wing with Chinese villagers who had rescued some of the airmen after they crash landed or parachuted into the nearby sea or China following the attack. Organized by a Red Wing–area resident who had led an expedition to China in 1990 to try to recover remains of raid bombers, the reunion also honors Doolittle, who is unable to attend. *See* March 30

MARCH 21

1864 George Edgar Vincent is born in Rockford, Illinois. A sociologist and a graduate of Yale University, he would serve from 1911 to 1917 as the third president of the University of Minnesota and an "academic house-cleaner" whose reforms during his energetic term would bring the institution into the modern era of education.

1913 After a wild chase early this morning in the North Minneapolis rail yards, railroad employees and armed police detectives capture Harry Christianson, who is suspected of attempting to rob boxcars. For a time Christianson manages to evade his pursuers by rolling under and jumping over and through coupled cars moving around the yards, but he eventually becomes confused and runs directly into the arms of the detectives.

MARCH 22

1882 A guilty verdict is rendered in the impeachment trial of Judge Eugene St. Julien Cox, who had been accused of conducting trial while drunk. His cause probably was not helped when ten bartenders were called to testify to his ability to hold liquor. Cox is removed from office, but later his allies in the Democratic Party help reverse the conviction.

1908 Maurice H. Stans is born in Shakopee. He would serve as secretary of commerce under President Richard M. Nixon.

1958 Movie producer Mike Todd, who won an Oscar for *Around the World in 80 Days* (Best Motion Picture, 1956), dies in an airplane crash in New Mexico. Todd was born in Minneapolis in 1909 as Avrom Hirsch Goldbogen.

1993 George O. Berry dies in Minneapolis. Born in St. Paul, the son of a railroad porter and a domestic worker and a federal meat and poultry inspector by profession, Berry was one of the first African Americans elected to public office in the city, winning a spot on the St. Paul school board from 1966 to 1973. During his tenure he worked for the creation of magnet schools.

MARCH 23

1823 Henry A. Swift is born in Ravenna, Ohio. He would serve as governor for six months during the Civil War, succeeding Alexander Ramsey, who left office for the U.S. Senate. Swift died on February 25, 1869, in St. Peter.

1860 Convicted of poisoning her husband, Stanislaus, Ann Bilansky is executed in St. Paul. Bilansky would be the only woman and the first white person to be legally executed in the state, although serious doubts about her guilt still persist.

1971 Minnesota is among the first states to ratify the twenty-sixth amendment to the U.S. Constitution, which gives U.S. citizens eighteen years of age or older the right to vote in local, state, and national elections. Both Minnesota and Delaware claim to be the initial actor on this important issue, although one Minnesota legislator who voted against ratifying calls his state's role a "dubious pleasure." Ratification by the necessary number of states would be completed later in the year.

MARCH 24

1858 The printing press of the *St. Cloud Visiter* is destroyed by a mob. The paper's editor, Jane Grey Swisshelm, a feminist and abolitionist, had angered local businessman and slave owner Sylvanus B. Lowry. Swisshelm soon obtains a new press and prints the story of her press's destruction and the names of the culprits, which re-sults in a libel case and the termi-

March 24, 1858

nation of the paper. A week later she begins publishing the *St. Cloud Democrat,* which she runs for eight years.

1999 The U.S. Supreme Court upholds the rights of the Mille Lacs Band of Ojibwe to fish and hunt in ceded lands without state regulation, as dictated by an 1837 treaty.

MARCH 25

1854 John Lind is born in Kanna, Småland, Sweden. In 1899 he would be the first Swede to be elected governor of Minnesota and the first Democrat to hold the office since Henry H. Sibley. He would also be the first Swede elected to Congress, where he served four terms, and in 1913 he would be President Woodrow Wilson's envoy to Mexico. He died in Minneapolis on September 18, 1930.

1886 The inaugural issue of the *Progress* is published at White Earth. The first English-language paper to be published on an Indian reservation, the *Progress* is edited by missionaries Gus H. and Theodore H. Beaulieu. The second issue is not published until October 8, 1887, because of interference by an Indian agent who was concerned about the intentions of the paper, in which the Office of Indian Affairs was often criticized.

1888 The *St. Paul Globe* publishes Eva McDonald Valesh's article recounting her observations as a worker in the Minneapolis garment industry. Using the pen name Eva Gay, Valesh would author a series of articles revealing women's lives in the Twin Cities workforce, and her work for the *Globe* would launch her career as a journalist.

1963 Karl F. Rolvaag is sworn in as governor, having beaten Elmer L. Andersen by ninety-one votes in the state's closest gubernatorial election. The recount of the election had taken four months.

MARCH 26

1804 Present-day Minnesota west of the Mississippi River is included in the District of Louisiana, to be governed by Indiana Territory. Nearly a year later, on March 3, 1805, this region would become part of Louisiana Territory.

1857 Inkpaduta (Scarlet Point) and his band of Dakota attack Springfield (now Jackson) in Jackson County. The settlers gather in two cabins to defend the settlement; during the battle one child dies and several adults are wounded. This incident is part of the so-called "Spirit Lake Massacre" (only one death actually occurred at Spirit Lake, Iowa). The failure of the government to capture Inkpaduta may have encouraged other Dakota to expect victory in the U.S.–Dakota War of 1862.

MARCH 27

1819 President James Monroe appoints Lawrence Taliaferro as Indian agent at St. Peter's (now Mendota). Taliaferro would move his operations across the river to Fort St. Anthony (later Snelling) when that post opened. Serving the territory for the next twenty years, he is remembered for his honesty toward and concern for the Indians, for maintaining peace between Dakota and Ojibwe tribes, and for enforcing laws governing relations between Indians and white settlers.

1905 The Aerial Bridge, spanning the Duluth Ship Canal, carries its first passengers across the harbor inside a carriage suspended from the bridge's framework. The system would be replaced with a lift bridge in 1930.

1912 The St. Olaf Choir, directed by F. Melius Christiansen, gives the opening concert of its first tour at the First Baptist Church, Minneapolis.

MARCH 28

1992 William Maupins, Duluth's premier civil rights leader, dies. He served as president of the Duluth NAACP chapter, and, when a black family was prevented from moving into a Duluth neighborhood, he launched the campaign that led to a city fair-housing ordinance. He also organized a food drive for poor blacks in Mississippi; when white truckers in the South tried to block the shipments, he persuaded Duluth teamsters to deliver the food.

MARCH 29

1823 William G. Le Duc is born in Wilkesville, Ohio. Moving to St. Paul in 1850, he would open a law office and bookstore and publish three yearbooks publicizing the territory. In 1857 he would move to Hastings, where his mill is the first to offer spring wheat flour. He would also become a general in the Civil War, serve as U.S. commissioner of agriculture, and help develop the Remington typewriter. Le Duc died in 1917.

1855 In St. Anthony, Minnesota's Republicans hold their first formal meeting, during which they discuss the group's strong antislavery stance.

1916 Eugene J. McCarthy is born in Watkins. He would serve in Congress for over two decades, as a representative from 1949 to 1959 and as a senator from 1959 to 1971. In 1968, McCarthy would challenge President Lyndon Johnson for the Democratic nomination. Running on an anti–Vietnam War platform, McCarthy would make a strong showing in the New Hampshire primary, convincing Johnson to drop out of the race. McCarthy would ultimately lose the party's bid to another Minnesotan, however: Hubert H. Humphrey.

1928 St. Paul's new 2,000-watt radio station KSTP inaugurates its illustrious broadcasting career in the North-

west with a seven-hour program that offers a "wide variety of entertainment" throughout the evening and
runs until 2:00 A.M. the following morning. With begin-
nings in local stations WAMD (launched by Stanley E.
Hubbard in 1923) and KFOY, KSTP would increase its
power to a potential 50,000 watts by 1935 and claim to
be the only high-fidelity, high-power radio transmitter
in the West and the first U.S. station to broadcast to
Australia. *See* April 27

1980 Walter H. Deubener, inventor of the handled
grocery bag, dies in St. Paul. Owner of the S. S. Kresge
store, St. Paul's first cash-and-carry (rather than delivery) grocery store, Deubener devised a bag with a string
around the bottom that would enable shoppers to carry
additional groceries to their destination.

1998 Ferocious tornado touchdowns strike a dozen
communities eastward from Nobles to Wabasha Counties in south-central Minnesota, causing at least one
death and numerous injuries, damaging Comfrey and St.
Peter, and carrying debris many miles away. Extensive
damage in Comfrey forces residents to evacuate from
their homes, while the devastation in St. Peter prompts
an eyewitness to remark that the city looks "decapitated" and a man in far-off Dakota County catches a
falling page from a Le Center school-library book.

MARCH 30

1844 Stillwater's first sawmill, owned by John McKu-
sick, cut its first board, the start of over sixty years of
milling in the city. Stillwater's mills cut primarily white
pine, a wood prized for ornamental carving.

1917 Mayor Louis A. Fritsche holds a meeting at the
New Ulm armory in support of U.S. neutrality in World
War I. Attendees send a peace delegation to Washington,
D.C., but the country declares war in April. *See* July 25

March 30, 1844 Crew of the McKusick-Anderson and Company sawmill, 1886

1924 Prominent Minneapolis industrialist Lewis S. Gillette dies at his winter home near Natchez, Mississippi. An 1876 graduate of the University of Minnesota with bachelor's degrees in both science and engineering, Gillette farmed for three years and then became involved in numerous businesses, including Gillette-Herzog Manufacturing Company (later absorbed by U.S. Steel) and Minneapolis Steel and Machinery Company, at one time the largest industry in the state.

1930 Aviator James H. "Jimmy" Doolittle, touring with his Shell Oil Company plane, visits St. Paul. In 1942, Lieutenant Colonel Doolittle of the U.S. Army Air Corps would command the first air attack on Japan during World War II, leading sixteen B-25 bombers, which had been prepped in St. Paul, from the deck of the aircraft carrier *Hornet*. *See* March 20

1992 Former governor Harold LeVander dies at age eighty-two. Born in Swede Home, Nebraska, LeVander served as governor from 1967 to 1971. During that time he led in the establishment of Minnesota's first state human rights department, a pollution control agency, and the Metropolitan Council for the Twin Cities area. LeVander also opposed establishing a state sales tax, but his veto was twice overridden.

MARCH 31

1810 Newspaper editor James M. Goodhue is born in Hebron, New Hampshire. In 1849 he would establish the territory's first newspaper, the *Minnesota Pioneer,* which promoted the territory both within its borders and beyond. Goodhue died in 1852, but in 1858 Jane Grey Swisshelm would use his press after hers was destroyed (*see* March 24).

March 31, 1810 *James Goodhue, Ernest Galvan, 1875*

1847 For the fourth and final time, Seth Eastman takes command of Fort Snelling. *See* September 30

1918 Roald Amundsen, the famed Norwegian polar explorer who had discovered the South Pole in 1911, addresses a large audience in Duluth about the on-going battle of World War I and appeals to the people of the United States, especially American labor, to "stand behind the President to the last ditch, and to work with 100 per cent efficiency to the end of the war." After remarking that "Norwegians in this country will be pleased to know after the war that they, too, have had a share in the liberation of mankind," Amundsen would continue on a speaking tour of Minnesota and later leave for Norway to prepare for a North Pole expedition.

1934 A shoot-out between outlaw John Dillinger and the Federal Bureau of Investigation occurs at the Lincoln Court Apartments in St. Paul. Dillinger escapes but a few months later is shot to death by F.B.I. agents in Chicago.

APRIL 1

1880 An act of Congress places Fort Ripley Military Reservation in the public domain, making the land available for settlement. The fort, located on the Mississippi River below the mouth of the Crow Wing River, had been established in 1849 and was abandoned by the army in 1878. *See* November 4

1923 Twin City Savings and Loan Association is chartered, a $7 million institution that would assist thousands of area families in becoming homeowners.

1924 Six hundred women attend a Women's Safe Driver Automobile School at the YWCA, sponsored by the *St. Paul Pioneer Press,* the St. Paul Association Safety Division, and the Dunwoody Institute.

APRIL 2

1849 Alexander Ramsey is appointed the first governor of Minnesota Territory. The third choice of President Zachary Taylor, Ramsey is selected after the first, Edward W. McGaughey, is rejected by the Senate, and the second, William S. Pennington, declines the post. Appointed while Congress is out of session, Ramsey is already in Minnesota before the Senate approves his nomination in January 1850.

1982 The last edition of the *Minneapolis Star* is printed, ending sixty-two years of publication. The following day marks the first publication of the *Minneapolis Star and Tribune,* which later becomes the *Minneapolis Star Tribune.*

APRIL 3

1859 In Wright County, Oscar F. Jackson is found not guilty of the murder of his neighbor, Henry A. Wallace. Although there was a good deal of evidence against Jackson, a forensic examination of Wallace's body had not offered sufficient proof of his guilt. After his acquittal, on April 25 an angry mob lynches Jackson in Wallace's house. Because the authorities in Wright County cooperate with the lynching, Governor Henry H. Sibley offers a $500 reward for their capture. These events mark the beginning of the "Wright County War." *See* July 31

1920 St. Paul's Union Station opens.

1970 The former Greyhound bus station in Minneapolis opens its doors as a music club, the Depot. Eight years later it would be renamed First Avenue by Steve McClellan, the booking agent of the club, and Jack Meyers, the club's financial manager. A cornerstone of the city's music scene, First Avenue hosts local and national acts and was featured in Prince's movie *Purple Rain.*

APRIL 4

1888 Abram Elfelt, Minnesota's first Jewish settler, dies.

1893 The Minnesota state flag is adopted, just in time to grace a state-sponsored exhibit at the World's Fair in Chicago. Designed by Amelia H. Center of Minneapolis, the flag depicts the state seal

April 4, 1893

ringed by a wreath of white lady slippers and surrounded by nineteen stars, representing Minnesota as the nineteenth state (after the original thirteen) to be admitted to the Union. The flag would be modified on March 18, 1957, when the white flowers are replaced with pink-and-white lady slippers.

1914 Frederick E. Weyerhaeuser, founder of the timber dynasty, dies in California. At one time he owned two million acres of forestland in Wisconsin, Minnesota, and the Pacific Northwest.

APRIL 5

1830 The first work of fiction set in Minnesota, a collection of stories about fur traders and Indians titled *Tales of the Northwest,* is published in Boston. The author, William J. Snelling, is the son of Josiah Snelling, for whom Fort Snelling is named.

1852 Minnesota goes dry! The citizens of the territory approve a prohibition bill by a vote of 853 to 662. The measure, which would have outlawed the manufacture and sale of alcoholic beverages, is declared unconstitutional in November.

1876 The Bohemian Reading and Educational Society of McLeod County orders a set of Czech readers. The society would meet regularly for more than sixty years, usually in Bohemian Hall, located between the towns of Silver Lake and Hutchinson.

1904 Richard Eberhart is born in Austin. A poet and teacher, he would win the Pulitzer Prize for his *Selected Poems: 1930–1965* in 1966.

1929 A tornado kills three individuals as it moves from Lake Minnetonka across to Minneapolis and Fridley and into Chisago County.

1937 The People's Lobby occupies part of the capitol while demonstrating for a depression relief bill. Two hundred protestors heckle legislators and spend the night in the Senate chamber.

April 5, 1937 The People's Lobby in the Senate
(*St. Paul Pioneer Press*)

APRIL 6

1808 John Jacob Astor forms the American Fur Company, headquartered in New York City. It operates trading posts on Rainy River, at Grand Portage and Grand Marais, as well as on Moose, Basswood, Vermillion, and Little Vermillion Lakes. The company would exist until 1842.

1851 The first known baptism in the upper Mississippi River occurs in St. Paul. Schoolteacher Harriet E. Bishop had written the Baptist Home Missionary Society requesting a preacher, and the Reverend J. P. Parsons arrived in May 1849. The First Baptist Church was organized soon after, holding meetings in the schoolhouse on Jackson Street.

1956 The ore boat *C. L. Austin* picks up the first load of taconite at Silver Bay.

1982 In the Metrodome's first professional baseball game, the Minnesota Twins lose to the Seattle Mariners, 11–7.

APRIL 7

1846 The St. Paul post office is established in Henry Jackson's store.

1866 In Washington, D.C., the Bois Forte Ojibwe sign a treaty ceding their lands in St. Louis and Koochiching Counties and establishing the Nett Lake Reservation.

1924 A warrant is issued for the arrest of Joseph Friedman, operator of the Tower Theater in St. Paul, where he had shown clips of the Dempsey-Gibbons fight. Tommy Gibbons, a St. Paulite who later became Ramsey County sheriff, went fifteen rounds with heavyweight champion Jack Dempsey in Montana on July 4, 1923. Because boxing was illegal in some states at this time, interstate shipment of such pictures was outlawed, and Friedman would be charged with "receiving and exhibiting fight films in violation of Federal law."

APRIL 8

1897 The Red River crests in Moorhead and the floodwaters drive 300 people from their homes.

1905 Christened by Rose Marie Schaller of Hastings, the battleship *Minnesota* is launched at Newport News, Virginia.

1911 Melvin Calvin is born in St. Paul. A biochemist, Calvin would discover the details of the photosynthesis process, for which he would be awarded a Nobel Prize in Chemistry in 1961.

1953 Responding to the first-ever sit-down strike at the Minnesota State Prison at Stillwater, warden Carl Jackson meets the prisoners' demands for nourishing, sanitary food by firing the prison's chef. During the strike, which began on April 7, the locked-down prisoners littered the corridors with trash and broke a number of windows.

APRIL 9

1789 Geographer David Thompson leaves the trading post of Jean Baptiste Cadotte on Red Lake River, beginning the last part of his 4,000-mile survey of the northern wilderness, the first scientific study of the state. Beginning in Grand Portage in August 1788, he had traveled to the upper Missouri River and then through Minnesota, where he wintered with Cadotte. He would complete his trip by returning to Grand Portage in June.

1839 Rose Ann Perry marries James Clewett in St. Paul's first Christian wedding, officiated by the Reverend J. W. Pope, a Methodist missionary at Kaposia.

1849 Minnesota receives word that it is a territory of the United States, a month after the bill is approved by President James K. Polk.

2000 The Andersen Library at the University of Minnesota opens, named in honor of Elmer L. Andersen, former governor, university regent, and bibliophile. Library materials from around the state are stored in two manmade caverns, each two stories high and two football fields long, carved into the sandstone bluffs along the Mississippi River.

April 8, 1905

APRIL 10

1855 Jacob Fjelde is born in Norway. He would sculpt the work *Hiawatha and Minnehaha,* displayed in Minnehaha Park, Minneapolis, and the statue of Ole Bull, located in Loring Park, Minneapolis.

1895 The ocean liner *St. Paul* is launched at last. The International Navigation Company had intended to launch the ship on March 25, inviting seventy dignitaries to Philadelphia for the occasion. After the champagne bottle was broken, however, the ship refused to budge.

APRIL 11

1680 Father Louis Hennepin, exploring the Mississippi River north from Illinois by canoe, is captured by a group of Dakota. During his captivity he is the first white man to see the Falls of St. Anthony, which he names for his patron saint. On July 25, explorer Daniel Greysolon, the Sieur Du Luth, would arrange for Hennepin's release.

April 11, 1680 *Father Hennepin at the Falls of St. Anthony,* Douglas Volk, 1905

APRIL 12

1923 St. Paul's first automatic traffic signal, on a pedestal about ten feet high, begins operating at Fifth and St. Peter Streets.

1937 Dennis J. Banks is born on Leech Lake Indian Reservation. An Indian activist, he would be one of the founders of the American Indian Movement (AIM) in 1968, along with Clyde and Vernon Bellecourt (from White Earth Reservation) and George Mitchell. Intent on raising awareness of the plight of Indians, the members of AIM would participate in the occupation of Alcatraz Island in San Francisco (*see* November 20), Wounded Knee in South Dakota, and the Bureau of Indian Affairs headquarters in Washington, D.C. For these activities, Banks would spend time in prison, after which he would remain active in Indian matters.

1976 A two-month strike by members of the Graphic Arts International Union is settled when several hundred bookbinders and four Twin Cities–area envelope companies reach an accord about a new two-year contract that provides hourly pay increases of 45 cents the first year and 50 cents the second year; the strikers had settled earlier with a fifth company. *See* February 13

APRIL 13

1849 The army officially occupies Fort Gaines, later renamed Fort Ripley. The post had been built to monitor the Winnebago (Ho-Chunk), recently transferred from Iowa, and to maintain peace between Ojibwe and Dakota bands.

1907 Harold E. Stassen is born in West St. Paul. Elected governor at age thirty-two, he would be the youngest individual to hold that office, from 1939 to 1943. He would resign as governor to serve as lieutenant commander in the navy during World War II. His long and distinguished career in public service would unfortunately be overshadowed by a string of defeats as he sought the Republican nomination for president. He died in 2001.

1967 Rod Carew plays his first major league baseball game with the Minnesota Twins, hitting a single.

1993 The North Stars professional hockey team plays its final game in the Met Center against the Chicago Blackhawks, losing 3–2. The team moves to Dallas later that year.

APRIL 14

1805 Pine City records a high temperature of 108 degrees.

1861 Minnesota is the first state to offer troops at the outbreak of the Civil War. Governor Alexander Ramsey is in Washington, D.C., when word of the attack on Fort Sumter arrives, and he meets with Simon Cameron, the secretary of war, and offers one thousand Minnesota soldiers for the country's defense. He then telegraphs Lieutenant Governor Ignatius Donnelly, who summons volunteers from across the state. This group of men becomes the famous First Minnesota Regiment. *See* July 2

1870 The St. Paul Academy of Natural Sciences is formed. The group would suspend activities after the capitol fire of 1883 destroys its collection, reorganize in 1890, and hand over its new collection to the St. Paul Institute of Science and Letters in 1907. The institute would evolve into the Science Museum of Minnesota.

1894 Organizer Eugene Debs calls a strike by the workers of the Great Northern Railway. The railroad had imposed three wage cuts despite profits of over five million dollars the previous year. As the strike progresses, other railroads—following the lead of the Great Northern in other strike situations—refuse to help company president James J. Hill move his stalled trains. On May 1 Charles A. Pillsbury negotiates an agreement between the strikers and Hill, who consents to restore seventy-five percent of the wage cuts made earlier.

1901 A poker game in Granite Falls ends in violence. After playing for several hours, local dentist S. Wintner notices that his two kings have lost to two aces held by St. Paul card sharp William Lenard, the "Irish Lord," eight times in succession. Wintner produces a revolver and, when Lenard proclaims his innocence, fatally shoots him. At the trial later that year Frank Nye, for the defense, makes the creative assertion that, gambling being a felony, Dr. Wintner had the right to stop such an act, with violence if necessary. The jury, perhaps unsympathetic to a crooked gambler, finds Wintner not guilty.

1977 The Minnesota Asian American Project (MAAP), an organization that promotes civil rights, affirmative action, and legal services for the Asian community, is officially incorporated by Dennis Tachiki, Gloria Kumagai, and Daniel Matsumoto.

APRIL 15

1892 The Lake Traverse Reservation—600,000 acres in the Dakotas, across the western Minnesota border from Browns Valley—is opened to white settlement. In a scene reminiscent of the Oklahoma land rush, a pistol is shot at noon and the stampede of prospective settlers begins.

1912 The schoolchildren of St. Paul select the city's official flower, the sweet pea, in an election sponsored by the city's women's clubs. Other choices included the coreopsis, marigold, petunia, and aster. News of their selection is overshadowed by reports of the *Titanic's* sinking.

1916 The first regulated trout season opens.

1944 The Farmer-Labor Party and the state Democratic Party agree to merge at their joint convention, and a slate of candidates is quickly chosen to meet the filing deadline two days later. The Democratic-Farmer-Labor (DFL) Party is unique to Minnesota.

APRIL 16

1901 While in Seattle on business, St. Paul rail tycoon James J. Hill learns that Edward H. Harriman, in New York, is buying up shares of the Northern Pacific Railroad, trying to wrest control of the company from Hill. Hill orders all trains to give right of way to his express train and heads east for New York, making the 1,800-mile trip from Seattle to St. Paul in 45 hours and 50 minutes, 21 hours under the average time. From there Hill continues to New York and thwarts the deal. During the buying frenzy, Northern Pacific shares rise from under $100 to a peak of $1,000 on May 9.

1917 The Minnesota Commission of Public Safety is formed by the legislature to "protect life and property and to aid in the prosecution of the war." Seeking to achieve one hundred percent patriotism, the commission uses its sweeping powers to harass non-English-speaking immigrants and members of the Nonpartisan League. *See* June 14 and August 25

1927 The Mesaba Railway Coach Company stops providing streetcar service between the towns of Hibbing and Gilbert. *See* December 17

1991 Marge Anderson becomes chief executive of the Mille Lacs Band of Ojibwe. Emphasizing traditional government, education, and cultural preservation, Anderson would be a leader in the successful nine-year battle to preserve rights granted by an 1837 treaty to hunt and fish in and around Mille Lacs. *See* March 24

APRIL 17

1856 The Minnesota Pioneer Guard, the state's first volunteer military company, is organized in St. Paul. This group would become Company A of the First Minnesota Regiment.

1895 Hasting's spiral bridge opens. It would carry horse and automobile traffic into the heart of the city for over fifty years and be replaced by a straight bridge in 1951.

April 17, 1895

1965 The Mississippi River crests in St. Paul at 25.8 feet, nearly ten feet above flood stage. Three days earlier, President Lyndon B. Johnson had visited St. Paul to survey damages from record flooding along the Minnesota and Mississippi Rivers. In the flood's wake, losses are estimated at $88 million and numerous counties across the state are declared federal disaster areas.

1990 The Minnesota State Lottery begins selling instant tickets, and within four months sales reach $100 million.

1997 The Red River crests at 39.5 feet, 22.5 feet above flood stage at Fargo, breaking a 100-year-old record. Continuing into Grand Forks, North Dakota, and East Grand Forks, Minnesota, on April 21 the flood pushes water levels to 54.2 feet, 26.2 feet above flood stage. The worst flooding in the area in over a century, it causes more than one billion dollars of damages and displaces 47,000 of the 50,000 residents of Grand Forks.

2000 George Morrison, abstract painter and sculptor, dies. Born at Grand Portage Indian Reservation in 1919, Morrison had pursued a career in art that took him to New York, Paris, Ohio, and Rhode Island. In 1970 he returned to Minnesota, where he taught American Indian studies and studio arts at the University of Minnesota for fifteen years. His works are in the collections of many galleries, including the Art Institute of Chicago, the Minneapolis Institute of Arts, the Walker Art Center, and the Whitney Museum of American Art.

APRIL 18

1807 The first recorded mention of farming by white Minnesotans is made in a letter written by George H. Monk, who notes crops of potatoes, oats, cabbages, beets, beans, pumpkins, and Indian corn being cultivated at the North West Company's fur trading posts on Sandy and Leech Lakes.

1820 Soldiers at Fort St. Anthony (later Snelling) view Minnesota's first officially recorded tornado, which damages the barracks roof.

1888 In an unprecedented move, two hundred and sixty female employees at the clothing factory of Shotwell, Clerihew & Lothman on Second Street in Minneapolis walk out, demanding that piece rates, which had been cut at the first of the year, be restored. Although the company agrees to make small reforms, few of the strikers return to work. Due to lack of workers or to a boycott by sympathetic community members, Shotwell, Clerihew & Lothman would close its doors a few months later.

APRIL 19

1858 The Yankton Dakota cede the area around their pipestone quarry in Pipestone County to the United States but retain free access to the quarry grounds.

1865 On a national day of mourning for President Abraham Lincoln, St. Paul businesses close and city officials wear black armbands. The courthouse is draped in black for thirty days.

1866 At Fort Wadsworth, South Dakota, Samuel J. Brown receives word that an Indian raid is headed for settlements in Minnesota. He rides sixty miles to alert the settlers, only to find that the report is erroneous. He then makes a return trip, riding through a blizzard to tell people that no attack is imminent. This ride cripples him for life. The Sam Brown monument in Traverse County preserves his memory.

1902 Duluth's public library opens.

1945 "Hail! Minnesota" becomes the state song. Written by two University of Minnesota students in 1904 and 1905, it is also the university's official song.

APRIL 20

1836 Wisconsin Territory is established, extending westward to the Missouri River, including the area of present-day Minnesota. Two years later the land west of the Mississippi River becomes part of Iowa Territory.

1891 Itasca State Park, the state's first, is established. Its 32,000 acres preserve more than 300 lakes as well as the headwaters of the Mississippi River.

1899 Minnesota passes the nation's first direct primary election law, which applies to candidates running for city and county offices in counties with a population of 200,000 or more (at the time, only Hennepin County qualifies). Wisconsin would be the first state to make statewide direct primaries the law in 1903; while Minnesota had drafted similar legislation applicable to city and county offices in 1901, the state's officers and U.S. senators would not be elected by direct primary until 1912.

1921 The legislature passes the Minnesota Lynching Bill, which stipulates that a law enforcement officer can be removed from duty for not stopping a lynching and that damages may be recovered by the victim's family. Authored by civic activist Nellie G. Francis, this bill is a response to the Duluth lynchings of 1920. *See* June 15

1949 Jessica Lange is born in Cloquet. In 1995 she would win an Oscar Award for best actress for her performance in the movie *Blue Sky.*

APRIL 21

1883 Clarence "Cap" Wigington is born in Kansas. Minnesota's first African American registered architect and the nation's first African American municipal architect, he would design civic and residential buildings in St. Paul and create six designs for St. Paul Winter Carnival ice palaces during his lengthy career. He died on July 7, 1967.

1891 James K. Hilyard, an early African American entrepreneur and intellectual, dies in St. Paul. In addition to being co-founder of the *Western Appeal,* one of Minnesota's first black-owned newspapers, Hilyard, by active recruitment through newspapers and personal connections, was largely responsible for the influx of African American professionals into the state in the 1800s.

1899 The legislature creates a state public library commission, which establishes a system of traveling libraries to serve rural areas.

1940 World famous soprano Lily Pons gives a concert as her husband, Andre Kostelanetz, conducts the Minneapolis Symphony Orchestra.

1961 The Minnesota Twins (formerly the Washington Senators) play their first game at Metropolitan Stadium, losing to the new Washington Senators, 5–3.

APRIL 22

1818 Cadwallader C. Washburn is born in Livermore, Maine. A pioneer in the state's flour-milling industry, Washburn would build his first mill at St. Anthony Falls in 1866 and his Washburn-Crosby Company would market Gold Medal flour. He died in 1882.

1903 Alexander Ramsey dies at age eighty-eight. During his distinguished political career, Ramsey served as Minnesota's first territorial governor and second state governor, negotiated major land sales from the Dakota and Ojibwe, and served in the U.S. Senate and as secretary of war. A founder of the Minnesota Historical Society, he was its president at the time of his death.

April 22, 1903

1911 Governor Adolph O. Eberhart signs a law abolishing the death penalty in Minnesota. *See* February 13

APRIL 23

1857 Samuel Medary takes office as Minnesota's third and final territorial governor. He steps down thirteen months later when Minnesota becomes a state and

Henry H. Sibley is elected governor. Medary would later become territorial governor of Kansas. He died in Columbus, Ohio, in 1864.

1881 A group of Belgian colonists, led by Angelus Van Hee, arrives at Grandview in Lyon County. The village is renamed Ghent in honor of these settlers, who had been invited to the state by Bishop John Ireland.

1897 The state government allocates $5,000 to open the Gillette State Hospital for Crippled Children in St. Paul. Named for Dr. Arthur J. Gillette, it is the first state-funded hospital of its kind in the nation.

1992 Governor Arne H. Carlson signs the HealthRight bill into law. Providing medical insurance for low-income Minnesotans, the program is now known as MinnesotaCare. *See* October 1

APRIL 24

1846 Seth Eastman becomes commander of Fort Snelling for a third time, holding the post until May 14. *See* March 31

1914 In a scene reminiscent of a biblical plague, thousands of frogs overrun Melrose. The *Melrose Beacon* explains that the frogs' annual migratory pattern runs through town.

1956 The first baseball game is played at Metropolitan Stadium, and the Wichita Braves beat the Minneapolis Millers, 5–3.

APRIL 25

1892 Maud Hart Lovelace is born in Mankato. She is remembered as author of the Betsy-Tacy books, a series of stories for young readers set in early twentieth-century Mankato. In 1979, the Mankato Friends of the

Library Association established the Maud Hart Lovelace Book Award for children's books.

April 25, 1892

1924 Λ race to break the world record for the longest distance traveled in a hot air balloon ends in Rochester as the winner, W. T. Van Orman, lands the *Goodyear III* just under the world record distance (1,179.9 miles). The race had begun in San Antonio, Texas, and the three top finishers would soon represent the United States at the international competition in Brussels, Belgium.

APRIL 26

1840 Father Lucien Galtier arrives in St. Peter's (Mendota) to organize a Catholic church. He soon builds a chapel down the river at the settlement that becomes known as St. Paul. *See* November 1

1877 Governor John S. Pillsbury appoints this day for prayer to relieve the state from the swarms of Rocky Mountain locusts that had plagued farmers for four years. The locusts linger until August, when they disappear. *See* June 12

1896 Edward J. Thye is born near Frederick, South Dakota. Thye would succeed Harold E. Stassen (*see* April 13) to become the twenty-sixth governor of the state and, notably, the first farmer to hold the office. During his term, he would reduce the state debt, increase old-age assistance, expand state institutions, establish a human rights commission, and approve a health-care plan for state employees. As a Republican senator from 1947 to 1958, he would be one of seven to sign Margaret Chase Smith's "declaration of conscience" against Joseph McCarthy. He died at his farm near Northfield on August 28, 1969.

1924 In a prohibition scandal, two agents are arrested for stealing $100,000 in confiscated liquor that had been stored in a Minneapolis warehouse. Eventually, four agents are suspended and warrants are issued for seven others.

1972 Vietnam War protestors stage a demonstration at Honeywell, Inc., which at the time manufactured fragmentation bombs.

APRIL 27

1915 A fire destroys the St. Paul Public Library at Seventh and Wabasha Streets. The library resides in the old House of Hope Presbyterian Church building at Fifth and Exchange Streets and later moves into its present building across from Rice Park.

1948 KSTP-TV makes the first commercial television broadcast in Minnesota, showing the Minneapolis Millers' baseball game from Nicollet Park for the approximately 2,500 owners of television sets in the Twin Cities. Station owner Stanley E. Hubbard had experimented with television since the 1930s. *See* March 29

1967 Dr. Martin Luther King, Jr., criticizes U.S. involvement in the Vietnam War during a speech at the University of Minnesota, St. Paul campus.

APRIL 28

1849 James M. Goodhue publishes the first issue of the *Minnesota Pioneer,* the territory's first newspaper.

1871 A lake monster is seen swimming in Lake Pepin.

1882 Frank McManus, charged with molesting a four-year-old girl, is lynched by a mob at the old Central High School, Minneapolis.

April 28, 1916

1916 Arbor Day is renamed "Loring Day," and over one thousand elms are planted in honor of Charles M. Loring, visionary of Minneapolis's park system. *See* November 13

APRIL 29

1816 Congress passes a law that extends fur-trading licenses to U.S. citizens only. Soon after, John J. Astor's American Fur Company pushes out its British rivals, the Hudson's Bay and North West Companies.

1858 Entertainer Daniel D. Emmett obtains a business license for his "Ethiopean Minstrels." Emmett visited the state often in the 1850s while his brother Lafayette served as chief justice of the Minnesota Supreme Court, and it is believed that while here he wrote an early version of "Dixie," which was performed at Russell C. Munger's music store in St. Paul.

April 29, 1816 *The Rival Companies Soliciting Trade*

APRIL 30

1803 The Louisiana Purchase is signed, transferring to the United States territory that includes present-day Minnesota west of the Mississippi River.

1853 Troops from the U.S. Sixth Infantry begin constructing Fort Ridgely, having arrived from Fort Snelling on the steamer *West Newton* the previous evening. The fort is built to watch over the Dakota reservation in the Minnesota River valley and would be a focal point during the U.S.–Dakota War of 1862. Secretary of War Jefferson Davis names the fort for three Ridgelys who were killed in the Mexican War.

1901 Charles Joy makes the first automobile ascent of St. Paul's Selby Hill, at a speed of eight to ten miles per hour.

1961 In his first home run for the Minnesota Twins baseball team, Harmon Killebrew hits the ball 467 feet.

1967 Nine tornadoes strike southern Minnesota, particularly the towns of Waseca, Owatonna, and Albert Lea, killing thirteen people.

MAY 1

1840 Joseph Haskell finishes constructing his farmhouse near Afton. His is the first commercial farm north of Prairie du Chien.

1873 St. Paul character "Old Bets" dies at age eighty-five. The Dakota woman was a familiar sight in early St. Paul and made her living by begging and charging tourists who photographed her.

1896 Three-quarters of Red Lake Indian Reservation land—the region north and east of Thirteen Towns (Badger, Brandsvold, Chester, Columbia, Eden, Fosston, Hill River, King, Knute, Lessor, Queen, Rosebud, and Sletten) in Polk County—is opened to white settlement.

1926 Sauk Centre's Sinclair Lewis declines the Pulitzer Prize for the novel *Arrowsmith,* saying that awards inhibit creativity and make writers lazy. He would, however, feel differently a few years later (*see* December 10).

1933 Prompted by Governor Floyd B. Olson, the legislature passes an emergency law stopping farm foreclosure sales. The Great Depression and the dust bowl had hurt farmers throughout the nation, and they had responded to foreclosures by organizing the Farmers' Holiday, which attempted to stop the sale of farm products until prices rose. Willmar's John Bosch, who revered the nonviolent ideas of Mohandas Gandhi, led the state's Farmers' Holiday movement.

1976 St. Paul's Frank Boyd Park is dedicated to a "fighter for his class, his race, and his union." Born in Kansas, Boyd moved to Minnesota in 1904 and joined the Brotherhood of Sleeping Car Porters Union in 1925, rising to secretary-treasurer in the organization. Active in DFL politics, he was one of the first two African Americans to cast votes in the Electoral College, in 1944. He died on May 2, 1962.

May 1, 1976 Frank Boyd in his home, 1951

MAY 2

1670 The Hudson's Bay Company is chartered in London. The company's territory is the Hudson Bay watershed, including northern Minnesota, but no posts would be established in present-day Minnesota until a century later, and the North West, XY, and American Fur Companies would play a larger role in the territory's fur trade.

1878 An explosion at the Washburn "A" flour mill in Minneapolis kills eighteen workers. Studies show that flour dust is highly explosive, and the company begins replacing millstones with rollers, which reduce the fire hazard and revolutionize the flour industry.

1903 Automobile license Number One is issued for a Packard owned by R. C. Wright of St. Paul.

1976 A baseball game is cancelled at Metropolitan Stadium due to snow accumulation of one inch, the latest snow-out in Twins history. True Minnesotans would have played the game!

1986 The Steger International Polar Expedition, led by Will Steger and Paul Schurke of Ely, reaches the North Pole, and team member Ann Bancroft of St. Paul is the first woman to cross the Arctic to the pole. *See* January 14

1992 Nobel laureate Rigoberta Menchú of Guatemala visits the Twin Cities as a guest of the Minneapolis American Indian Center.

May 2, 1878 Explosion at the Washburn "A" mill

MAY 3

1865 John Campbell, head of an outlaw band that had murdered the Jewett family of Garden City, is hanged by a crowd of eight hundred angry men in Mankato. Caught in Mr. Jewett's clothes, Campbell claims during his mock trial that Indians had committed the crime, captured him, and forced him to wear the victim's clothes. The "jury" finds him guilty but recommends waiting for a real trial before handing down his punishment. The mob persists, however, and Campbell eventually confesses to the crime.

1959 After passing through the St. Lawrence Seaway, which had opened on April 25, the British freighter *Ramon de Larrinaga* becomes the first deep draft ocean ship to enter Duluth's harbor.

1989 Charlotte Day, founder of the Red School House (St. Paul), dies. A member of the Bois Forte Band of Ojibwe, Day founded the school to meet the needs of American Indian children, teaching Indian languages and culture as well as English reading and math skills in Indian contexts.

MAY 4

1863 In response to a federal law mandating that all Dakota be removed from the state as punishment for the U.S.–Dakota War, 1,310 captives at Fort Snelling, mostly women and children, are loaded onto two steamboats to be transported to a reservation on Crow Creek in southeastern Dakota Territory. Soon after arriving at the reservation, many would die of disease and hunger.

1888 The Catholic Archdiocese of St. Paul is established.

1925 St. Paul's Ford Motor Company plant assembles its first car, which St. Paul mayor Arthur E. Nelson, Minneapolis mayor George E. Leach, and Ford executives A. W. Bendick and V. E. Nystrom ride in during a ceremony. The plant soon produces five hundred cars each day.

May 4, 1925

1975 The Minnesota Twins retire number 3 in honor of Harmon Killebrew.

1984 During a Minnesota Twins baseball game, Dave Kingman hits a ball into the roof of the Metrodome, where it is lodged in a pocket. He is awarded a ground-rule double.

MAY 5

1820 After a terrible winter in which forty of his one hundred men die, probably from scurvy, Colonel Henry Leavenworth moves his soldiers to Camp Coldwater, about a mile northwest of the proposed site of Fort St. Anthony (later Snelling), which the troops would soon construct.

1880 Lightning strikes the Faribault gasworks, destroying 1,000 gallons of naphtha, used to power the city's gaslights.

1884 Charles Albert "Chief" Bender is born in Brainerd. The Ojibwe pitcher would be the first Minnesotan inducted into the Baseball Hall of Fame. He would pitch in five World Series for the Philadelphia Athletics, and his career record is 212 wins and 127 losses.

1973 Father Frank F. Perkovich celebrates Minnesota's first polka mass at Resurrection Catholic Church in Eveleth. Drawing on his Slovenian and Croatian roots, Perkovich had arranged traditional folk music and adapted hymns in English, bringing the polka mass to the Iron Range and later celebrating it in venues around the world.

1974 In the Heart of the Beast Puppet Theater presents its first Minneapolis May Day Parade. Part peaceful protest, part carnival, the parade is a South Minneapolis tradition, occurring every year on the first Sunday of May.

May 5, 1974 *Community,* Gaylord Schanilec, 1990

MAY 6

1834 Two Presbyterian missionaries from Connecticut, Samuel W. and Gideon H. Pond, arrive at Fort Snelling and soon begin working with the Dakota on the shores of Lake Calhoun. The Ponds would develop a Dakota alphabet, publish a Dakota newspaper, and record many traditional Dakota practices during their years as missionaries in Minnesota.

1840 Soldiers expel Selkirker squatters from the Fort Snelling military reservation and burn their cabins. Although the Selkirkers had moved to escape the fort's boundaries the year before, a new survey showed that they remained within the military's jurisdiction. The settlers then relocate to the site that would become the city of St. Paul. *See* August 30

1865 A group of Cutlerites, a branch of the Mormon Church that had faced discrimination elsewhere, arrive at Clitherall Lake and lay the foundations for the first permanent settlement in Otter Tail County.

1896 Groundbreaking ceremonies are held for the present capitol building.

1965 Windstorms in northern Twin Cities suburbs kill fourteen people and cause $57 million in damages.

May 6, 1896

MAY 7

1800 Eastern Minnesota is organized as part of Indian Territory by an act of Congress. *See* February 3

1850 The *Anthony Wayne* is the first steamboat to reach the Falls of St. Anthony, winning a prize of $200.

1900 Two days after arriving in Faribault with his new locomobile, an expensive two-seat roadster, Dr. R. N. Jackson is involved in an accident, breaking his ribs and collarbone.

MAY 8

1881 Encouraged by Bishop John Ireland and sponsored by John Sweetman, visionary leader of the Irish-American Colonization Company, a group of Irish farmers settle in Currie, Murray County.

1910 Governor Adolf O. Eberhart declares Minnesota's first Mother's Day holiday.

1924 Ice in Duluth's harbor traps thirteen ships, confining 400 individuals aboard.

1968 Future baseball hall-of-famer James Augustus "Catfish" Hunter, pitching for the Oakland Athletics, throws a no-hitter against the Minnesota Twins. The final score is 4–0.

MAY 9

1887 The Flint Furniture factory in Faribault burns. Built in 1856, the factory was the first in the state to manufacture items for wholesale trade.

1918 Orville Freeman is born in Minneapolis. He would serve as the state's governor from 1955 to 1961 and later as U.S. secretary of agriculture. While governor, he would respond to the 1959 strike at the Wilson & Company packinghouse in Albert Lea by declaring martial law and closing the plant. *See* November 3

1921 Daniel Berrigan is born in Virginia (Minn.). An author and a radical Catholic priest, Berrigan would write about social responsibility and play an active role in the antiwar movement during the Vietnam era and later protest nuclear armament. His brother Philip, also a radical priest, was born October 5, 1923.

2001 The Dalai Lama Tenzin Guyatso, head of state and spiritual leader of the Tibetan community worldwide, visits the Twin Cities and shares his message of compassion, tolerance, kindness, and peace.

MAY 10

1823 The *Virginia* is the first steamboat to reach Fort St. Anthony (later Snelling), having made the 729-mile-trip from St. Louis in twenty days. Among the *Virginia*'s passengers is Italian adventurer Giacomo C. Beltrami. *See* August 31

1827 William Windom is born in Belmont City, Ohio. Settling in Winona in 1855, Windom would represent Minnesota in the U.S. Congress as both a congressman and a senator, and he would be secretary of the treasury under Presidents James A. Garfield and Benjamin Harrison. His likeness appears on the 1891 two-dollar bill, and Windom in Cottonwood County is named for him. He died in 1891.

1902 The St. Paul Saints minor league baseball team beats the Indianapolis Indians 4–0 in the first American Association game at Lexington Park.

1941 Charles A. Lindbergh, Jr., is the featured speaker at a large America First rally in Minneapolis. The America First Committee promoted U.S. isolationism during the years leading up to World War II. Lindbergh's antiwar activity reduced his stature in many people's eyes, but after war was declared he would dedicate himself to the battle for victory, flying fifty missions in the Pacific. *See* May 20

1993 Ralph Ware, Jr., who played an instrumental role in creating the Heart of the Earth School, dies in Oklahoma. Founded in 1972, the Heart of the Earth School at the Center for American Indian Education in Minneapolis was the nation's first alternative school for Native Americans. It still emphasizes individual learning styles and parent and community involvement in education. Ware, a Kiowa, was born in Lawton, Oklahoma.

2000 St. Augusta Township in rural Stearns County becomes the city of Ventura as five new city officials take the oath of office to serve this community, which was named for Governor Jesse Ventura as part of a political strategy to prevent annexation attempts by St. Cloud, the county seat. The former township clerk comments,

"We are about to form the newest city in the state of Minnesota." In November voters would overwhelmingly choose to change the city's name from Ventura to St. Augusta.

MAY 11

1844 Samuel R. Van Sant is born in Rock Island, Illinois. The state's fifteenth governor, serving from 1901 to 1905, he would establish the State Board of Control to handle issues affecting criminals and the mentally disabled. He died on October 3, 1936, in Attica, Indiana.

1858 Minnesota becomes the thirty-second state. The enabling act for statehood had been passed on February 26, 1857, and the state's constitution (*see* August 29) was written that summer and ratified in October. Full statehood had been held up by southern senators who wanted Kansas to enter the Union as a slave state. Finally approved by Congress, the bill is signed by President James Buchanan. Word of statehood would not reach St. Paul until May 13.

1869 The Lindbergh colony of Swedish settlers, headed by Måns Olsson Lindbergh, arrives in St. Paul. The group would eventually settle in Sherburne County.

MAY 12

1806 James Shields is born in Ireland. He would be a U.S. senator for three different states: Illinois, Minnesota, and Missouri. After moving to Faribault in 1855, he would be one of the first two senators selected by the state's legislature, and while in office he would encourage Irish immigration to Minnesota. Shieldsville in Rice County is named for him. He died in 1879.

MAY 13

1824 General Winfield Scott arrives to inspect Fort St. Anthony. Impressed with what he sees, he suggests that the fort be renamed for Colonel Josiah Snelling, supervisor of its construction.

1858 The survey for a road from St. Cloud to Breckenridge begins, following the East Plains trail of the Red River oxcarts. Today that road is Highway 52.

1956 Elvis Presley performs at the Minneapolis Auditorium for a crowd of 3,000.

MAY 14

1852 After weeks of rain, a mudslide covers much of Stillwater, destroying barns, shops, homes, and three rafts of lumber but injuring no one. Two cows in a barn keep their feet during the slide, and afterwards they walk out of a second-story window. In all, the slide covers five acres of ground to a depth of one to twenty feet. Prior to the slide, this land had been low and boggy, selling for about $1.25 an acre. After the slide the land is more useable, and its value rises to $500 an acre. Most of the business area of present-day Stillwater is built on this location.

1988 The University of Minnesota Law School's one hundredth class graduates with 234 candidates: 98 women and 136 men. *See* June 6

MAY 15

1896 The St. Paul Saints, at the time a Western League professional baseball team, play their first home game at Aurora Park, beating the Grand Rapids Yellow Jackets 17–0.

MAY 16

1850 The Reverend Edward D. Neill's Presbyterian chapel is destroyed in St. Paul's first fire.

1898 The Twelfth, Thirteenth, and Fourteenth Regiments of the Minnesota Volunteer Infantry depart for training to fight in the Spanish-American War. Only the Thirteenth Regiment would see combat, in the Philippines. *See* August 7

1938 The sewage disposal plant on Pig's Eye Island in St. Paul is dedicated. Originally considered progressive, it later becomes a Superfund site.

MAY 17

1837 Methodist missionary Alfred Brunson arrives at Fort Snelling. He would establish the first Methodist mission in Minnesota at Kaposia (now South St. Paul). *See* October 15

MAY 18

1905 Five doctors at St. Paul's Ancker Hospital strike to protest the tyrannical ways of hospital director Dr. Arthur Ancker, who had suspended Dr. William Frost on "unsubstantiated grounds." The striking doctors are later dishonorably discharged from their duties. On May 15, 1923, Ancker would die of a heart attack while screaming at two surgeons he accused of not properly washing their hands. The Minnesota History Center now stands on the site of his hospital.

1931 Minneapolis-born aviator Charles "Speed" Holman is killed during an air show in Omaha. A pioneer of aviation, his best-known aerial stunt was looping and he had won the U.S. air speed trials in 1930. At his funeral, four 109th Air Squadron planes flew in the first recorded Missing Man formation, a vacant spot reserved in Holman's memory. Holman Field at the St. Paul Downtown Airport is named in his honor.

May 18, 1931 Speed Holman in his Laird biplane, ca. 1930

MAY 19

1857 Duluth is incorporated as a town, having been platted (surveyed and mapped) and named the previous year.

1860 Alexander Ramsey and other Republican notables travel from Chicago to Springfield, Illinois, to formally offer Abraham Lincoln the Republican presidential nomination.

1968 Adolf Dehn, printmaker and artist, dies in his studio in New York. Born in Waterville, he was known for his satirical lithographs of high society.

MAY 20

1882 Ten thousand trout and salmon are planted in Rice County's Cedar Lake.

1902 The State Federation of Afro-American Women's Clubs is organized in St. Paul, with the goal of uniting clubs for better communication and productivity. Representatives from clubs in St. Paul, Minneapolis, and Duluth attend the meeting.

1927 Little Falls native Charles A. Lindbergh, Jr., begins his famous trans-Atlantic flight to Paris, which takes thirty-three and one-half hours. *See* May 10

May 20, 1927

MAY 21

1839 Donald McDonald receives the first steamboat shipment of cargo to the settlement that would become St. Paul. Six barrels of whiskey are delivered to McDonald's shop, the "Half-Way House," in Fountain Cave.

1882 Mark Twain visits St. Paul while compiling research for his book *Life on the Mississippi,* which he publishes the following year.

1934 During the Minneapolis teamsters' strike, violence erupts between picketers blocking trucks driven by non-unionists and an army hired by the Citizens Alliance, a union of local employers. Thirty Minneapolis policemen and a number of army deputies are hospitalized after the brawl. *See* July 20

1961 In Metropolitan Stadium's first sellout, the Minnesota Twins baseball team loses a doubleheader to the Cleveland Indians before a crowd of 30,999.

1972 Forestville State Park is formally dedicated, having been open to the public since 1968.

MAY 22

1888 Minneapolis architect LeRoy S. Buffington, the "Father of the Skyscraper," patents a construction method involving a steel skeleton that allows structures to be built to any height.

1945 The Rice County Historical Society acquires the Alexander Faribault House, which it maintains as a historic site in Faribault. The house was the first built in Rice County, at the confluence of the Cannon and Straight Rivers.

MAY 23

1857 Twelve counties are created. Six are named for individuals important to the state's history: Aitkin is for William A. Aitkin (also spelled Aitken), who ran an American Fur Company post on Sandy Lake; Carlton honors Reuben B. Carlton, a Fond du Lac pioneer; Jackson is for either pioneer merchant Henry Jackson (*see* February 11) or President Andrew Jackson; Martin is for either Connecticut investor Henry Martin, who owned land in the area, or Wisconsin territorial delegate Morgan L. Martin, who introduced legislation to create Minnesota Territory; Murray County commemorates St. Paul attorney and politician William P. Murray; Nobles is for wagon maker, road builder, and politician William H. Nobles.

Six are translations of native names or refer to landscape features: Anoka is the Dakota word for "on both sides," because the city after which the county is named is on both banks of the Rum River; Cottonwood is for the river and its trees; Crow Wing is from the French *rivière à l'Aile de Corbeau,* which is a translation of the Ojibwe place name; *Mille Lacs* means "thousand lakes"; Pipestone refers to the quarry within its boundaries, and Rock to the county's quartzite formation. The names of Pipestone and Rock Counties originally are transposed, and the legislature would correct the error on February 20, 1862.

1879 James J. Hill, Norman W. Kittson, and others combine several troubled railroads into the St. Paul, Minneapolis and Manitoba Railroad, totaling 560 miles of track. This railroad would become the Great Northern Railway on February 1, 1890, and would eventually be part of the Burlington Northern, later the Burlington Northern Santa Fe.

1884 Cannon Falls' first fire starts in A. Sayer's store and, despite a bucket brigade formed by the village's residents, much of the downtown is destroyed.

1908 After a ten-year campaign by the Minnesota Federation of Women's Clubs, the Minnesota National Forest (now Chippewa National Forest) is created. *See* July 5

MAY 24

1841 Christopher Carli, the first non-military doctor to settle permanently in the territory, and his wife Lydia move to the site that is now Stillwater. He helps build the town's first log cabin and opens the town's first pharmacy and bank.

1858 The first group of state officers, including Henry H. Sibley as governor, is installed.

1941 Robert Zimmerman is born in Duluth. He would become iconic singer and songwriter Bob Dylan, his surname borrowed from Welsh poet Dylan Thomas. Originally a folk singer, this versatile artist would also shift between rock and gospel. An inductee to the Rock and Roll Hall of Fame, Dylan has written over 500 songs and earned a number of Grammy Awards. After

achieving fame, he did not perform in Duluth until
October 22, 1998.

MAY 25

1850 The *Governor Ramsey* takes the first steamboat trip
on the Mississippi River above the Falls of St. Anthony.
Built in St. Anthony, the steamboat makes a twice-
weekly run from the falls to Sauk Rapids.

1859 Author Bayard Taylor lectures in Minneapolis. A
portion of the proceeds from his talk funds the Young
Men's Literary Association, which would buy the books
that form the original collection of the Minneapolis
Public Library.

1867 *The Minneapolis Daily Tribune* is first published.

1877 During the grasshopper plague, the state declares
a bounty of one dollar for each bushel of grasshopper
eggs collected by this date. *See* April 26

1926 The Ku Klux Klan burns a cross at Mounds Park
in St. Paul, probably in response to an alleged assault of
a seventeen-year-old white female by a black male the
previous day.

1997 The Minnesota Twins retire number 34, worn by
fan favorite Kirby Puckett.

MAY 26

1780 Chief Wabasha, serving as a general in the British
Army, leads 200 Dakota in an attack on Spanish positions at St. Louis. This is the only known involvement
of Minnesotans in the Revolutionary War.

1861 Author and naturalist Henry David Thoreau,
traveling west to preserve his health, arrives in St. Paul
and spends two weeks exploring the flora and fauna of
the surrounding area.

1900 Dr. Justus Ohage donates Harriet Island, named for schoolteacher Harriet Bishop, to the city of St. Paul.

MAY 27

1858 The army withdraws troops from Fort Snelling, having decided that the fort is no longer an essential outpost. Military personnel would return in 1861 to train recruits for the Civil War. *See* July 19

1858 In Eden Prairie, about 150 Ojibwe attack and defeat Shakopee's band of Dakota in the Battle of Shakopee, the final major battle between these tribes in Minnesota.

1902 The Mille Lacs Ojibwe are offered $40,000 to move to the White Earth Reservation so that their land can be sold to developers. In August, seventy-four males (of 125 eligible) sign the agreement, and by 1914 1,152 individuals would move to White Earth while 276 remain at Mille Lacs.

1930 A patent is issued to 3M for its transparent cellophane tape, which becomes known as Scotch™ Tape. Richard G. Drew of St. Paul had developed the product from his earlier invention, a pressure-sensitive masking tape used as a border when repainting cars.

MAY 28

1827 Dakota warriors shoot into an Ojibwe camp outside Fort Snelling, killing several people, and Ojibwe warriors make reprisal attacks over the next few days, killing four Dakota. Although a peace treaty had been negotiated in 1825, battles between the two groups would continue for decades.

1859 Anticipating a delightful lecture by Bayard Taylor, 300 passengers board the steamboat *Equator* at Afton for a trip up the St. Croix River to Stillwater. However, forty-mile-per-hour winds force water into the hatches and drown the boilers, and Captain Asa Green and his crew are compelled to ground the ship near Hudson, unloading the passengers just before a wind gust rips the cabin off the boat. Unfortunately, the passengers miss Taylor's lecture, "Life in the North."

1866 The Twin Cities fete General William T. Sherman, who is on a tour of army forts in Minnesota and the Dakotas as commander of the Division of the Mississippi.

1896 Minneapolis celebrates John H. Stevens Day. Stevens had built the first house on the west side of the Mississippi River in 1849, and on this day schoolchildren pull the house to a location in Minnehaha Park.

1903 St. Paul's first automobile fatality occurs when a child is struck on Selby Avenue between Dale and St. Albans Streets.

1936 A statue depicting five Indians with sacred pipes seated around a fire and a "god of peace" emerging from the smoke is dedicated in the Ramsey County Courthouse. Sculpted by Swedish artist Carl Milles and later named *Vision of Peace,* the sixty-ton, thirty-six-foot-tall revolving onyx statue cost $75,000.

May 28, 1936

MAY 29

1848 Wisconsin is admitted to the Union, leaving present-day Minnesota east of the Mississippi River, which had been part of Wisconsin Territory, without a government until the establishment of Minnesota Territory on March 3, 1849.

1896 Luther W. Youngdahl is born in Minneapolis. As the state's governor from 1947 to 1951 he would attack gambling practices across the state, even at the level of church raffles. President Harry S. Truman would later appoint him judge of the U.S. district court for the District of Columbia. He died in 1978.

1897 The *St. Paul Dispatch* runs a photograph of the first automobile in the Twin Cities. The owner, cigarmaker H. J. Schley, used the car to advertise his business.

May 29, 1897 (St. Paul Dispatch)

1916 James J. Hill, the Empire Builder, dies in St. Paul. A man of enormous influence, he moved to St. Paul in 1856 from his native Ontario, began work in the shipping business, and became owner of the Great Northern Railway and Northern Pacific Railroad Companies. His interests were widespread: he helped develop the Iron Range, had a fleet of ships on the Pacific Ocean, pushed for modern farming techniques in the Northwest, and helped float the bonds that supported the democracies of Europe against the Central Powers in World War I.

1919 Charles Strite of Stillwater applies for a patent for a pop-up toaster for use in his company's cafeteria.

1935 High-speed rail service between the Twin Cities and Chicago begins with the train Hiawatha.

MAY 30

1871 The steamer *St. Paul* carries the first shipment of grain from the port of Duluth.

1889 Memorial Day becomes a legal holiday in Minnesota.

MAY 31

1819 William W. Mayo is born in England. A pioneer of medicine in Minnesota and one of the first doctors to use a microscope to aid in diagnosis, he would arrive in the territory in 1855 and settle in Rochester in 1863. *See* August 21

1853 Isaac I. Stevens and his surveying crew leave Minneapolis to plot a rail route to Puget Sound. In 1870 the Northern Pacific Railroad would follow this route.

May 31, 1819

JUNE 1

1849 Minnesota Territory is legally organized when territorial governor Alexander Ramsey signs a proclamation written by Judge David Cooper.

1859 The steamboat *Anson Northup* begins working on the Red River. In an effort to cash in on the lucrative Red River valley trade and to improve connections with Fort Garry (now Winnipeg), St. Paul businessmen offered a $2,000 prize to the first boat to deliver a cargo to Fort Garry. Mr. Anson Northup traveled with his Mississippi steamer *North Star* up the Crow Wing River as far as possible. Then he dissembled the 90-by-24-foot boat and began the overland trip with sixty-four horses and a crew of sixty men. Losing their way near Detroit Lakes, they were found by a

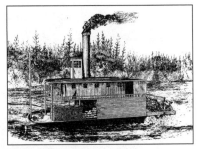

June 1, 1859

rescue party from Georgetown and led to Lafayette on the Red River. Northup's boat, renamed for its owner, reaches Fort Garry on June 5 and, subsequently sold and renamed the *Pioneer,* remains in service until 1861.

1927 Harper and Brothers publishes the first English edition of Ole E. Rølvaag's *Giants in the Earth,* a novel of Norwegian settlement on the Great Plains. Rølvaag, a professor at St. Olaf College, wrote the original text in Norwegian.

1979 Adventurer Gerry Spiess departs from Chesapeake Bay in his ten-foot sailboat *Yankee Girl,* built in his White Bear Lake garage in 1977. After a solo voyage across the Atlantic, Spiess arrives in Falmouth, England, on July 24, 1979.

June 1, 1979 (poster, Northwestern National Bank of St. Paul)

JUNE 2

1838 St. Paul's founder Pierre Parrant builds the city's first structure, known as the "whiskey seller's cabin," in Fountain Cave. Nicknamed "Pig's Eye" because one of his eyes was surrounded by a "white-ish ring," Parrant had been expelled from the Fort Snelling grounds for selling liquor. The name is also applied to the community when people begin having their mail sent to "Pig's Eye." At Father Lucien Galtier's suggestion, the town's name would be changed to St. Paul on November 1, 1849.

1924 Congress passes a law extending citizenship to all Indians in the United States.

JUNE 3

1836 Charles Nathaniel Hewitt is born in Vermont. He would lead the state legislature to create the state board of health in 1872, making Minnesota the third state to do so. Dr. Hewitt died in 1910.

1839 Liquor was a constant plague to the officers at Fort Snelling: forty-seven soldiers are confined to the guardhouse for violating orders about visiting the saloon of Henry Menk, near modern Fort Road and Munster Avenue, in St. Paul.

1859 Logs driven by floodwaters knock down the second and third bridges built over the Mississippi River, in Minneapolis.

1916 Forty miners on the Mesabi iron range walk off the job at the start of a massive strike, coordinated by the ethnically diverse rank and file, with help from experienced organizers from the Industrial Workers of the World. Scab workers undermine the strike, and the strikers concede defeat after three and a half months. However, by December, Oliver Mining Company, a subsidiary of U.S. Steel, compromises with pay raises and other small reforms. The company would maintain its anti-union stance until 1943.

1990 Soviet president Mikhail Gorbachev spends a few hours in the Twin Cities.

1999 Duluth's Ed Hommer is the first double amputee to reach the top of Mount McKinley (20,320 feet). He had lost his legs to frostbite after a plane crash on the mountain in 1981.

JUNE 4

1869 John S. and Charles A. Pillsbury buy a third interest in the Frazee and Murphy Flour Mill. The Pillsbury Company marks this date as its birthday.

1993 "Jim Ed Poole" (Tom Keith) and Dale Connelly celebrate their tenth year as hosts of *The Morning Show* on Minnesota Public Radio with a broadcast from the World Theater in St. Paul.

2000 A statue is unveiled in Periers, Normandy, France, of four American soldiers who died trying to free the town from the Germans during World War II. Citizens of the town and veterans of the Ninetieth Division raised funds for the monument. Two Minnesotans are commemorated in the statue: Virgil Tangborn of Bemidji and Richard Richtman of Minneapolis. It is unusual for statues dedicated to the memory of common soldiers to be of specific individuals.

JUNE 5

1806 John McDonald, who would be the first permanent settler in Wright County, is born in Maine. In 1847 he would move to St. Anthony and help build the dam at the falls. He would work in the mills there until July 31, 1852, when he took a land claim in Otsego, where he would establish a ferry and serve as postmaster, county commissioner, and justice of the peace. He would also plan a portion of County Road 39, now part of the Great River Road.

1873 A delegation of German Mennonites from Russia arrives in St. Paul to assess the state for settlement. Mennonite settlers soon establish homesteads around Mountain Lake in Cottonwood County.

1885 The *Western Appeal* (later the *Appeal*), the first Minnesota-published African American newspaper to gain national readership, premieres under the editorship of Frederick D. Parker. *See* August 6

JUNE 6

1736 Twenty-one French fur traders are killed in a fight with Dakota warriors on an island in the Lake of the Woods. The men were part of a post set up by the Sieur de La Vérendrye. *See* August 26

1849 Major Samuel Woods leads a group of cavalry from Fort Snelling to map the Red River valley and select a site for a new fort. Captain John Pope drew the map. Pope would later lead the Union Army to defeat at Second Manassas in the Civil War, after which he would return to Minnesota to oversee federal forces during the U.S.–Dakota War of 1862. His personality was summed up by one of his peers: "Pope is an ass." He did, however, make a good map.

1877 The Minneapolis Base Ball Association is organized, and two days later the team plays Fairbanks of Chicago, winning 4–3.

1889 The University of Minnesota Law School graduates its first class, a total of three men. The following year's graduates number forty-five. *See* May 14

1910 Paper milling in International Falls begins as eighteen tons of newsprint are manufactured. Paper production remains a major business of the city today.

1945 In a horrifying multiple-murder, Robert Doan of Mahtowa clubs to death his wife and three of his four children. He also sets fire to the house, killing the remaining child. Doan had "lost his temper" after being fired from his job as a bulldozer operator at the Duluth Williamson-Johnson Municipal Airport and then getting into an argument with his wife. His first trial closes with a 9–3 deadlock because, according to the defense, Doan had signed a confession under extreme duress and he later denied the murders during the trial. At a second trial Doan is sentenced to life imprisonment for second-degree murder.

JUNE 7

1838 Edward Phelan (variously spelled), recently discharged from Fort Snelling, stakes out a claim in St. Paul near Ryan and Hill Streets. Lake Phalen and Phalen Creek are named for him.

1892 The Republican National Convention meets in Minneapolis and renominates Benjamin Harrison to the office of president. Harrison had defeated Grover Cleveland four years before but would lose to him in November. Two women from Wyoming attend the convention as alternates, the first female delegates to a national political convention.

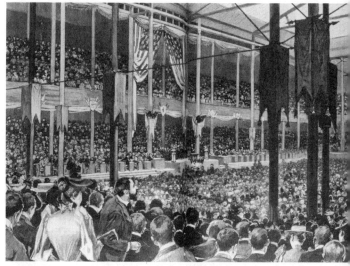

June 7, 1892

1902 The steamer *Hadley* rams the whaleback freighter *Thomas Wilson* near the entry to the Duluth harbor. The *Wilson* sinks quickly, and nine crewmembers drown.

1921 The Minnesota Cooperative Creameries Association, now known as Land O'Lakes, is formed.

MINN. CO-OPERATIVE CREAMERIES ASSN.

June 7, 1921

1958 Musician Prince Nelson is born in Minneapolis. He is perhaps best known for the song and movie *Purple Rain*. Nelson first took the name "Prince" as his stage name but for a time adopted a symbol as his name, leading people to refer to him as "the artist formerly known as Prince."

1987 August Wilson's play *Fences* wins four Tony Awards, including one for best play. Born in Pittsburgh, Wilson moved to St. Paul in 1978 and soon began writing his award-winning plays, which chronicle African American experiences during the twentieth century.

JUNE 8

1848 A group of Winnebago (Ho-Chunk) are moved from a reservation in Iowa to a new one in present-day Minnesota, on land that had been purchased from the Ojibwe. Along the way they wish to buy some Dakota land from Chief Wabasha but are prevented from doing so by Captain Seth Eastman of Fort Snelling, who enforces the terms of their treaty. The move is complete on June 30. *See* September 9

1854 Former president Millard Fillmore visits St. Paul as part of a Grand Excursion celebrating the completion of the Rock Island Railroad from Chicago to Rock Island, Illinois. The group had journeyed up the Mississippi River by steamboat. Although not a Minnesota railroad, the rail connection between the river and Chicago would provide a great boost to Minnesota's economy.

1880 The flour of the Washburn-Crosby Company wins a gold medal at an exhibition in Cincinnati, launching the Gold Medal brand. Washburn-Crosby would eventually become General Mills.

1898 The body of a "petrified man" is found in Bloomer, Marshall County. The gullible believed he was a voyageur, but the wise knew he was made of plaster.

1910 Cartoonist C. C. Beck, who drew Captain Marvel, is born in Zumbrota.

1927 Popular artist LeRoy Neiman, known for his wildly colored sports scenes, is born in St. Paul.

JUNE 9

1871 A court orders an injunction against construction of the Duluth Ship Canal, which Duluth was building in order to divert traffic from Superior, Wisconsin, which has the natural mouth of the harbor. Duluth mayor J. B. Culver orders the excavation into high speed, completing the work on June 13, just before the formal court order is delivered. Duluth's reply to Superior is "You can stop the water if you can. We can't." The Aerial Lift Bridge now crosses the canal.

1892 Ira S. Field dies at age seventy-eight. He and his partner, John Wesley North, co-founded Northfield.

1894 The steamer *North West,* built in Cleveland for James J. Hill's Northern Steamship Company, arrives in Duluth, completing its maiden voyage.

1921 The Cottonwood Oil Company, the first oil cooperative in the United States, is incorporated.

1979 Governor Albert Quie calls out the National Guard to protect truck drivers who continue to work during a nationwide strike.

JUNE 10

1864 At Brice's Cross Roads in Mississippi, Confederate forces led by Nathan Bedford Forrest capture 233 soldiers from the Ninth Minnesota Regiment. The captives are sent to Andersonville prison in Georgia, where 119 of them die.

1902 Faribault's first passenger train arrives.

1922 Frances Gumm, later known as actress and singer Judy Garland, is born in Grand Rapids. She died in London on June 23, 1969.

JUNE 11

1835 Thomas Williamson and Alexander Huggins organize a church at Fort Snelling, probably the first Protestant church in Minnesota. Although Gideon H. and Samuel W. Pond had started their Dakota mission the year before, they had not yet organized a church. The French had a Catholic mission on Lake Pepin in the 1700s, and Father Lucien Galtier would establish a Catholic church in Mendota in 1840. The First Presbyterian Church of Minneapolis descends from the fort's church.

1849 Minnesota Territory is divided into three judicial districts. The first district, the region between the Mississippi and St. Croix Rivers, holds court in Stillwater and is presided over by Aaron Goodrich. The second, the lands north of the Minnesota River and west of the Mississippi River, holds court in St. Anthony, with

Bradley B. Meeker as judge. South of the Minnesota River is the territory of Judge David Cooper, whose court is in Mendota.

1858 Wadena County, named for a trading post on the Crow Wing River, is formed.

1877 The Tom Brown Foot Ball Association, an exclusive club for football players, is formed in Minneapolis.

1899 In an effort to control speeding bicyclists, the St. Paul police department establishes a squad of twelve bicycle officers to patrol the roads and sidewalks, keeping the public safe from "scorchers." The speed limits are set at six miles per hour on sidewalks and eight on streets.

1945 Nellie Stone Johnson, union organizer and activist, is elected to the Minneapolis library board, the first African American ever elected to a citywide post in Minneapolis.

JUNE 12

1838 Iowa Territory is formed, including in its claim present-day Minnesota west of the Mississippi River, which was called Clayton County. Henry H. Sibley serves as justice of the peace for the county, but this part of Minnesota would be left without a government when Iowa became a state in 1846.

1873 Rocky Mountain locusts cross into Minnesota and begin destroying crops in the southwestern part of the state. Relief efforts are organized to keep the settlers from starving. The locusts return for the next four years, finally leaving in August 1877. *See* April 26

June 12, 1873

June 12, 1905

1905 Visiting the Twin Cities for the dedication of the new capitol, William Colvill dies in his sleep at the Old Soldier's Home in Minneapolis the night before the ceremony, at which he was to carry the battle flag of his regiment. Born in New York in 1830, Colonel Colvill had led the First Minnesota's famous charge at Gettysburg (*see* July 2). After the war, the Red Wing resident served as state attorney general.

1914 The last commercially cut logs pass through Stillwater's boom on the St. Croix, marking the end of large-scale logging in the St. Croix valley. The boom was a chain of logs stretching across the river. Logs floated from upstream, each carrying their owner's brand, were sorted and measured so that each logging company got credit for what they had cut.

JUNE 13

1820 John H. Stevens is born in Brompton Falls, Quebec. A farmer, merchant, editor, and legislator, he would build the first house on the west bank of St. Anthony Falls in 1849. *See* May 28

1838 Captain Frederick Marryat, author of numerous sea tales, most memorably "Mr. Midshipman Easy," visits Fort Snelling while on a trip to investigate American democracy. The next year he publishes *Diary in America,* which contains several chapters on his Minnesota experiences.

1886 A four-mile logjam closes the St. Croix River at Taylors Falls. The jam is so spectacular that excursion trains travel from Duluth to see it.

1968 A tornado kills nine in Tracy, Lyon County.

June 13, 1886

JUNE 14

1671 In a ceremony at Sault Ste. Marie, the Sieur de St. Lusson formally claims the territory that would become northeastern Minnesota for France.

1868 The first Ojibwe to relocate to the White Earth Reservation arrives. An annual ceremony and reunion is held to commemorate the event. *See* March 19

1918 A picnic held by the Nonpartisan League in Wegdahl draws 14,000. The Nonpartisan League was a farmers' association organized in North Dakota in 1916. It advocated several ideas considered radical, including public ownership of the nation's food distribution system and a draft of capital to finance World War I. The organizers of the league sought to avoid charges of antipatriotism by selling war bonds at their rallies, but Governor Joseph A. A. Burnquist's Commission of Public

Safety still restricted them, supporting nineteen Minnesota counties as they banned the league from meeting in their jurisdictions.

1959 The St. Paul Housing and Redevelopment Authority condemns the few remaining homes in the area known as "The Levee." The Upper Levee Flats had long been the location of poor immigrant neighborhoods for various ethnic groups, including Poles, Bohemians, and Swedes. Around 1900, Italians settled there in such numbers that it earned the name "Little Italy." Upper Levee Flats was prone to flooding, leading the city to condemn the neighborhood.

1981 A tornado travels from Edina to Minneapolis to Roseville, killing one, injuring eighty-three, and causing $47 million in losses.

JUNE 15

1838 The U.S. Senate ratifies treaties with the Ojibwe and Dakota that formally transfer ownership of the land between the Mississippi and St. Croix Rivers to the federal government. Squatters quickly claim land in St. Paul and Marine on St. Croix.

1851 Artist Frank Blackwell Mayer arrives in St. Paul from Baltimore to make drawings of the pending treaty negotiations at Traverse des Sioux. These drawings and his diary, published as *With Pen and Pencil on the Frontier in 1851,* provide a valuable record of frontier and Indian life.

1892 An odd and deadly freak of nature: a windstorm traverses Jackson and Martin Counties, then splits into two parts near Winnebago City in Faribault County. One part travels northeast into Freeborn County, the other southeast, passing near Albert Lea. About fifty are killed in the 85-mile path of the storm.

1909 The St. Paul police activate motorcycle patrols, with two plainclothes officers watching traffic on Summit Avenue.

1920 One of the ugliest days in Minnesota history: three African American workers for the John Robinson circus are lynched in Duluth. The men were accused of raping a white woman. Ignoring the pleas of a priest and a judge, a mob of 5,000 breaks into the city jail and hangs the men from a lamppost.

1933 Brewer William Hamm, Jr., is kidnapped at Minnehaha Street and Greenbrier Avenue in St. Paul. He is released after a ransom of $100,000 is paid. Gangster Roger Touhy is brought to trial but acquitted, and investigators later learn that the real culprits were the Barker-Karpis gang. *See* January 17

1939 Crown Prince Olav of Norway dedicates Duluth's Enger Tower, which offers spectacular views of Duluth Harbor and Lake Superior. Bert Enger (1864–1931) was a Norwegian-born businessman who ran a successful furniture store in Duluth. He donated much of his estate to the city after his death.

June 15, 1909

JUNE 16

1854 Arriving in St. Paul, the steamer *Galena* delivers cholera along with its passengers. Cholera's last occurrence in Minnesota would be in 1873.

1863 Amid fears that another Indian war is imminent, General Henry H. Sibley and his troops leave Camp Pope, near present-day Redwood Falls, on their campaign against the Dakota.

1931 The bones of "Minnesota Man" are uncovered by a road crew near Pelican Rapids. Despite its name, this glacial-age human skeleton is likely that of a teenage girl.

1945 The last navy tanker built at the Cargill shipyards in Savage is launched. The *Wacissa* is one of eighteen ships manufactured there for the war effort.

1955 Mary Grant, the youngest of Sauk Centre's fabled Grant Sisters, is born. She would eventually play the French horn in venues around the world.

1999 Kathleen Soliah, a fugitive since 1974, is arrested in St. Paul. Having lived under the name Sarah Jane Olson, Soliah was a presumed member of the Symbionese Liberation Army, the group that kidnapped Patty Hearst, and was wanted for the attempted bombing of two police cars. She had been featured on the television show *America's Most Wanted* a few months before her arrest.

JUNE 17

1673 Father Jacques Marquette and Louis Jolliet, French explorers traveling down the Wisconsin River, enter the main stream of the "Mechassipi." They are the first Europeans to travel on the upper river.

1889 Frederick L. McGhee becomes the first African American admitted to practice at the bar of the state supreme court. Born a slave in Mississippi in 1861,

McGhee would take on civil rights cases and serve as an emissary to Catholic prelates in Minnesota. In 1905 he would help develop the organizational precursor to the NAACP, the Niagara Conference. He died September 19, 1912, in St. Paul.

1890 The U.S. marshal from St. Paul arrests seven census takers in Minneapolis, the opening salvo of the "Twin Cities Census War." St. Paul's leaders accused Minneapolis of cooking the books in order to claim the title "most populous city." The accusation is proven true; however, St. Paul is also found to be padding its numbers. A new count completed in August gives Minneapolis 164,581 and St. Paul 133,156.

1909 Elmer L. Andersen is born in Chicago. During his term as governor, from 1961 to 1963, he would pioneer progressive legislation in civil rights, special education, mental health care, and metropolitan governance and establish numerous state parks.

1913 The first "Minnesota Good Roads Day" is declared. The national Good Roads Movement was spurred by two forces: bicyclists who wanted to ride on better surfaces than muddy country lanes, and Rural Free Delivery, the post office's promise to deliver mail to and from farms that were easily accessible by road.

JUNE 18

1847 William Willim receives the first known citizenship papers granted in Minnesota. An English-born building contractor in Stillwater, Willim also builds the first limekiln in the state this year.

1855 St. Mary's Falls Canal opens at Sault Ste. Marie, Michigan. It connects Lake Superior to Lake Huron and the lower Great Lakes, eventually permitting the mass transport of wheat, coal, and iron ore from Minnesota to points east.

1892 Little Mamie Schwartz is kidnapped in St. Paul. Her disappearance causes a sensation, with the legislature offering $500 for her return. The police find her the next year in Superior, Wisconsin.

1893 The towns of Virginia, Merritt, and Mountain Iron are destroyed in a forest fire.

June 18, 1893 Floyd T. Ryan, Executive Secretary of Keep Minnesota Green, Inc., inspects a forest fire danger sign north of Virginia, 1961

1934 Congress passes the Indian Reorganization Act, which allows Native Americans to govern themselves on a tribal basis, to manage natural resources on reservations, and to incorporate as a tribe to facilitate business ventures.

1939 A tornado kills nine and injures 222 in the Anoka area.

JUNE 19

1816 Twenty-four people are killed in the "Seven Oaks Massacre" near Winnipeg, Manitoba. The battle is between settlers of the Selkirk Colony and an army of métis (mixed-bloods) hired by the North West Company to prevent the settlers from destroying the fur market. The colony's founder, Thomas Douglas, the fifth Earl of Selkirk, owned a large interest in the Hudson's Bay Company, a rival to the North West Company. The massacre is a factor in the Selkirkers' decision to leave the Red River and move to the Fort Snelling military reservation. Forced by the army to move downriver in 1839, they would form the small settlement that grew into the city of St. Paul.

1852 By an act of Congress, the St. Peter's River is renamed with its original Dakota name, "Minnesota," translated as either "sky-colored waters" or "muddy water." The river had been known as "St. Pierre" for 150 years, since the days of the explorer Pierre Charles Le Sueur.

1873 The first graduation ceremony for the University of Minnesota is held at the Academy of Music in Minneapolis to honor both graduates, Warren Eustis and Henry Williamson.

JUNE 20

1823 Jesse Reno is born in Wheeling, West Virginia. In 1853 General Reno would survey the military road from Council Bluffs, Iowa, to Mendota, a route of 279 miles. He was killed in the Civil War.

1887 William A. Hazel, a black architect, files suit because the Clarendon Hotel in St. Paul had refused to rent him a room.

1970 Dave and John Kunst and their mule, Willie-Make-It, set out from their Waseca home to walk around the earth. In Afghanistan, bandits attack the brothers, killing John and wounding Dave. Dave's brother Pete then joins him until they reach the Indian Ocean.

Dave returns to Waseca on October 5, 1974, the first person to walk around the earth, 14,450 miles in all.

JUNE 21

1839 Hundreds of Dakota and Ojibwe are at Fort Snelling for payments of treaty annuities. On this neutral ground the usually hostile parties participate in dancing and foot races.

1867 Minneapolis's thriving theatrical scene begins in earnest with the dedication of the Pence Opera House at Second Street and Hennepin Avenue. The opening performance is a joint concert by the Minneapolis Musical Union and the St. Paul Musical Society. The first play—*The Hunchback*—opens three days later.

1899 Robert Kennedy dies at age eighty-eight in St. Paul. He was vice president of the Stillwater Convention, which initiated the creation of Minnesota Territory. *See* August 26

1925 Noted socialist and labor leader Eugene Debs speaks at a rally in Camden Park, Minneapolis. Praising Russia's Soviet government, he encourages the crowd of 5,000 to support unions and set their sights on industrial democracy.

1973 The United States Hockey Hall of Fame opens in Eveleth, the capital of American hockey.

JUNE 22

1806 Alexander Faribault, future fur trader and Minnesota pioneer, is born in Prairie du Chien, Wisconsin.

1861 The First Minnesota Regiment departs Fort Snelling for Washington, D.C., eventually finding both glory and death in the Civil War.

1919 Three windstorms hit Fergus Falls on the same day, leaving fifty-nine dead.

JUNE 23

1870 Adolph O. Eberhart is born in Sweden. He would become Minnesota's seventeenth governor upon the death of John A. Johnson in 1909 and would be elected to the office in 1910. During his tenure he would sign into law a direct primary bill. He died on December 6, 1944.

1911 Duluth celebrates its first *Svenskarnas Dag,* the Swedish midsummer festival, with a parade, music, and speeches. St. Paul would follow suit in 1933.

1927 Captain Gerhard Folgero and his 42-foot Viking ship *Leif Erickson* sail into Duluth, completing a voyage from Norway. The ship is now displayed in a Duluth park.

1975 The *Discoverer,* a Danish passenger ship, calls at Duluth. No international passenger ships would return to Minnesota for twenty-two years. *See* October 3

JUNE 24

1924 Herbert Huse Bigelow, of the Brown and Bigelow publishing firm, is sentenced to three years in prison for income tax evasion. He had long argued that an income tax punished initiative, and he had expected to be fined rather than jailed for his transgression.

1948 African American leaders in the Twin Cities reject an offer to establish an "all-Negro" unit of the Minnesota National Guard. The group tells state adjutant general Ellard A. Walsh that it cannot accept the offer as a matter of principle. Walsh had proposed forming a truck company so that Minnesota's African Americans could take advantage of a provision in the draft law that exempted guardsmen from the draft.

1996 At the federal courthouse in St. Paul, White Earth tribal leader Darrell "Chip" Wadena and others are convicted of corruption and vote-buying charges. Wadena is sentenced to four years in prison.

JUNE 25

1849 Territorial governor Alexander Ramsey arrives in St. Paul with his wife Anna, their son, and a nurse. The governor had stayed in Mendota with Henry H. Sibley for about a month before moving to the capital. Ramsey, who was thirty-four, found a town of 800 people and no preparations for his arrival. The family set up house in an abandoned saloon.

1977 The first Grandma's Marathon is run from Two Harbors to Duluth. Named for its first major sponsor, the Duluth-based Grandma's restaurants, this race now draws over 8,500 contestants annually.

JUNE 26

1834 Congress appropriates $7,000 to survey the boundary line between the Ojibwe and Dakota tribes, which had been agreed upon in the treaty of 1825 at Prairie du Chien. The line is eventually drawn from the Chippewa River to Otter Tail Lake.

1851 A young woman wearing "bloomers," or Turkish-style pants, steps onto the St. Paul levee. She creates quite a sensation, with James M. Goodhue, editor of the *Minnesota Pioneer,* noting that "the girl looked remarkably well, as far as we could see." Thus Amelia Bloomer, who on the east coast was attempting to reform the style of women's clothing, made her influence known in the Midwest.

1948 Sweden's Prince Bertil unveils a tablet to Jacob Fahlstrom, first Swede in Minnesota. A fur trader who arrived in Minnesota in the 1820s, Fahlstrom settled near Afton and died there in 1859. The plaque is at the intersection of Robert Street and Kellogg Boulevard in St. Paul.

1953 Bemidji native Jane Russell and Marilyn Monroe, her costar in *Gentlemen Prefer Blondes,* immortalize their handprints in the "Forecourt of the Stars" at Grauman's Chinese Theatre, Hollywood, California.

1959 President Dwight D. Eisenhower and Queen Elizabeth open the St. Lawrence Seaway in an official ceremony in Montreal. The seaway connects the Great Lakes to the Atlantic Ocean, making Duluth and other lake cities international ports.

1993 Sunrayce 93 concludes in Apple Valley, near the Minnesota Zoo. The six-day race of solar-powered one-passenger cars on a route from Texas to Minnesota was a competition between engineering students from schools across the country. Activities at the finish include solar-powered boat races on Lake Nokomis.

JUNE 27

1928 Rudolph G. "Rudy" Perpich is born in Carson Lake, near Hibbing. The Iron Ranger would become one of Minnesota's most colorful governors, serving from 1976 to 1979 and 1983 to 1991. He would send National Guard troops to Austin to quell tensions during the Hormel strike in 1986, and he would sign a law returning the state's drinking age to twenty-one. During his terms the state lottery would be established and education heavily funded. He died on November 21, 1995.

1975 The taxicab drivers of the Twin Cities split from the International Brotherhood of Teamsters to establish their own union, the Guild of Taxi Drivers and Associated Workers.

1977 Heiress Elizabeth Congdon and her nurse are murdered at Glensheen mansion in Duluth. In a sensational trial, Congdon's son-in-law, Roger Caldwell, is convicted of the murders. New evidence in the case sets him free a year later but incriminates his wife Marjorie. Acquitted of these murders but found guilty in two arson cases, Marjorie is now in an Arizona prison.

JUNE 28

1818 Congress extends the area of Michigan Territory, bringing present-day Minnesota under its domain. So things would stand until the creation of Wisconsin Territory in 1836.

1849 Amherst Willoughby begins stagecoach service between St. Paul and St. Anthony.

1862 St. Paul mayor John Prince joins the crowd on the first train trip from the capital to Minneapolis. This railroad, the St. Paul and Pacific, would eventually become part of the Great Northern Railway.

1880 Dr. H. S. Tanner of Minneapolis begins a forty-day fast in New York in an effort to prove his theory that neither the human stomach nor food is required in order to sustain life. He resides in a room in Clarendon Hall that had been carefully searched for any morsel. Dropping fifty pounds and shrinking two inches, he makes it to the end, breaking his fast on a meal of milk and watermelon. Dr. Tanner moved to California and died in 1919 at the age of 87.

JUNE 29

1837 Elizabeth S. Hamilton, widow of Alexander, visits Fort Snelling and views points of interest including Lake Calhoun, Minnehaha Falls, and the Falls of St. Anthony. She is one of the first female tourists of the area.

1854 Congress establishes the principle of offering land grants to railroads. Federal land grants eventually total 10 million acres, 18.5 percent of the state's land, ranking Minnesota fourth among the states in acreage granted.

1863 A group of Dakota who had avoided capture after the 1862 war attack the Dustin farm near Howard Lake in Wright County, killing four settlers.

1905 Chisholm's Archibald "Moonlight" Graham plays his only game as a major leaguer, with the New York Giants. He would be celebrated in W. P. Kinsella's novel *Shoeless Joe,* later translated to the screen as *Field of Dreams.*

1916 Reflecting nationwide attitudes about prohibition, Duluth adopts a ban on alcohol sales within the city.

1922 John Vessey is born in Minneapolis. Vessey would lie about his age to join the Minnesota National Guard in 1939. In World War II he would fight in North Africa and at Anzio, Italy, where he would win a Bronze Star and earn a battlefield commission as an officer. He would win a Distinguished Service Cross in Vietnam and serve as chairman of the Joint Chiefs of Staff under President Ronald Reagan from 1982 to 1985.

JUNE 30

1853 Minnesota's first real-estate advertisement—for a land salesman—appears in the *Minnesota Pioneer.*

1888 Alexander McDougall launches the first whale-back freighter onto Lake Superior.

1992 A train derailment in Superior, Wisconsin, sends a tanker car of benzene into the St. Louis River. The resulting cloud of possibly toxic smoke leads to the evacuation of 50,000 residents of Superior and Duluth.

JULY 1

1922 A nationwide walkout by railroad shop craft and other employees includes 8,000 workers in the Twin Cities. The strike ends in defeat for the workers, with scab labor permanently replacing many of them, but the new Farmer-Labor Party's assistance during the strike encourages the workers' support of the party in later elections, making the Farmer-Labor Party, rather than the Democratic Party, the principal opposition party in Minnesota for many years.

1931 The Interstate Bridge in Stillwater opens, replacing a wooden one built in 1876.

1974 The Raptor Center at the University of Minnesota opens. The facility treats injured birds of prey and helps to rehabilitate them for release into the wild.

JULY 2

1679 Explorer Daniel Greysolon, the Sieur Du Luth, attaches the coat of arms of King Louis XIV to a tree on the shore of Mille Lacs Lake, thereby claiming the land for France.

1863 At Gettysburg, 262 members of the First Minnesota Regiment charge a much larger Confederate force, succeeding in slowing their advance but resulting in 215 casualties, a stunning eighty-two percent. The next day the remaining soldiers help repel Pickett's charge, capturing the flag of the Twenty-eighth Virginia Regiment in the process. Today, the First Minnesota's regimental flag, along with the state's other civil war regimental flags, resides in the state capitol. The flag of the Twenty-eighth Virginia is held by the Minnesota Historical Society. In 1999, the state of Virginia requested

July 2, 1863 Twenty-eighth Virginia regimental flag captured at Gettysburg

the return of the Virginia battle flag. Governor Jesse Ventura turned them down, noting with indisputable logic, "we won." He might have also mentioned that the captured flag is as much a part of Minnesota's heritage as it is Virginia's.

1882 James J. Hill's Hotel Lafayette opens at Minnetonka Beach.

JULY 3

1839 Dakota and Ojibwe warriors engage in two battles: one in Stillwater in an area called Battle Hollow, the other at the mouth of the Rum River in Anoka. The Dakota attacks kill about 100 Ojibwe people, and during the next month the Dakota hold celebratory dances with Ojibwe scalps at Lake Calhoun.

1863 Little Crow (Taoyateduta), leader of the Dakota during the U.S.–Dakota War of 1862, is killed while picking berries with his son in Meeker County, near Hutchinson. He is shot by Nathan and Chauncey Lamson, who are unaware of his identity. The Lamsons collect a bounty of five hundred dollars for their deed.

1863 Minnesota's first railroad fatality: a train strikes a wagon driven by Captain Abraham Bennett at the Como Road crossing in St. Paul. There had been talk of building a bridge at the site, but, ironically, Bennett himself had opposed it.

1917 The *Dandelion* is the first ship to pass through the Minneapolis locks, which connect the upper Mississippi to water traffic from below St. Anthony Falls.

1941 Charles Haralson dies in Excelsior at the age of seventy-eight. The first resident superintendent of the University of Minnesota's Fruit Breeding Farm (now the Horticultural Research Center) at Excelsior, the Swedish-born Haralson served as superintendent from 1908 to 1925, an especially creative period during which several outstanding hardy trees and fruits were developed and introduced, including his namesake Haralson apple (1922), a tart, long-keeping, winter variety that remains popular with both home and commercial growers.

JULY 4

1836 Major Lawrence Taliaferro, Indian agent at Fort Snelling, arranges a one-day truce between the Dakota and Ojibwe by promising them a visit from a prominent medicine man and a twenty-one-gun salute. The ruse is successful, as painter George Catlin plays the medicine man and the salute to the colors would have been fired regardless. The Indians spend the day playing lacrosse in the area now known as the polo fields.

1859 The temperature falls below freezing.

1862 During a raucous Independence Day celebration, downtown Winona catches fire. Hannibal Choate keeps members of the fire department near his store by supplying them with whiskey, and his business is the only one saved.

1868 Dr. Thomas Foster nicknames Duluth "Zenith City of the Unsalted Seas" during a rousing Independence Day speech at Minnesota Point.

1875 The first settlers from Iceland arrive in Lyon County, having traveled by oxcart from Iowa. Their leader, Gunnlaugur Petursson, sets up camp near modern Minneota.

1896 The *Minneapolis Journal* is the first American newspaper to use halftones, black-and-white illustrations in which gradations of light and dark are created by dots photographed through a screen.

July 4, 1896 First halftone photograph reproduced in the *Minneapolis Journal*, captioned "A summer home at Minnetonka"

1999 A giant windstorm causes heavy damage to the Boundary Waters Canoe Area Wilderness. The 100-mile-per-hour winds blow down trees on a ten- to twelve-mile front for a stretch of thirty miles. One person is killed.

JULY 5

1876 Fairmont's first passenger train arrives.

1928 The Minnesota National Forest is renamed the Chippewa National Forest.

JULY 6

1849 Bavarian immigrant Anthony Yoerg opens Minnesota's first brewery, located in St. Paul below what is now the River Center parking ramp.

July 6, 1849 Yoerg brewery wagon, ca. 1890

1883 Mule cars begin carrying passengers on Superior Street in Duluth.

1889 Police and strikers clash in Duluth. Three are mortally wounded before Mayor John B. Sutphin leads in the militia and empties the streets.

1974 The comedy, music, and variety show *A Prairie Home Companion* makes its first live broadcast from Macalester College in St. Paul. The show's first national broadcast would follow nearly four years later, in February 1978.

JULY 7

1849 Minnesota Territory is divided into seven "council districts." Territorial Governor Alexander Ramsey also declares that elections will be held August 1.

1862 One hundred and thirty gold miners, including a group from St. Paul led by James L. Fisk, set out on oxcarts from Fort Abercrombie on the Red River for the Montana gold fields. The federal government encouraged the expedition in an effort to find gold to finance the Civil War.

1871 Lumbermen from Stillwater descend the St. Croix River at dawn to remove pilings placed in the river to support a railroad bridge at Hudson, Wisconsin. Lumber interests in Stillwater had obtained a court injunction requiring a 200-foot clearance between the pilings to allow timber rafts to float through, but the order had been ignored. The lumberjacks return to Stillwater with about 100 pilings, and the event becomes known as the "Battle of the Piles."

JULY 8

1775 Alexander Henry the elder, one of the first Englishmen to journey west to present-day Minnesota, travels up the Pigeon River to Partridge Portage.

1887 A police officer is shot while trying to break up a riot at the saloonkeepers picnic in St. Paul.

1889 The federal government and the Red Lake Ojibwe sign a treaty that cedes 2,905,000 "surplus" acres from the reservation. Rather than distributing the remaining reservation land to individual tribe members as allotments, this treaty allows the Red Lake Ojibwe to hold the land in common, thereby protecting it from piecemeal sale.

1939 The final day of operation for Duluth's streetcars, which are replaced by trolley buses.

JULY 9

1823 Major Stephen H. Long leaves Fort St. Anthony (later Snelling) to explore areas of present-day Minnesota then unknown to the United States. Giacomo C. Beltrami joins Long as he travels up the Minnesota River and then down the Red River to Lake Winnipeg.

1832 Lewis Cass, territorial governor of Michigan, forbids the sale of liquor on Indian lands under his control, including the area around Fort Snelling.

1835 Dr. Thomas S. Williamson and Alexander Huggins establish the Lac qui Parle mission to the Dakota, which operates for twenty years.

1902 The National Afro-American Council, a precursor to the NAACP, holds a meeting at the state capitol, and business, social, education, and religious leaders discuss strategies for improving the position of African Americans nationwide.

1932 Carl F. Hirte sets up a homestead claim in the middle of St. Paul's Union Depot rail yard. Hirte had discovered that a nearly five-acre tract in the middle of the yard had never been claimed, and, in

July 9, 1932

accordance with the Homestead Act, he builds a shack for housing. His attorney values the land at $1,000,000.

1975 The reassembly of steam engine 201—once operated by Casey Jones and the last of its kind in existence—is complete and ready for display on the grounds of the Owatonna Tool Company. Reuben Kaplan and his son, "Buzz," brought the engine from Peoria, and they would move the beautiful old Owatonna Union Depot building to the same site the following year.

JULY 10

1823 Major Joseph Delafield and his party arrive at Grand Portage to run the first survey of the international boundary in the region.

1930 Golf great Bobby Jones plays a round at the Interlachen Country Club in Edina on the first day of the U.S. Open Championship. At the end of the two-day tournament, he wins the title for the fourth time.

JULY 11

1999 Duluth's state representative Willard Munger dies. He had served over forty years in the Minnesota House and was known as an advocate for environmental protection.

JULY 12

1829 Lieutenant Colonel Zachary Taylor ends his command at Fort Snelling, which had begun May 24, 1828. He would later lead the U.S Army in the war against Mexico, and "Old Rough and Ready" would take that fame to the White House. Taylor is the only U.S. president to have spent a significant amount of time in Minnesota.

1869 Norwegian newspaperman Paul Hjelm-Hansen leaves Alexandria to travel to the Red River by oxcart. Hjelm-Hansen had been hired by the State Board of Immigration to publicize the advantages of settling in western Minnesota. His letters, published in a number of Norwegian newspapers, encourage many emigrants to settle here. In 1924 the Norwegian-Danish Press

Association of America presented the Minnesota Historical Society with a plaque in his memory.

JULY 13

1787 Congress passes the Northwest Ordinance. Authored by Thomas Jefferson, it set up the rules of government for the Northwest Territory of the United States, which included present-day Minnesota east of the Mississippi River. Slavery was outlawed, the land was to be surveyed into townships, and each township was to set aside land for a school. In addition, the ordinance stated that "the utmost good faith shall always be observed toward the Indians, their land and property."

1832 Ozawindib (Yellow Head), an Ojibwe guide, shows Henry Rowe Schoolcraft that Lake Itasca is indeed the source of the Mississippi River. Schoolcraft would name the lake from the Latin words *Veritas Caput* (True Head), using the last syllable of *veritas* and the first of *caput.* The Ojibwe name for the lake is *Omushkos,* meaning "Elk Lake." *See* February 4

1862 The Third Minnesota Regiment suffers one of the great embarrassments of the Civil War when it surrenders to a smaller Confederate force led by Nathan Bedford Forrest, who convinced the Minnesotans that his force was much larger than theirs. The men would be paroled and eventually return to action, fighting well under new officers. *See* July 14

1881 Faribault begins requiring dog licenses.

1890 The steamer *Sea Wing,* carrying a large party and towing a barge, capsizes in a sudden storm on Lake Pepin. Twenty-five individuals manage to clamber back on the boat, but, a few hours later, the boat turns turtle again, throwing the survivors back in the water. By the time the boat and the barge are driven ashore, ninety-eight individuals had drowned. Surprisingly, no one on the barge was hurt.

1977 The city of Kinney, St. Louis County, secedes from the United States. The city council, frustrated by unsuccessful attempts to obtain a grant from the federal government for a water project, decides to secede and apply for foreign aid because "there is less paperwork." Passports are issued by sympathizers in New Haven, Connecticut. Although the United States did not recognize Kinney as a foreign country, Duluth's frozen food king Gino Palucci did, giving Kinney a used Ford to replace the city police car (which no longer ran) and ten cases of frozen pizza for good measure.

JULY 14

1864 Four Minnesota regiments finally defeat their old nemesis, Nathan Bedford Forrest, in battle at Tupelo, Mississippi. The Seventh Minnesota plays the largest role and loses sixty-two men. Colonel Alexander Wilkin of the Ninth Minnesota Regiment is killed, making him Minnesota's highest-ranking casualty in the Civil War. *See* July 13

1901 By special act of the legislature, Jim and Cole Younger are released from the Minnesota State Prison at Stillwater. They had been incarcerated for the murder of an employee during a Northfield bank robbery. Jim would commit suicide in St. Paul, but Cole would tour on a Wild West show with Frank James, lecturing on "What My Life Has Taught Me." He died in 1915, his body still holding seven bullets. *See* September 7

1903 Benson plays Willmar in a doubleheader on a hot summer's day, the second game stretching into extra innings. Willmar's Thielman opens the tenth with a single, which O'Toole follows with a long drive. Running ahead of O'Toole, Thielman collapses on third base. O'Toole, knowing he can't pass the runner ahead of him, picks up Thielman and carries him to home plate before touching it himself, literally bringing the runner home. Only then does O'Toole discover that Thielman had suffered a massive heart attack and that a dead man had scored the winning run.

1924 Lawrence S. Donaldson, founder of the first department store in the Northwest, dies in Minneapolis.

1948 Hubert H. Humphrey gives a rousing speech on the subject of civil rights for African Americans at the Democratic National Convention in Philadelphia. Humphrey opposed an effort by Harry S. Truman's supporters to put a weak civil rights plank in the Democratic platform in order to carry the southern states. The speech marks the beginning of Humphrey's rise to national attention and is a turning point in the Democratic Party's shift from a generally segregationist party to one advocating full legal rights for minorities.

1991 The Twins retire number 6, formerly worn by slugger Tony Oliva, who was 1964 American League Rookie of the Year and three-time American League batting champion.

JULY 15

1856 The celebrated Norwegian violinist Ole Bull performs in the capitol building in St. Paul, a heady concert for a territorial capital.

1872 The Twin Cities' first streetcar, a horse-drawn affair, begins operation.

1881 A tornado kills six in New Ulm. It also blows through Palmyra, Wellington, and Cairo in Renville County, killing eleven more.

1917 Fred Brown of Melrose kills a wolf with his bare hands. While walking to Ward Springs he finds a wolf hunting frogs, its back to him. Brown, momentarily forgetting that he has a hunting knife in his pocket, grabs the wolf by its tail and wrestles with it until he breaks open its head. When five or six other wolves approach him, Brown draws his knife and prepares to fight, but the wolves retreat.

July 15, 1856 Statue of Ole Bull, sculpted by Jacob Fjelde

1929 African American lawyer William T. Francis, appointed U.S. minister to Liberia by President Calvin Coolidge in 1927, dies of yellow fever in Monrovia, Liberia. Born in Indianapolis in 1869, Francis moved to Minnesota in 1888 and later took over Frederick McGhee's law practice (*see* June 17). As a well-known St. Paul attorney, Francis participated in many racially charged trials, including the 1920 appeal of the Duluth lynchings trial, in which he represented the defendants (*see* June 15).

1951 Jesse Ventura is born in Minneapolis. His given name is James Janos, but he would adopt the Ventura moniker at the start of his professional wrestling career. As an actor, wrestler, talk-show host, and governor, he's challenged many in the political and business elites.

JULY 16

1817 While charting the Mississippi River for the army, Major Stephen H. Long discovers St. Paul's Fountain Cave. The cave, located a few blocks west of present-day Randolph Avenue near Shepard Road, had many curious rooms and a cold crystal spring. Lewis Cass and Henry Rowe Schoolcraft visit the cave on August 2, 1820, and Schoolcraft, noting the number of names written on the walls, comments that the cave is a popular site for tourists. Later, Pig's Eye Parrant operates a saloon inside the cave. In 1955 the cave would be filled in during construction of the Archer-Daniels-Midland elevator and Shepard Road.

1858 The state seal is adopted. Modifying the territorial seal, the design includes the slogan *L'Etoile du Nord* (Star of the North) and depicts a white man plowing eastward and looking over his shoulder at an Indian on horseback riding toward the setting sun. Minor changes have been made to the seal since then, including the addition of Norway pines in the background and a shift of the Indian's route so that he rides toward the farmer.

July 16, 1858

1862 Bishop Henry B. Whipple lays the cornerstone for the Cathedral of Our Merciful Savior in Faribault, the first Episcopalian cathedral built in the United States. On the following day Whipple sets the cornerstone of the nearby Seabury Divinity School. The cathedral is dedicated on June 24, 1869.

1992 William K. Finney is sworn in as St. Paul's chief of police, the first African American to hold the position.

JULY 17

1817 Cree and Ojibwe leaders in the Red River valley make a treaty with Lord Thomas Douglas Selkirk, who hopes to re-establish his colony of Scottish settlers. *See* June 19

1854 Congress passes an act to settle the legal mess of the "Half-Breed Tract," a reservation for mixed-bloods in Wabasha and Goodhue Counties. Land titles had been confused, with many whites settling in the area, unaware that it was a legal reservation, and some of the mixed-bloods selling deeds to parcels of land, although there was no individual ownership of reservation land. Further complications arose with land speculators, and the settlers formed vigilante groups to watch the land office and prevent speculators from claiming existing farms. The matter is settled in 1858, with the squatters receiving full rights, as was standard practice on public domain land.

JULY 18

1840 A second post office is established in the region that would become Minnesota: "Lake St. Croix, Wisconsin Territory," which today is Point Douglas.

1847 Harriet E. Bishop arrives in St. Paul to open her public school. She wastes no time, starting school the next day. Although Bishop is usually remembered as Minnesota's first public school teacher, Matilda Runsey had taught for several months before Bishop's arrival, and there had been a number of missionary teachers. In addition to teaching for many years, Bishop would write two books, *Floral Home* and *Dakota War Whoop*. Harriet Island (formerly Devil's Island) is named in her honor. She died August 9, 1883.

1908 St. Paul's Lexington Park is the site of an international balloon race, sponsored by the Northwest Aero Club. Weather conditions are good, but the showing is poor: the winner is aloft for sixteen hours and forty minutes and travels only seventy-five miles.

July 18, 1908

1913 Karl F. Rolvaag is born in Northfield. He would serve as governor from 1963 to 1967. He died December 20, 1990. *See* March 25

1918 Sergeant Louis Cukela, a Croatian-born Minneapolitan serving in France, performs a feat of heroism that earns him two Congressional Medals of Honor, one from the navy and one from the army. Cukela, a member of the Fifth Marine Regiment, was pinned down with his company by machine-gun fire. Cukela worked his way around the side of the emplacement and used his bayonet to kill or capture members of the crew. He then threw a grenade into another machine gun nest, capturing it as well. A number of Minnesotans have won the nation's highest honor for bravery, but only Cukela has won two.

1962 Harmon Killebrew and Bob Allison each hit a grand slam in the same inning, leading the Twins to a win over Cleveland.

JULY 19

1815 The Dakota, having sided with the British during the War of 1812, agree to end their hostilities with the United States.

1850 The Catholic Diocese of St. Paul is created.

1858 Franklin Steele formally takes possession of the Fort Snelling military reservation, which he had bought from the government for $90,000. Although Steele envisions a city on the grounds of the fort, this idea fails and Steele is unable to keep up the payments. During the Civil War the government reasserts its claim to the fort, which would remain in government hands until after World War II.

1967 Minneapolis experiences some of the unrest in African American communities nationwide as an off-and-on riot—a crowd throwing rocks and setting fires, mostly along Plymouth Avenue—starts at about 11:30 P.M. and lasts for two nights. By 2:00 A.M. things seem to quiet down, but a second wave of rioting begins that night after Samuel Simmons, an African American, is shot during an argument in a northside bar. Governor Harold LeVander calls in 150 national guardsmen to maintain the peace, and the toll for both nights is three people shot, two policemen and one fireman injured, thirty-four people arrested, and four businesses burned to the ground.

1982 Robert Asp sails his replica Viking ship *Hjemkomst* into Bergen, Norway, completing a journey from the Great Lakes. The ship now resides in the Heritage Hjemkomst Interpretive Center in Moorhead.

1987 The Twins retire number 19 in honor of hall-of-famer Rod Carew.

JULY 20

1837 Chief Hole-in-the-Day, Chief Flat Mouth, Lawrence Taliaferro, Henry H. Sibley, Wisconsin governor Henry Dodge, and others meet at Fort Snelling to negotiate the sale of Ojibwe lands east of the Mississippi River. About 1,400 Ojibwe camp near the fort during negotiations. In the treaty, signed on July 29, the Ojibwe agree to sell the land to the federal government for $215,000. This treaty is notable for two reasons: it marked the first opening of Minnesota land to white settlers, and it allowed Indians to retain their right to hunt, fish, and gather foods in the ceded lands. The fishing clause would lead to a lengthy dispute in the 1990s.

1858 Polk County is established, named for James K. Polk, who was president when Congress authorized creation of Minnesota Territory.

1907 The Western Federation of Miners calls a strike on the Mesabi iron range. Two hundred union men had been laid off from Mountain Iron Mine, owned by the Oliver Mining Company, a subsidiary of U.S. Steel. Although layoffs on the range were common, at issue was recognition of the union, which was threatened by the discharge of only union workers. Within two months a large number of imported scabs undermine the union's efforts and the strike is broken.

1934 Two are killed and sixty-seven are injured in a clash between strikers and police during the trucker's strike in Minneapolis. After federal mediation fails, Governor Floyd B. Olson declares the city under martial law, and the National Guard takes control of the streets. *See* May 21

1940 Minneapolis holds its first Aquatennial, a festival celebrating Minnesota's summers.

JULY 21

1820 Captain Stephen Kearny's expedition to find a road from Council Bluffs, Iowa, to Fort St. Anthony (later Snelling) arrives at Lake Pepin, having lost their way. Kearny then marches his men north to the fort.

1820 Lewis Cass, governor of Michigan (which at the time included present-day Minnesota), reaches what he erroneously believes to be the source of the Mississippi River. Today this body of water is known as Cass Lake.

1856 James J. Hill arrives in St. Paul to work as a shipping clerk for J. W. Bass and Company. He would eventually find his fortune as a railroad baron and business tycoon.

July 20, 1940 Uncle Sam at the Minneapolis Aquatennial parade, ca. 1945

1879 Joseph A. A. Burnquist is born in Dayton, Iowa. During the war years of 1915 to 1921 he would serve as the nineteenth governor of the state. He died in Minneapolis on January 12, 1961.

JULY 22

1850 The steamboat *Yankee* proves that the Minnesota River is navigable by traveling for 300 miles upstream from Fort Snelling.

JULY 23

1838 Father Francis Pierz, a Slovene priest, arrives at his post in Grand Portage. He remains there for a few months and then returns in 1841 to establish a mission on the Pigeon River. His later writings encourage Germans and Slovenes to immigrate to the "earthly paradise of Minnesota."

1851 Wahpeton and Sisseton Dakota bands sign the treaty of Traverse des Sioux, near St. Peter. Cloud Man and Sleepy Eyes are among the Dakota signers, while Alexander Ramsey and Luke Lea represent the United States, with missionary Stephen Riggs interpreting. Henry H. Sibley acts as agent for the fur traders, who had accumulated debts from the Indians. In the treaty, the Dakota relinquish title to their lands west of the Mississippi River, about 24 million acres, for $1,665,000 and a reservation for the Indians is set up in the Minnesota River valley. Soon, a similar treaty with other Dakota bands is signed at Mendota. Problems with treaty payments would be one of the causes of the U.S.–Dakota War of 1862.

1872 A mob attacks the Brainerd jail, where two half-Ojibwe brothers, Te-be-ke-ke-sheck-wabe and Go-go-once, are being held for allegedly murdering a woman.

The men are taken to a nearby pine tree and hanged in front of a crowd of 1,000. After the lynching, a rumor spreads among Brainerd's residents that angry Indians are planning to attack the town. Sheriff John Gurrell telegraphs Governor Horace Austin for help. Three companies of troops are sent out, arriving on July 25. The troops find the Indians in the woods picking blueberries, and the entire incident becomes known as the "Blueberry War."

1924 St. Paul's horse-drawn fire engines make their final run.

July 23, 1924

1943 Princeton-area farmer O. J. Odegard is the first to utilize the labor of Axis prisoners of war when he requests 100 Italian POWs for farm work due to the acute labor shortage in Mille Lacs County. Odegard is forced to pay the average wage for farm work, $3.00 per prisoner per day, and the prisoners and forty armed guards arrive from Camp Clark, Missouri, on September 5. Provided with kitchen facilities, the prisoners prepare their own food, and, in fact, they are such skilled cooks that their guards prefer their meals over standard army fare.

JULY 24

1786 Geographer Joseph N. Nicollet is born in France. After traveling by canoe to Lake Itasca in 1836 and to the pipestone quarry in 1838, he would publish an excellent map of the upper Mississippi drainage in 1843.

1998 Pitcher Ila Borders of the Duluth-Superior Dukes is the first woman to win a men's regular season professional baseball game. The Dukes beat the Sioux Falls Canaries 3–1, in Duluth.

JULY 25

1847 A Baptist church in St. Paul holds Minnesota's first known Sunday school session.

1917 In New Ulm, a group of at least 6,000 attend a rally at Turner Park to protest the policy of sending draftees of German descent to fight in the European War. *See* August 25

1990 The U.S. Senate votes 96–0 to denounce David Durenberger for "reprehensible" conduct as a senator, making him one of only seven members to be publicly condemned by the Senate in the twentieth century. Durenberger is censured for financial misconduct, including evading the limit on outside earnings.

JULY 26

1820 Colonel Henry Leavenworth performs a marriage ceremony for Lieutenant Green, one of the officers at Fort St. Anthony, and Miss Gooding. Leavenworth has legal authority to perform marriages not as post commander, but as Indian agent for the lands east of the Mississippi, so he and the happy couple cross the river for the ceremony.

1892 Almost eight inches of rain fall in St. Paul, causing Lake Como to rise fourteen inches.

1895 Pierre Bottineau, the "Kit Carson of the Northwest," dies. Bottineau, the son of an Ojibwe woman and a French trader, was born in the Red River valley about 1817. Fluent in Ojibwe, French, Dakota, and English, he worked for Henry H. Sibley in the fur trade beginning in 1837. From 1850 to 1870 he led expeditions to Montana and British Columbia and was a guide for Isaac Stevens's transcontinental railroad survey of 1853. During an attack by Dakota forces at Fort Abercrombie in 1862, Bottineau slipped through the lines and went to get help. After retiring in 1870, he spent the rest of his life at Red Lake.

1896 A bicycle built for thirteen—requiring twelve people to peddle and one person to steer—tours St. Paul.

1937 Governor Elmer A. Benson refuses to give a business license to the Pinkerton Detective Agency, a notorious union-busting group.

JULY 27

1898 Alexander Ramsey, who had served as governor during the Civil War, sets the cornerstone of the present state capitol building. Designed by Cass Gilbert, the capitol is a memorial to Minnesota's Civil War soldiers.

1972 Virginia Piper, wife of investment banker Harry C. Piper, Jr., is kidnapped. The Minneapolis woman is released near Duluth after a ransom of one million dollars is paid, at the time the highest such payment ever made.

JULY 28

1861 John A. Johnson, Minnesota's first homegrown governor, is born in St. Peter. A Horatio Alger success story, Johnson would work his way up from poverty to become editor of the *St. Peter Herald*. A popular figure statewide, he would be elected governor in 1905, and his oratorical skills would attract nationwide attention. He died in office on September 21, 1909, cutting short plans to make him the Democratic Party's presidential nominee in 1912.

JULY 29

1827 John S. Pillsbury is born in Sutton, New Hampshire. Arriving in Minnesota in the 1850s, he would eventually find success and wealth in the flour-milling trade. He would serve as the state's eighth governor, arranging for the state to repay bondholders for the $5 million loan, which the railroads had defaulted on in 1858 (*see* March 9), and using his own funds to support operations at the state penitentiary, which the legislature had neglected to include in the budget. He would ensure the success of the University of Minnesota, being one of three regents who put the university on firm financial footing, and he would visit the campus almost daily for the last forty years of his life. He died on October 18, 1901.

1856 Missionary Stephen R. Riggs and his converts at the Upper Sioux Agency in Yellow Medicine County form the "Hazelwood Republic," a system of self-government by the Christianized Indians. The republic has a president, secretary, and judges, and its members would save many lives during the U.S.–Dakota War of 1862. Unfortunately, although they had not participated in any battles, the Christian Dakota would also be expelled from the state after the war.

1887 A runaway wagon strikes a streetcar traveling down Walnut Street on St. Paul's Ramsey Hill, causing the streetcar to lose control and rocket to the bottom of the hill. Surprisingly, given the hill's steep incline, there are no injuries.

1927 Beardsley sets a state record for high temperature: 114 degrees. Moorhead would equal it on July 6, 1936.

1974 Minnesota's Jeannette Piccard, who had once piloted hydrogen balloons into the stratosphere, is one of the first women to be ordained a priest in the Episcopal Church. *See also* October 23

JULY 30

1805 Lieutenant Zebulon M. Pike receives orders to seek the headwaters of the Mississippi River and to buy from the Indians land for a fort somewhere on the upper reaches of the river. Pike would not locate the source of the river, but he did purchase land for what would become Fort Snelling. *See* September 21

1835 Army Lieutenant Albert Lea, commanding a group of U.S. Dragoons, arrives at the site of his namesake city.

1884 The state's first rail shipment of iron ore, from the Soudan Mine, reaches Two Harbors.

JULY 31

1859 A mob threatens State Attorney General Charles Berry and frees Aymer Moore from the Rockford jail. Moore had led the mob that lynched suspected murderer Oscar Jackson earlier that year (*see* April 3). Learning that Moore had been freed and Berry threatened, Governor Henry H. Sibley declares Wright County to be in a state of insurrection and calls out three companies of militia to establish order and begin an investigation. He recalls the troops only when three members of the mob, including Moore, are turned over. That October, a Wright County grand jury fails to indict anyone for Jackson's murder, a sorry conclusion to the Wright County War.

1866 Major Gouverneur Kemble Warren opens the first St. Paul office of the Army Corps of Engineers. Warren's duties include bridging the Mississippi River and installing a shipping channel from St. Louis to the Falls of St. Anthony.

1873 Amherst Wilder signs his will, donating $2.5 million to help the needy in St. Paul. Born July 7, 1828, in Lewis, New York, Wilder moved to St. Paul in 1859 and soon found his fortune in various business ventures, including railroads, steamers, banks, real estate, and merchandising. He died November 11, 1894.

1910 The Split Rock Lighthouse opens. Built in response to a 1905 storm that sank twenty-six ships on Lake Superior, at first it can be reached only by boat.

1928 The St. Paul Southern Electric Railway ends fourteen years of service between St. Paul and Hastings.

July 31, 1910

AUGUST 1

1820 Lewis Cass, governor of Michigan Territory, negotiates a peace treaty between the Dakota and Ojibwe at Fort St. Anthony.

1849 Henry H. Sibley is elected delegate to Congress and other state officers are chosen in Minnesota's first territorial election.

1870 The Lake Superior and Mississippi Railroad inaugurates rail travel between St. Paul and Duluth.

1989 Duluth holds its first Bayfront Blues Festival. Originally a small, one-day regional event, it has grown into one of the major blues festivals in the country, attracting fans from all over the world, hosting over 200 blues performers of national and regional acclaim, and growing in attendance from about 1,000 the first year to nearly 60,000 over a three-day period in 1998.

AUGUST 2

1847 The U.S. government and several Ojibwe bands sign a treaty establishing the Long Prairie Reservation (between the Watab and Crow Wing Rivers) for the Winnebago (Ho-Chunk). Originally from Wisconsin, the Winnebago had been pushed to a reservation in Iowa and then were moved again to Long Prairie. This reservation would not be a good fit, however, and in 1855 they would move to Blue Earth Reservation.

Following the U.S.–Dakota War of 1862, they would be forced to move again, this time to a reservation in Dakota Territory.

1873 The Canadian government negotiates with Canadian tribes on U.S. territory when the lieutenant governor of Manitoba meets with 1,000 Indians at Harrison's Creek in the Northwest Angle.

1874 George W. Nims, a student at the Seabury Divinity School in Faribault, attempts to assassinate Bishop Henry B. Whipple. During a church service, Nims rises from the congregation, walks into the chancel, and points his pistol at Whipple. Luckily, he had forgotten to cock the hammer, giving bystanders enough time to tackle and subdue him. Whipple had turned him down for ordainment with his class as he had shown signs of being mentally unbalanced. Judged insane, he is sent to the asylum in St. Peter.

1928 President Calvin Coolidge visits Virginia and tours the iron mines.

1956 Albert Woolson, the last surviving Union veteran of the Civil War, dies in Duluth at age 109. Woolson had enlisted in the First Minnesota Heavy Artillery when he was sixteen, serving as a drummer boy. He was the model for a bronze figure on the Memorial to the Grand Army of the Republic at Gettysburg, although he did not fight there. Woolson moved to Duluth in 1905 and remained active in the GAR for decades.

August 2, 1956

AUGUST 3

1794 Minnesota's first labor dispute? French Canadian canoe paddlers at the North West Company's post at Rainy Lake threaten to quit unless they are given a raise.

AUGUST 4

1854 Congress approves legislation guaranteeing pre-emption for Minnesota settlers squatting on lands that had not been surveyed. Technically, the land could be sold only after being surveyed, but settlers had poured into lands purchased from the Indians, sometimes making substantial improvements before the surveyors completed their work. This act, sponsored by delegate Henry H. Sibley, allows the settlers to purchase their land after the fact of settlement.

1857 One of a series of arson fires in St. Paul destroys virtually all the buildings between Market, St. Peter, St. Anthony (Third), and Fourth Streets. These fires become occasions for looting, and citizens form a vigilance committee to patrol the streets.

1892 On St. Paul's West Side, heavy rains create a lake behind the landfill near Page and Brown Streets. When the "dam" gives way, three die in the resulting flood.

1916 Amos Owen is born on Sisseton Reservation, South Dakota. He would move to the Prairie Island Indian Reservation at age sixteen and later become a prominent spiritual leader, tribal chairman, and pipe carrier of the Dakota, working to broker understandings between Indian and non-Indian peoples. He died June 4, 1990.

AUGUST 5

1851 The Mdewakanton and Wahpekute bands of Dakota sell most of their lands in the southern part of the state when the Treaty of Mendota is signed. Governor Alexander Ramsey and Luke Lea represent the United States, and Little Crow, Medicine Bottle, Good Thunder, Six, and Wabasha sign for the Dakota. Other bands had sold their lands in the Treaty of Traverse des Sioux. *See* July 23

1945 Actress Loni Anderson is born in St. Paul. She would achieve fame for her role on the television show *WKRP in Cincinnati,* and, later, her divorce from actor Burt Reynolds would provide reams of material for the tabloids.

1957 The Cincinnati Reds and the Detroit Tigers play an exhibition game at Metropolitan Stadium in Bloomington, drawing a record crowd of 21,783. The Tigers win 6–5.

August 5, 1957 Aerial view of Metropolitan Stadium during the 1965 all-star game

AUGUST 6

1886 John Quincy Adams, journalist, intellectual, and civil rights proponent, arrives in St. Paul to begin his new post as editor of the *Western Appeal* (later the *Appeal*), through which he championed civil rights and supported the Republican Party. Born to free parents in Louisville, Kentucky, in 1848, he was also a member of the National Afro-American Council and president of the Afro-American Newspaper Association. He died in St. Paul on September 3, 1922.

1945 Fighter pilot Richard Bong dies in an airplane explosion in California. Bong had shot down forty Japanese planes during the war, making him America's top ace. The Bong Bridge, which opened October 25, 1984, connects Duluth with Bong's birthplace, Superior, Wisconsin.

1969 A windstorm whips through the resort town of Outing, Cass County, killing fourteen.

AUGUST 7

1898 The Thirteenth Minnesota Volunteers arrive at Paranaque, Luzon, the Philippines, to fight in the Spanish-American War and, later, to combat Filipino patriots led by Emilio Aguinaldo. Upon their return home a year later, the regiment's casualties number forty-four killed and seventy-four wounded.

1915 Towed by the *Ottumwa Belle,* the last log raft passes Winona. The sawmills downstream soon cease operations as the lumbering era draws to a close.

1942 Humorist Garrison Keillor is born in Anoka. *See* July 6

AUGUST 8

1849 The Grand Master of the Masonic Lodge in Ohio names Charles K. Smith, a founder of the Minnesota Historical Society, the master for the first Masonic Lodge in Minnesota. An organizational meeting is held on September 8 in the Central House on Bench Street, St. Paul.

1857 Organized baseball teams square off for the first time in Minnesota when members of the Base Ball Club meet on a field in Nininger.

AUGUST 9

1820 The Dakota transfer land on Pike Island to Pelagie Faribault, wife of Jean Baptiste Faribault. The Faribaults build a house and live on the island until 1826, when they are evicted because, although the land grant was part of a treaty negotiated by Colonel Henry Leavenworth, Congress had never ratified it.

1823 Edward D. Neill is born in Philadelphia. A Presbyterian minister, Neill would arrive in St. Paul in 1849, where he would be a leader in the city's intellectual and religious life until his death in 1893. In addition to founding the First Presbyterian Church, he would help establish public schools in St. Paul, serve as superintendent of instruction in Minnesota Territory, found the Baldwin School and Macalester College, and serve as chancellor of the University of Minnesota. During the Civil War he would fulfill duties as chaplain of the First Minnesota and as private secretary to Presidents Abraham Lincoln and Andrew Johnson. After the war he would serve as U.S. consul in Ireland and as secretary of the Minnesota Historical Society.

1842 The Webster-Ashburton Treaty, which set the boundary between Canada and the United States, is signed by the United States and Great Britain. The boundary had been in dispute since the end of the American Revolution. Minnesota's curious Northwest Angle is a result of this treaty. *See* February 24

AUGUST 10

1853 The Chicago *Landverein,* or land society, which would eventually establish the town of New Ulm, is formed by a group of German immigrants. At first, lawyers and preachers are banned from membership.

1887 The first edition of the *Prison Mirror,* newspaper of the state penitentiary, is published. The paper continues to this day.

1909 Mailcarrier John Beargrease dies. Born in 1858, the son of an Ojibwe leader and a white woman, Beargrease grew up in Beaver Bay and delivered mail along the north shore of Lake Superior from 1887 to 1904, his route being Two Harbors to Grand Marais. During open water the trip took him three days by rowboat, and in the winter he used a dogsled.

AUGUST 11

1900 All thirteen of the cars in Minneapolis race from the Hennepin County courthouse to Wayzata to demonstrate to the county commissioners the need for better roads. Harry Wilcox arrives in Wayzata first, making the twelve-mile run in forty-two minutes.

1906 The statue *Mississippi, Father of Waters* is unveiled in Minneapolis City Hall. An allegorical representation of the Mississippi River, the statue was carved from a single block of marble by Larkin Goldsmith Mead and weighs almost 14,000 pounds.

August 11, 1906

1992 The Mall of America opens to a gala ceremony, an unexpected parking crunch, and an estimated 150,000 shoppers, who, as the *Star Tribune* would comment, "took a vacation from recession and bought." Standing on what was the site of Metropolitan Stadium, the "megamall" is the largest in the United States.

AUGUST 12

1940 A tractor truck made by the Minneapolis-Moline Power Implement Company receives nationwide attention during army battle maneuvers at Camp Ripley. Soldiers would call it the "jeep."

August 12, 1940

1981 International Business Machines (IBM) introduces the first personal computer, which the company's plant in Rochester had helped design.

1983 The first WeFest takes place in Detroit Lakes, featuring performers Alabama, Merle Haggard, Tammy Wynette, Jerry Lee Lewis, and others. The biggest country music and camping festival in the nation, it attracts tens of thousands of country music enthusiasts annually.

1984 Harmon Killebrew is the first Twin inducted into the Baseball Hall of Fame. He blasted 573 home runs over the course of his career.

AUGUST 13

1849 Minnesota Territory's first court session is held in Stillwater. Reportedly, only one man on the jury wore boots. All the rest had moccasins.

1893 The biggest fire in Minneapolis history burns twenty-three square blocks of the city and more than 150 buildings, leaving 1,500 people without shelter.

AUGUST 14

1830 The council house of the Indian agency at St. Peter's (later Mendota) is destroyed by arson. Arsonists strike again on February 24, 1831, burning the agency home. Indian agent Lawrence Taliaferro was unpopular with corrupt traders, who disliked his strict enforcement of federal rules.

1848 Residents of the land that would become St. Paul, nearly all of whom are squatters, send Henry H. Sibley to a land sale at St. Croix Falls where, as their agent, he formally purchases their lots for them.

AUGUST 15

1933 The Barker-Karpis gang robs South St. Paul's Swift and Company of its $30,000 payroll. Police officer Leo Pavlak dies in the ensuing shoot-out.

AUGUST 16

1909 Author Marchette Chute is born in Minneapolis. She would publish several award-winning children's books, including *Shakespeare of London, Geoffrey Chaucer of England,* and *Ben Jonson of Westminster.*

1964 Australia defeats Chile as Minneapolis hosts the Davis Cup tennis tournament.

AUGUST 17

1862 Five young Dakota men, on a dare, murder the Baker family on a farm near Acton in Meeker County. Upon hearing this news, Dakota leaders decide to launch a general attack on settlers near the Lower Sioux Agency, thus beginning the U.S.–Dakota War. In terms of civilian lives lost, the conflict proves to be one of the nation's bloodiest Indian wars. In the first weeks, 400 to 800 whites are killed, and, in the months ahead, untold numbers of Dakota perish. The conflict launches a series of Indian wars on the northern plains that continue until 1890, ending with the Battle of Wounded Knee in South Dakota.

1946 A tornado kills eleven and injures sixty individuals in Mankato and North Mankato, and a second tornado injures 200 people in Wells an hour later.

AUGUST 18

1929 A 350-pound bear is killed in the Hotel Duluth's lounge. The bear had followed truck driver Arvid Peterson and his shipment of fish into the city, and, attracted by the smell of food in the Hotel Duluth's

August 18, 1929

coffee shop, broke through the window of the lounge. The hotel's night watchman, Albert Nelson, and a local unnamed drunk confront the bear, hitting it with a chair and a hammer. Others call the police, and Sergeant Eli LeBeau shoots the bear after trying first to corner it unharmed to return it to the woods. The bear is the third killed in Duluth that year.

1993 Dan and Steve Buettner of Roseville complete the first north-to-south bicycle ride across Africa. They set their rear wheels in the Mediterranean Sea 272 days and 11,836 miles before rolling their front wheels into the Indian Ocean. In addition to such natural obstacles as the Sahara Desert, jungles, and mountains, the men faced malaria, civil war, thieves, and a lack of supplies.

AUGUST 19

1862 During the U.S.–Dakota War, the Dakota make their first attack on New Ulm, and Governor Alexander Ramsey appoints Henry H. Sibley general of the Minnesota Volunteers. Although Sibley had no military experience, Ramsey selected him because the settlers trusted him and because he had a long history with the Dakota and their leaders.

1863 Count Ferdinand von Zeppelin, inventor of the airships that would be used to bomb London in World War I, enjoys a more conventional balloon ascension in St. Paul.

1957 The air force launches the ultra-high-level balloon *Man-High II* in Crosby. Pilot David Simons reaches a record 101,516 feet (almost twenty-one miles) before setting down in Elm Lake, South Dakota. The flight takes thirty-two hours and ten minutes, but Simons occupies the balloon's capsule, from pre-launch to landing, for forty-four hours, a period longer than Charles Lindbergh's solo flight across the Atlantic.

AUGUST 20

1892 On St. Paul's East Side, a five-story building collapses into Swede Hollow. The structure, home to twelve stores and twenty-five families, had been built on a landfill. Luckily, the tenants manage to evacuate the building before its slide into the hollow.

1904 A tornado with 110-mile-per-hour winds blows down St. Paul's High Bridge and kills fourteen in the Twin Cities and Stillwater.

1928 A tornado strikes Austin, killing five.

AUGUST 21

1833 The Reverend William T. Boutwell leaves La Pointe, Wisconsin, to begin his mission to the Pillager Ojibwe at Leech Lake. *See* February 4

1860 A group of abolitionists in Minneapolis persuade Judge Charles E. Vanderburgh to issue a writ of habeas corpus or an order to bring to court Eliza Winston, a slave of a visiting southern family. Vanderburgh then declares her to be free, as she is living in a free state. Her freedom provides a boost to the antislavery cause at the same time that it discourages Southerners from traveling to Minnesota, much to the dismay of the state's tourism industry.

1883 A tornado sweeps through Dodge County, killing five, and then lands in Rochester, killing thirty-one. Mother Alfred Moes and the Sisters of St. Francis convert their school into an emergency hospital, with Dr. William Mayo supervising. Realizing the need for a permanent hospital in the city, Moes establishes St. Mary's Hospital on October 1, 1889. This facility would evolve into the Mayo Clinic.

August 21, 1883 Operating room at St. Mary's Hospital, 1893

1893 A tornado strikes the city of Rochester and Olmstead County, killing thirty-eight people in fifteen minutes. The force of the winds is enough to drive a picket through a spruce tree and to pick up boxcars full of flour and then gently set them back down on the track.

1965 The Beatles perform at Metropolitan Stadium to an estimated crowd of 4,000 teenagers, mostly girls, turning the event into what one writer described as "Shrieksville, U.S.A." With the continued popularity of Beatles's recordings long after their breakup in 1970, the irony of early panning is shown in sharp relief by a *Pioneer Press* comment on the performance: "The Twin Cities was visited Saturday by some strange citizens from another world. They wore long hair and wide grins and were easily identified as Ringo Starr, John Lennon, George Harrison and Paul McCartney. They were the Beatles—alleged musicians."

August 21, 1965 "Shrieksville, U.S.A."

1995 Robert Blaeser, co-founder of the Native American Bar Association, is sworn in as the Twin Cities' first judge of American Indian descent.

AUGUST 22

1888 The Minnesota [Farmers'] Alliance and the Knights of Labor hold a conference to organize the Farm and Labor Party, nominating Ignatius Donnelly as their gubernatorial candidate. Donnelly would, however, withdraw from the race, and the nascent party would collapse. From the ashes of their false start, the members and organizations associated in the Farm and Labor Party would eventually become the Nonpartisan League and the Minnesota Federation of Labor, the direct ancestors of the Farmer-Labor Party, organizing the new party thirty years later, on August 24–25, 1918, and nominating David Evans as their gubernatorial candidate.

1912 Coya Knutson is born in Edmore, North Dakota. In 1954 she would become the first female member of Congress from Minnesota, and she would be respected nationwide for her stance on agriculture issues and her championing of the family farmer. In 1958, however, members of her own party conspired with her husband Andy Knutson to keep her from winning a third congressional term. Known as the "Coya Come Home" episode, this scandal is unfortunately what most people remember about Knutson, rather than her political record as a congresswoman.

1999 Governor Jesse "The Body" Ventura returns to his roots, refereeing a professional wrestling match at the Target Center in Minneapolis.

AUGUST 23

1852 Joseph R. Brown arrives at the site of Henderson, which he would name for his mother's family. Brown had been involved in various ventures, serving as a soldier, explorer, farmer, lumberman, legislator, and Indian agent in the early years of the territory.

1862 Twenty-four townspeople are killed at the second Battle of New Ulm during the U.S.–Dakota War. Although the Indians come close to victory, the barricaded defenders, led by Judge Charles E. Flandrau, manage to hold the town's center. Among the dead is Captain William Dodd, who had founded St. Peter in 1853 and laid out the Dodd Road from St. Paul to Mankato.

1899 Interurban streetcar service between St. Paul and Stillwater begins. The ride costs thirty cents and lasts about an hour and fifteen minutes.

AUGUST 24

1819 Colonel Henry Leavenworth and the Fifth Infantry arrive in Mendota to build a fort at the confluence of the Mississippi and St. Peter's (later the Minnesota) Rivers on land purchased from the Dakota by Lieutenant Zebulon M. Pike in 1805. The following August, Colonel Josiah Snelling takes command of the fort, which is known as Fort St. Anthony until 1825.

1839 Lewis S. Judd and David Hone open the Marine Lumber Company on the St. Croix River.

AUGUST 25

1827 Minnesota's first post office is established at Fort Snelling.

1901 Elmer Engstrom is born in Minneapolis. He would be involved in the development of color television during his career with the RCA Corporation.

1917 Reacting to protests in New Ulm over the use of draftees in the European War, the Commission of Public Safety, under orders from Governor Joseph A. A. Burnquist, suspends Mayor Louis A. Fritsche from office. Other city officials and the president of Martin Luther College are also removed from their positions. These actions effectively end the protests, although Fritsche would later be reelected. *See* July 25

1937 Congress establishes the state's first national monument: Pipestone National Monument in southwestern Minnesota. Pipestone, or catlinite, named for painter George Catlin, who visited the quarry in 1836, is still used by Indians to make calumets (peace pipes).

AUGUST 26

1731 French explorer La Vérendrye and his voyageurs land at Grand Portage to begin an expedition into the region west of the Great Lakes. La Vérendrye eventually establishes a trading post, Fort St. Charles, on Lake of the Woods. *See* June 6

1848 The Stillwater Convention petitions Congress to establish the Territory of Minnesota. Wisconsin's recent admission into the Union meant that settlers in the area between the Mississippi and St. Croix Rivers were without a government. Minnesota Territory would be officially recognized on March 3, 1849. *See* October 30

1919 The state legislature ratifies the nineteenth amendment to the Constitution of the United States, granting women the right to vote. Prior to this federal amendment, the state's women had been permitted to vote only in elections for school officials and for library officials, since 1876 and 1898 respectively.

2000 On Women's Equality Day, the Minnesota Woman Suffrage Memorial is dedicated at the state capitol. Titled "Garden of Time: Landscape of Change," the memorial is planted with native grasses and flowers and features a 100-foot trellis imprinted with the names of important suffrage leaders in the state's history.

AUGUST 27

1979 A UFO sighting in Marshall County? In the early morning Sheriff's Deputy Val Johnson is driving his car when he sees a bright light and then loses consciousness. An investigation by Sheriff Denis Brekke finds the car's windshield inexplicably damaged. The Ford Motor Company determines that the windshield cracked due to a combination of high pressure inside the car and low pressure outside. Later it is discovered that Johnson's wristwatch and the car's clock are both fourteen minutes slow. No further explanations of the event have come to light.

AUGUST 28

1857 The one-day "Cornstalk War" occurs between a group of six Ojibwe and the St. Paul Light Cavalry Company, which had been summoned after reports of thefts by the Indians. Each side loses one man after exchanging shots in a cornfield near Sunrise.

1883 Jacob A. O. Preus is born in Wisconsin. Founder of the Lutheran Brotherhood fraternal society, he would serve as state governor from 1921 to 1925. He died on May 24, 1961. For information on his son, also named Jacob, *see* January 8.

1977 Lake City's Ralph Samuelson, the "father of water-skiing," dies. In 1922 Samuelson had successfully tested water skis on Lake Pepin, having fashioned the skis by boiling and curving the tips of boards purchased at a local lumberyard.

AUGUST 29

1857 The Constitutional Conventions for the soon-to-be state of Minnesota agree to a compromise document as the state's constitution. The convention had split into two parts, Republican and Democrat, shortly after it convened. While the groups were unable to bring themselves to work together formally, they manage to produce nearly identical documents that form the state's constitution. No change in cooperation has been noted since.

1857 Minnesota experiences the first ripple of the panic of 1857 as the William Brewster and Company bank goes out of business, soon followed by the Marshall and Company bank on October 3 and the Truman M. Smith bank on October 4. The first depression in the territory, the panic is caused in part by the unsound land speculation of the territory's boom period and by the August 24 collapse of the New York branch of the Ohio Life Insurance and Trust Company, which brings down banks across the country, causing a nationwide depression that lasts three years.

1860 St. Paul's first telegraphed message is delivered to William H. Seward, governor of New York and Republican presidential hopeful.

AUGUST 30

1812 The first of the Selkirk colony members reach the Red River valley, where the Earl of Selkirk had claimed land covering much of present-day Manitoba and parts of present-day North Dakota and Minnesota. Rivalries between fur companies, grasshoppers, and a flood in 1826 lead to the colony's failure, and many of the settlers would move to the Fort Snelling grounds. *See* June 19

1813 Martin McLeod is born in Montreal. Arriving at Fort Snelling in 1837, he would trade furs in the Minnesota Valley for twenty years, be instrumental in persuading the Dakota to sign the treaties of Mendota and Traverse des Sioux, and, as a member of the legislature, write the law that put Minnesota schools on firm financial footing. He died in 1860.

1924 H. F. Pigman, a "human fly," loses his grip and falls seventy feet from the courthouse tower in Albert Lea. He survives the fall but sustains serious injuries. Said the *Minneapolis Tribune* of human flies, "When he meets with disaster his title to sympathy is decidedly clouded."

1968 A race riot begins during a dance at Stem Hall in St. Paul. Ignited by an alcohol violation, the riot continues through the next day, resulting in twenty-six arrests, numerous police and civilian injuries, and thou-

sands of dollars in property damage from fire and van-
dalism, mostly in St. Paul's Selby-Dale neighborhood.

AUGUST 31

1823 Giacomo C. Beltrami reaches and names Lake
Julia, which he incorrectly declares to be the source of
the Mississippi River.

1929 The Foshay Tower is dedicated in Minneapolis.
Hiring John Sousa to write and perform a march for
the occasion, Wilbur Foshay throws a splendid grand-
opening party, a final display of extravagance before the
1929 crash and subsequent depression that ruins him.

August 31, 1929 Dedication ceremonies for the Foshay Tower

SEPTEMBER 1

1851 Cass and Chisago Counties are created. Cass is named for Lewis Cass, governor of Michigan Territory, who explored the upper Mississippi in 1820 and negotiated several Indian treaties (*see* July 21). Chisago is named for the lake, a contraction of the Ojibwe name for the lake, *Ke-chi-sago,* meaning "large and lovely."

1857 Wendelin Grimm moves to Carver County. Grimm begins experimenting with what he called *Ewiger Klee,* or "everlasting clover," in the next year, developing a winter-hardy strain of alfalfa. Fed to cows, this alfalfa would be critical to the dairy boom in the Upper Midwest. Local schoolteacher Arthur Lyman describes Grimm alfalfa in a speech to the State Agricultural Society on January 12, 1904; with this publicity it soon becomes a major American crop and the leading variety of alfalfa until the 1940s. A monument to Grimm was erected on his old farm in Laketown Township in 1924.

1894 A forest fire kills 413 people and burns 160,000 acres of timberland around Hinckley. Railroad engineer James Root saves more than 100 people by loading them onto train cars and driving through the blaze. The devastation of this fire convinces many of the importance of forest conservation.

1918 Residents of Hibbing begin moving its buildings so that the iron ore deposit located beneath the town can be mined.

1941 Workers begin dismantling the Duluth and Northeastern Railroad, the last logging line to operate in Minnesota.

SEPTEMBER 2

1844 French Canadian voyageur, trader, and farmer Benjamin Gervais founds Little Canada. His gravestone describes him as "the first settler of St. Paul."

1862 In the Battle of Birch Coulee, Dakota warriors surround a detachment of 160 soldiers and fight them for thirty hours. Casualties for the soldiers number ninety-eight before relief troops from Fort Ridgely arrive. Dakota losses are unknown.

1868 Oliver H. Kelley organizes Minnesota's first permanent grange, the North Star Grange of St. Paul. Kelley had helped found the National Grange—a political movement and social organization for farmers—in Washington, D.C., the year before. Kelley's farm is now a historic site operated by the Minnesota Historical Society.

1873 The Anti-Monopoly Party, headed by Ignatius Donnelly, is established during a state convention at Owatonna. The party opposes protective tariffs, monopolies of wood and coal, and extravagant corporate salaries. The Democratic and Republican Parties would absorb the anti-monopolist platform, and the party itself survives only one election.

1924 Eleven hundred Ku Klux Klan members from all over the Midwest and 13,000 spectators pack the Fairmont fairgrounds in a massive rally to initiate 400 Minnesota candidates as members of the KKK.

1952 Doctors Floyd Lewis and C. Walton Lillehei perform the first hypothermic open-heart surgery, at the University Hospital in Minneapolis. During the procedure, the patient, a five-year-old girl, has her body temperature lowered to 79 degrees. She recovers, leaving the hospital eleven days later.

SEPTEMBER 3

1783 The Treaty of Paris is signed, ending both the Revolutionary War and, in theory, British control of what is now eastern Minnesota. In fact, British trading posts remain in the region until after the War of 1812.

1849 For its first meeting, the territory's legislative assembly convenes in the Central House, located at Minnesota and Bench Streets in St. Paul. The Reverend Edward D. Neill gives the invocation, and the council meets in the parlor while the house sits in the dining room.

1860 The state's first normal school opens in Winona with two teachers and twenty students. Normal schools were two-year colleges dedicated to training teachers.

1883 A celebration in St. Paul marks the impending completion of the Northern Pacific Railroad from St. Paul to the Pacific Coast. The road is actually completed on September 8. Guests include railroad president Henry Villard, President Chester A. Arthur, Ulysses S. Grant, and General Phil Sheridan.

September 3, 1883

SEPTEMBER 4

1839 Today is the birthday of Bazil Gervais, who claimed to be the first white child born in St. Paul.

1882 Oliver Crosby and Frank Johnson open the Franklin Manufacturing Company. Renamed Amhoist in 1892, the derrick crane company would be a major St. Paul employer until 1985, when it relocated to Wilmington, North Carolina.

1884 An attempt on Sitting Bull's life occurs at the Grand Opera House in St. Paul. Sitting Bull is there as part of a program, where, incidentally, he meets Annie Oakley.

1908 A forest fire burns Chisholm, causing millions of dollars in damage and leaving 6,000 homeless.

1939 Duluth's Incline Plane Railway makes its final trip. Built in 1891 for $400,000, it had carried passengers up Seventh Avenue from Superior to Ninth Street, a distance of 2,749 feet.

September 4, 1939

SEPTEMBER 5

1882 The city council establishes the St. Paul Public Library. Located on the fourth floor of the Ingersoll Building, it opens on January 2 with a collection of 8,000 books.

1893 Bohemia's renowned composer Antonín Dvořák visits Minnehaha Falls and performs for the Czecho-Slovanic Benefit Society (at CSPS Hall) in St. Paul.

Inspired by his view of the falls, Dvořák later bases a composition on his "Minnehaha theme": the *Sonatina* for violin and piano.

1917 In response to anti-draft activity, particularly in New Ulm, the "drafted men of Brown County" pass a resolution supporting both the United States' entry into the Great War and the draft law itself. *See* August 25

SEPTEMBER 6

1877 The Minnesota Chapter of the Woman's Christian Temperance Union is formed. Temperance unions were dedicated to ending drunkenness.

1889 Bob Younger dies in the Minnesota State Prison at Stillwater, where he was serving a life sentence for his role in the Northfield bank robbery.

1952 Presidential candidates Dwight D. Eisenhower and Adlai E. Stevenson address a crowd of 125,000 at the first national Soil Conservation District Field Day and Plow Match, held at a field renamed "Plowville," near Rochester.

SEPTEMBER 7

1876 The Younger gang tries to rob the First National Bank in Northfield. Bookkeeper Joseph Lee Heywood delays the robbery by refusing to open the vault and pays with his life. A gunfight in the streets of Northfield follows; two of the robbers die and two more are wounded in the fight. A posse catches up with the gang at Madelia a few days later, killing one additional member and capturing all three of the infamous Younger brothers, Cole, Bob, and Jim, who would be sentenced to life in prison. Two of the gang members escape. As the Younger brothers often worked with Frank and Jesse James, it was assumed that they took part in this crime, but their guilt has never been proven. *See* July 14

September 7, 1876 Clockwise from top: Joseph Lee Heywood, Sheriff James Glispin, Bob Younger, Charley Pitts, Jim Younger, Cole Younger, and citizen August Suborn. Center: Bill Chadwell and Clell Miller

1885 Minnesota celebrates its first Labor Day. The state legislature would declare the first Monday in September a legal holiday in 1893.

1885 The Minnesota State Fair opens for the first time on its present grounds in St. Paul. The Twin Cities had battled about which one would host the fair, but Ramsey County's donation of two hundred acres for a permanent fairgrounds clinched St. Paul's victory. The site had been the Ramsey County poor farm.

1996 "Kirby Puckett's Salute to You" draws 51,000 baseball fans to the Metrodome. On July 12 Puckett had announced his impending retirement. He would be inducted into the Baseball Hall of Fame on August 5, 2001.

SEPTEMBER 8

1884 A tornado moves through Hennepin, Ramsey, and Washington Counties, killing nine. White Bear Lake is hardest hit.

1906 The celebrated trotting horse Dan Patch paces a mile in 1:55 at the State Fair, setting the world's record.

1975 Deborah Montgomery is the first woman admitted to the St. Paul police academy, and she would eventually rise to the rank of lieutenant.

1991 Philanthropist Eleanor Lawler Pillsbury dies at age 104. She had been involved with the Women's Association of the Minneapolis Symphony Orchestra, the National Society of Colonial Dames of America, Minnesota Planned Parenthood, and the Friends of the Minneapolis Institute of Arts.

SEPTEMBER 9

1849 A group of Winnebago (Ho-Chunk), unhappy with the new Long Prairie Reservation in Minnesota, attempt to return to their native Wisconsin. Troops from Fort Snelling block their movements near St. Paul. *See* June 8

1861 The steamboat *Alhambra,* towing a barge carrying railroad track, cars, and the locomotive William Crooks, arrives in St. Paul. Operation of William Crooks, the first steam locomotive in the state, begins on June 28, 1862, with a trip to St. Anthony. The locomotive, named for the chief engineer of the St. Paul and Pacific Railroad, now rests at the Lake Superior Railroad Museum in Duluth.

1863 In Faribault, five students attend the first classes held at the Minnesota School for the Deaf.

1884 A tornado strikes the lumber mill at Marine on St. Croix, blowing away a million board feet of cut lumber.

1903 Respected judge Charles E. Flandrau dies in St. Paul. He was a hero in the defense of New Ulm during the U.S.–Dakota War. *See* August 23

1933 Joe Hauser hits two home runs for the Minneapolis Millers minor league baseball team, setting an American Association record of sixty-nine homers in a season. Hauser had also set the International League record mark at sixty-three, with the Baltimore Orioles in 1930.

SEPTEMBER 10

1820 Colonel Josiah Snelling lays the cornerstone of Fort St. Anthony, which would later bear his name. Snelling had chosen to build a stone fort rather than the typical wooden structure, in part because there was not enough wood available in the immediate area and in part because the fort was to sit on a limestone bluff. His choice would prove troublesome: while

September 10, 1820 *Fort Snelling, Minnesota, George F. Fuller, 1853*

many of his soldiers were familiar with carpentry, few had any experience with stonemasonry.

1863 In the Civil War, the Third Minnesota Regiment is involved in the capture of Little Rock, Arkansas. A painting of their entry into the city hangs in the governor's office in the state capitol.

1934 Baseball slugger Roger Maris is born in Hibbing. In 1961 he would hit sixty-one home runs for the Yankees, breaking Babe Ruth's single season record, which had stood for thirty-four years. Maris's record would be broken thirty-seven years later by Mark McGwire and Sammy Sosa.

1988 The Minneapolis Sculpture Garden opens. Designed by modernist architect Edward Larrabee Barnes in collaboration with landscape architect Peter Rothschild, it is the home of the famous *Spoonbridge and Cherry* by Coosje van Bruggen.

SEPTEMBER 11

1835 English traveler George Featherstonhaugh reaches Fort Snelling. He had been hired by the U.S. War Department to explore the geology of the Upper Midwest. He continues up the Minnesota River to Lake Traverse, and in 1847 he would publish the book *A Canoe Voyage up the Minnay Sotor.*

1888 The University of Minnesota Law School opens with thirty-two students and one faculty member, Dean William S. Pattee.

1896 A special train brings ten carloads of Minnesota Ojibwe to see the Buffalo Bill Wild West show in Ashland, Wisconsin, which in turn causes many whites to come see the Indians.

1900 How strong was the Galveston, Texas, hurricane of 1900? The remnants of the storm drop 6.65 inches of rain on Minnesota from September 9 to 11.

1971 The first Minnesota Renaissance Festival opens at Lake Grace in Jonathan. One of the largest of its kind, the festival now operates from a permanent encampment near Shakopee.

September 11, 1971

SEPTEMBER 12

1881 The balloon *Great Northwest,* piloted by Samuel A. King and carrying eight passengers, ascends from Minneapolis. Their plan to travel to the Atlantic Coast garners national attention, but the flight is a failure, with a forced landing before the balloon reaches St. Paul.

1883 Theodore Christianson is born in Lac qui Parle Township. From 1925 to 1931 he would serve as the twenty-first governor, but he was only the second one to be born in the state. He would also write a five-volume history of Minnesota. He died on December 10, 1948.

1883 The Little Sisters of the Poor establish their convent in St. Paul. The Sisters began as a Hospitallers Order in Saint Servan, Brittany, France, dedicated to serving the elderly poor and infirm, and they maintain convents and hospitality houses all over the world.

SEPTEMBER 13

1900 The Chicago Electric Vehicle Company test-drives its first car, in Faribault.

1930 Duluth's municipal airport is dedicated and a crowd of 15,000 attends the ceremony and air show.

1956 Commercial production of taconite at the Reserve Mining Company's plant in Silver Bay begins. Taconite had been developed in 1919 in Babbitt, but large-scale production wasn't begun until Edward W. Davis had perfected a method to process it and the richer parts of the iron ranges had been mined out.

SEPTEMBER 14

1871 Newspaper editor Horace Greeley gives the principal address at a Hennepin County agricultural fair held in Minneapolis. In his speech he advocates federal and state regulations for the protection of farmers.

1996 The first Northshore Inline Marathon is held in Duluth. Inline skates, or rollerblades, are a Minnesota creation: Scott and Brennan Olson designed them so hockey players could practice when there was no ice.

SEPTEMBER 15

1801 Alexander Henry II arrives at the Pembina River to begin his trading business.

1834 Indian agent Lawrence Taliaferro suspends the license of fur trader Alexis Bailly. An employee of the American Fur Company, Bailly had broken trade rules, including those forbidding the sale of liquor. Bailly's replacement, Henry H. Sibley, would play a major role in Minnesota history.

1862 The state of Minnesota and the Ojibwe living near Crow Wing sign a peace treaty. Negotiated to alleviate settlers' fears that the Ojibwe would join in the U.S.–Dakota War, in truth the agreement was void because the state does not have the power to make treaties.

1869 St. Cloud State Teachers College, Minnesota's third such institution, opens in a remodeled hotel, the former Stearns House.

SEPTEMBER 16

1885 Macalester College opens its St. Paul campus. Originally known as Baldwin School, it had been renamed for Charles Macalester, owner of the Winslow House, a hotel in Minneapolis where classes were first held. Macalester agreed to donate the hotel to the college in 1874.

1928 At the grand opening of a co-op in Mississippi (Minn.), forty-five gallons of Red Star coffee and eighty-five dozen biscuits are consumed.

1995 Henry Charles Boucha is inducted into U.S. Hockey Hall of Fame. An Ojibwe Indian born in Warroad on June 1, 1951, Boucha had been a star player on the U.S. Olympic team and had played professional hockey for the Detroit Red Wings and the Minnesota North Stars. After an eye injury forced him to retire, he served as coordinator of the Warroad Public Schools Indian Education Department.

SEPTEMBER 17

1727 Réné Boucher, the Sieur de La Perrière, lands on Lake Pepin's western shore with plans to build a military post. Fort Beauharnois is built and the Mission of St. Michael the Archangel, the first Christian mission in Minnesota, is established on a site near present-day Frontenac.

1885 Civil War veterans of Company B of the First Minnesota Regiment form the Last Man's Club, meeting yearly at the Sawyer House in Stillwater. They preserve a bottle of wine to be opened by the last survivor, who would be Charles M. Lockwood, the sole attendee of the 1930 banquet.

1887 A near-riot occurs in the grandstand of the Minnesota State Fair during a Civil War reenactment. The

September 17, 1885 Three surviving members of the Last Man's Club in 1924: John S. Goff, Peter O. Hall, and Charles M. Lockwood

mock battle breaks all previous attendance records for a grandstand event, with 80,000 people in the stands (and 20,000 more on Machinery Hill). The event is fraught with fears of the grandstand collapsing, fights for seats, and injuries from the mock battle itself. Agricultural Society secretary H. E. Hoard justifies the expense and chaos of the event by describing its educational value: "For most of the [audience] it was their first real conception of . . . the awfulness of . . . war."

1907 Warren E. Burger is born in St. Paul. As chief justice of the Supreme Court from 1969 to 1986, his major opinions would include the decision requiring President Richard Nixon to turn over the Watergate tapes and his dissent in the Bivens case, attacking the exclusion of illegally seized evidence.

1961 The Minnesota Vikings football team plays its first game, beating the Chicago Bears 37–13 at Metropolitan Stadium in Bloomington.

SEPTEMBER 18

1844 Captain Seth Eastman becomes commander of Fort Snelling for a second time. *See* April 24

1923 Al (Albert H.) Quie is born near Dennison in Rice County. Beginning in 1958, he would represent the state in Congress for ten consecutive terms, during which he advocated legislative bills relating to education, agriculture, anti-poverty, and labor issues. In 1979 he would be elected governor as an Independent Republican.

SEPTEMBER 19

1857 Gaslights illuminate the streets of St. Paul for the first time.

1865 Governor Stephen Miller announces that gold has been found near Vermilion Lake, based on a rock collected by state geologist Henry H. Eames. A gold rush begins but comes to nothing, as no sizeable amount of gold is ever found in the area. The exploitation of the rich iron ore of the region would begin twenty years later.

1926 The Duluth Eskimos professional football team defeats the Kansas City Cowboys 7–0 in their only home game of the season. The Eskimos had been designated a "road team," but they still compiled a 19–7–3 record in two years of play. Players Ernie Nevers, Johnny McNally, and Walt Kiesling are now in the Pro Football Hall of Fame. Before taking the name "Eskimos" the team was known as the Kelly-Duluths after their sponsor, Kelly Duluth Hardware Store.

1930 Dieudonne Coste and Maurice Bellonte, Frenchmen who had made the first east-to-west trans-Atlantic flight, are celebrated at Wold-Chamberlain field in Minneapolis.

1970 Fictional television character Mary Richards moves to Minneapolis, throws her hat into the air, and the popular *Mary Tyler Moore Show* begins its run.

SEPTEMBER 20

1863 At the Battle of Chickamauga in Georgia, the Second Minnesota is one of the few Union units on hand to repel a fierce Confederate attack. Casualties claim one-third of the regiment, with forty-five dead, 103 wounded, and fourteen captured out of the 382 engaged in battle.

1891 August Schell, founder of August Schell Brewing Company in New Ulm, dies. Born in Durbach, Germany, in 1828, Schell had moved to Minnesota in 1856 and four years later, with Jacob Bernhardt, founded a small brewery on the banks of the Cottonwood River. The brewery is still run by the Schell family, producing award-winning beers in the German tradition.

1939 First Lady Eleanor Roosevelt is the keynote speaker at the first meeting of the Women's Institute in St. Paul.

SEPTEMBER 21

1805 Lieutenant Zebulon M. Pike, reaching the mouth of the Minnesota River, stops at what is now known as Pike Island and raises the Stars and Stripes inside present-day Minnesota for the first time.

1836 Fur trader Alexander Faribault contracts with mason Michel Le Laire to build a house in Mendota. The house still stands. *See* May 22

SEPTEMBER 22

1895 Elmer A. Benson is born in Appleton. He would serve as governor from 1937 to 1939, representing the Farmer-Labor Party. Under his watch, the state's first workers' compensation law would be passed. His sympathy for communist principles would lead to distrust among members of his party, but he would retain control of the Farmer-Labor Party until 1944, when it merged with the Democratic Party. Increasingly radical, Benson would become a marginal figure in politics and return to farm in Appleton until his death on March 13, 1985.

1968 Cesar Tovar plays all nine positions during a Twins game.

SEPTEMBER 23

1805 The Dakota, led by Little Crow (grandfather of the warrior of 1862) and Way Aga Enagee, sell two pieces of land, a total of 100,000 acres, to Lieutenant Zebulon M. Pike for $2,000 and sixty gallons of whiskey. This agreement marks the first land cession by the Dakota and the first land purchase in what would become the state of Minnesota. Fort Snelling is built on one site, while the other is named Pike Island.

1857 In a homemade balloon, William Markoe lifts off from St. Paul and lands near Cannon Falls—Minnesota's first balloon ascension. A second flight on October 8, a feature of a territorial fair, reaches White Bear Lake.

1862 Soldiers under General Henry H. Sibley defeat the Dakota in the Battle of Wood Lake in Yellow Medicine County. Although this battle traditionally marks the end of the U.S.–Dakota War, Sibley and General Alfred Sully would undertake punitive expeditions against the Dakota the following year.

1897 The library of the Ramsey County Medical Society is established when Dr. Eduard Boeckmann donates the profits from his development of an improved method of preparing catgut for surgical use.

SEPTEMBER 24

1848 Photographer Edward A. Bromley is born in New Haven, Connecticut. Considered the first regular newspaper staff photographer in the United States, Bromley would be connected with the *Minneapolis Journal* and the *Minneapolis Times* and would emphasize the importance of photographs in illustrating news stories and chronicling historic events. He died in 1925.

1867 In the first State Baseball Championship, the St. Paul North Stars beat the Hastings Vermillion 43–35.

1886 Dr. Justus Ohage performs the nation's first successful gall bladder surgery, at St. Joseph's Hospital in St. Paul.

1924 Louis Warren Hill, second son of James J. Hill, is sued by seven of his nine siblings over his inheritance of the family's North Oaks farm and Burlington Northern railroad bonds totaling $750,000, all a gift from his mother, Mary T. Hill, shortly before her death. The "Allied Siblings" allege that their mother was not of sound mind and that Louis had intimidated her into bequeathing the legacy. The suit is eventually dropped because it could be proved that Mrs. Hill was competent when she made the gift.

1934 Arne Carlson is born in New York City. He would serve as the state's thirty-seventh governor. Among his achievements would be an innovative solution to the school voucher issue: a $1,000-per-child tax credit for families earning less than $35,000 per year. *See* October 28

1963 President John F. Kennedy speaks at the University of Minnesota at Duluth on the subject of high unemployment in the northern Great Lakes area, where joblessness was about twice the national average.

SEPTEMBER 25

1867 Horace Goodhue, Jr., opens a prep school in Northfield with twenty-three students attending. The institution is first known as Northfield College, but a generous donation from William Carleton of Charlestown, Massachusetts, would inspire its current name, Carleton College.

1896 Generals Oliver O. Howard, Daniel Sickles, Alexander Stewart, and Russel Alger speak against the silver standard, a Populist platform, and in support of William McKinley, to an audience of about 6,000 at St. Paul's Auditorium. On their speaking tour of the Northwestern states, the generals also stop in Le Sueur, Little Falls, Mankato, St. Peter, and Willmar.

1937 Ironton thug John Henry Seadlund and accomplice James Atwood Gray kidnap Charles Sherman Ross in Chicago. The kidnappers demand a $50,000 ransom from their hideout near Emily, Minnesota. In the end, Seadlund murders Ross and Gray at a location north of Spooner, Wisconsin. Seadlund would be captured at a racetrack in California and executed by order of the state of Illinois in 1938.

SEPTEMBER 26

1862 Dakota who had opposed the 1862 war gain control of 269 white captives and release them to General Henry H. Sibley at a location marked by Camp Release Monument in Lac qui Parle County.

1992 The Minnesota Vietnam Veterans Memorial is dedicated in St. Paul.

SEPTEMBER 27

1862 The legislature allows Minnesota's Civil War soldiers to vote by passing the state's first absentee ballot law.

1888 John Ireland is named Archbishop of Minnesota. Born on September 11, 1838, in Burnchurch, Kilkenny County, Ireland, he had arrived in St. Paul in 1852. After his ordination in 1861, he served as chaplain of the Fifth Minnesota Regiment during the Civil War, organized an abstinence society, and helped bring many immigrant groups to the state. He would also establish a black Catholic church and build the Cathedral of St. Paul, one of the city's most visible landmarks. A prominent Republican, he argued against the prevailing wisdom that Catholicism was compatible with democracy.

1894 Theodore Hamm holds an open house at his St. Paul brewery, which he had owned since 1865 and which would be incorporated in 1896. Hamm's beer has long been a popular Minnesota product, advertised with its catchy slogan— "from the land of sky-blue waters"— and recognizable image—the Hamm's bear.

1996 A statue of F. Scott Fitzgerald, author of the novel *The Great Gatsby*, is unveiled in Rice Park, St. Paul. Sculpted by Michael Price, a Merriam Park resident and teacher at Hamline University,

September 27, 1996 F. Scott Fitzgerald, ca. 1920

the statue is dedicated during a centennial celebration of Fitzgerald's birthday (September 24, 1896) and unveiled by his granddaughter, Eleanor Lanahan. This event is part of the Literature Festival, organized by Garrison Keillor, which brings together aspiring writers and professional authors to talk about their craft.

SEPTEMBER 28

1839 Early St. Paul resident Edward Phelan is arrested for the murder of his partner, Joe Hays. He would be acquitted, but his character was so unsavory that many considered him guilty. Hays's was the first death and the first murder in the city's history.

1908 Republican presidential candidate William Howard Taft campaigns briefly in Melrose as part of a whistle-stop tour of Minnesota that includes Minneapolis, St. Cloud, and Sauk Centre. Introduced by Congressman Charles A. Lindbergh, Sr., Taft urges voters not to take a chance on Democratic candidate William Jennings Bryan.

1935 Joan Growe is born in Minneapolis. She would serve as Minnesota's secretary of state from 1975 to 1998, the first woman elected to statewide office without first having been appointed. A member of the Democratic-Farmer-Labor Party, she would champion voter and election reform, including such programs as vote by mail and motor voter registration.

1955 The final game at Nicollet Park: the Minneapolis Millers play the Rochester Redwings, winning the Junior World Series 9–4. After Nicollet Park is demolished, the Millers' home would be Metropolitan Stadium until the Minnesota Twins replace them.

September 28, 1955

SEPTEMBER 29

1837 Dakota leaders sign a treaty in Washington, D.C., selling their lands east of the Mississippi River for about $500,000 in cash and goods. This treaty, along with the Ojibwe treaty of the same year (*see* July 20), opens eastern Minnesota to white settlement. Representatives for the United States are Joel R. Poinsett and Lawrence Taliaferro, while Tahtapesaah, Big Thunder, and Grey Iron sign for the Dakota.

1964 St. Paul's first McDonald's Restaurant opens on Fort Road. A burger costs fifteen cents.

1983 James Jenkins and his son Steven Jenkins (now Steven Jenkins Anderson) lure Ruthton bankers Rudy Blythe and Toby Thulin to their ten-acre dairy farm, which had been repossessed by Blythe's bank, and kill them both. The murders spur a nationwide manhunt, ending with Steven Jenkins's surrender and James Jenkins's suicide in northern Texas. Steven Jenkins, barely eighteen years old at the time, professes his innocence but is convicted of the murders. Seventeen years later he would admit in an interview that he had killed the bankers.

SEPTEMBER 30

1841 Captain Seth Eastman begins the first of his four commands at Fort Snelling, this one lasting until October 26. An artist and former instructor of drawing at West Point, Eastman would record in his paintings images of the fort, traditional Indian ways, and frontier life. *See* September 18

1854 At La Pointe, Wisconsin, a number of Ojibwe bands sign a treaty transferring Minnesota's "Arrowhead" region to the U.S. government for about $400,000. Signers for the Grand Portage band include Little Englishman and Like a Reindeer; Balsom and Loon's Foot sign for the Fond du Lacs; and Hole-in-the-Day and Berry Hunter sign for the Mississippi River band. Henry C. Gilbert and David B. Herriman represent the United States, and Henry M. Rice and Richard Godfroy act as witnesses.

1876 The Czecho-Slovanic Benefit Society, known as CSPS, a free-thought fraternal organization, is formed in St. Paul.

1887 The South St. Paul livestock market opens, and 363 cattle are sold the first day.

1892 The Oliver Mining Company is organized to work the Iron Range. It would eventually own nearly all of the mines in the range. *See* June 3 and July 20

1924 Bandits rob the Exchange State Bank at Wykoff. The bandits enter the town in the middle of the night, cut all telephone and telegraph wires, and then blast open the bank's safe. Apparently frightened during the burglary, the thieves leave hurriedly, taking only $500 and leaving another $500 as well as some of their tools behind.

1981 The Twins play their final game at Metropolitan Stadium. The Mall of America now occupies the site.

OCTOBER 1

1700 On his second visit to the region, French explorer Pierre Charles Le Sueur arrives at the mouth of the Blue Earth River. At this site he builds Fort L'Huillier, named for a chemist in France who had told Le Sueur that the blue clay found at this location on his first trip was rich in copper. Le Sueur travels with two tons of the clay to New Orleans, leaving nineteen men to continue operations. Unfortunately, further testing shows that the clay contains no copper, and when Le Sueur returned to the Blue Earth River the fort had disappeared. In 1907 A. Mitchell would find on his farm seventeen decapitated skeletons and many arrowheads about a mile and a half from the fort's site. The bodies had been arranged in a straight row, buried in European fashion, leading to the conclusion that two men had survived an attack and buried their comrades. Their fates are unknown.

1847 Ard Godfrey arrives at the Falls of St. Anthony to build his sawmill. His house, Minneapolis's first frame building, still stands at the corner of University and Central Avenues.

October 1, 1847 Godfrey House, 1936

1908 At the urging of Dr. Richard O. Beard, the Board of Regents for the University of Minnesota authorizes a nursing curriculum, the first college-associated school of nursing in the country. The school opens March 1, 1909, with Bertha Erdmann as director.

1929 The first celebration of Kolacky Day in Montgomery occurs. A kolacky is a Czechoslovakian pastry filled with fruit. At first the festival was only a day long, but in 1975 the celebration was scheduled for late July and extended into Kolacky Days, complete with music, dancing, art displays, and a parade.

1946 Author Tim O'Brien is born in Austin. His novel of the Vietnam War, *Going After Cacciato,* would win the National Book Award in 1979.

1992 The MinnesotaCare health program, benefiting uninsured low-income Minnesota residents, goes into effect. MinnesotaCare is financed by state tax dollars, provider taxes, and premiums paid by enrollees. According to the Institute for Southern Studies' "Gold and Green 2000" report, Minnesota boasts the lowest number of people without health insurance in the country.

OCTOBER 2

1843 The St. Croix County Board of Commissioners licenses Henry Jackson to open a tavern "at St. Paul's" and also names him justice of the peace. Jackson Street runs from the site of his store.

1863 The Red Lake and Pembina bands of Ojibwe sign the Old Crossing treaty, ceding to the U.S. government three million acres of land in the Red River valley. Senator Alexander Ramsey and Indian agent Ashley C. Morrill represent the United States, and Moose Dung, Crooked Arm, Little Rock, and Little Shell are among the Ojibwe signers. The treaty is named for a ford in the Red Lake River, near Red Lake Falls. A monument would be dedicated at the treaty site, in Huot, in 1933.

1900 William Jennings Bryan, presidential candidate, orator, and future participant in the Scopes trial on teaching evolution in public schools, speaks in St. Peter.

1900 The *St. Paul Dispatch* runs a photograph of all the automobiles owned by city residents: two cars and two trucks.

1950 The "Peanuts" comic strip of St. Paul's Charles Schulz begins national syndication in seven newspapers. *See* February 12

1968 Congress passes the National Wild and Scenic Rivers Act, naming the upper St. Croix River as one of eight rivers protected by this legislation. The lower fifty-two miles of the river is preserved on October 25, 1972.

OCTOBER 3

1887 Horsecars begin hauling passengers in St. Cloud.

1951 Dave Winfield is born in St. Paul. He may be the most versatile athlete the state has produced. Based on his performance at the University of Minnesota, professional teams in three different sports—basketball, football, and baseball—would draft him. His choice would be baseball and he would play for several teams, including the Twins, accumulating twelve all-star game appearances, 3,110 career hits, and 465 home runs. He was inducted into the Baseball Hall of Fame in 2001.

1977 Rosalie Wahl is the first female justice appointed to the state supreme court.

1997 International passenger ship traffic returns to Minnesota when the *Columbus,* carrying a load of German passengers, visits the Duluth-Superior harbor. *See* June 23

October 3, 1977

OCTOBER 4

1869 A tunnel being built under Hennepin Island to provide waterpower for additional mills gives way. The 2,000-foot collapse threatens to divert water from the main falls and cut the power source for mills along the river. Local citizens work to plug the hole until the river freezes, and then a dam is built to allow for more permanent measures. The repair job would require ten years to complete.

OCTOBER 5

1898 The Battle of Sugar Point occurs on Leech Lake. Soldiers from the Third Infantry had accompanied U.S. Marshal R. T. O'Connor to arrest Bugonaygeshig, or "Old Bug," of the Bear Island Pillager Indians. Bugonaygeshig had protested practices of lumber companies on the reservation, and he was in turn accused of illegal liquor sales. When O'Connor came to arrest him, Bugonaygeshig was rescued by a group of Ojibwe. O'Connor then requested assistance from General John M. Bacon at Fort Snelling, who traveled with eighty soldiers on a steamer to Sugar Point on Leech Lake, where Bugonaygeshig and his friends were living. Six soldiers are killed in the ensuing battle, while Bugonaygeshig escapes and is never arrested.

OCTOBER 6

1860 Joseph R. Brown's steam wagon, a horseless carriage that debuted in Henderson on July 4, is permanently mired near Three Mile Creek en route to Fort Ridgely. Brown would build another tractor in 1862, but he died before perfecting it.

1972 James Griffin becomes the first African American deputy chief of police in St. Paul.

OCTOBER 7

1794 Construction begins on Ash House, a Hudson's Bay Company trading post at the mouth of Rainy River. The two-story log house, with oiled parchment windows and a clay and stone chimney, is completed a month later.

1910 Forest fires destroy Baudette and Spooner, killing twenty-nine people and burning over 220,000 acres of land. During this dry year over 900 fires had burned in twenty-nine counties, causing forty-two deaths. Graceton, Pitt, Cedar Spur, and Williams also burned.

1935 Amelia Earhart speaks to the Women's City Club in St. Paul. Formed in 1921, the club valued social, cultural, political, and intellectual pursuits and also hosted speakers Gertrude Stein and T. S. Eliot.

OCTOBER 8

1858 Center City, the county seat of Chisago County, is established, and a number of Swedish immigrants settle in the area. Reflecting the ethnic makeup of the county, residents would later attempt to change the name of Chisago Lake to Swede Lake.

1910 Gus Hall, chairman of the Communist Party, U.S.A., is born in Virginia (Minn.). His given name is Arvo Kusta Halberg. Hall would join the Communist Party at age sixteen and, despite his stated political views, serve in the navy in World War II. He would run for president four times and spend over eight years in prison for his activities. At its peak in the 1930s, the Communist Party had about 100,000 members. Hall died October 13, 2000.

1956 Southdale Shopping Center, the first fully enclosed shopping mall, opens in Edina. Austrian war refugee and architect Victor Gruen designed the mall, which he hoped would become "the town square that has been lost since the coming of the automobile. It should become the center of this civilization." Later realizing that civilization was in fact crystallizing around the mall in a commercial rather than in his utopian way, Gruen would retire from architecture in 1967 and become one of the most ardent critics of commercialized mall culture until his death in 1980.

OCTOBER 9

1846 Jacob Schmidt is born in Bavaria. Schmidt would open a major regional brewery in St. Paul. The Jacob Schmidt Brewing Company, Inc., would be bought by G. Heilemann Brewing Company, which in turn would sell the brewery to Landmark Brewing in 1992.

October 9, 1846 Schmidt brewery, bottling department, 1933

1876 At a Kandiyohi County rally to support greenbacks rather than gold as the national currency, candidate for Congress Ignatius Donnelly gives a speech.

1933 The bones of Browns Valley Man are found in a Traverse County gravel pit that was likely a Paleo-Indian burial site between 8,000 and 12,000 years ago.

1949 A statue of Leif Erikson, titled "Discoverer of America" and sculpted by John K. Daniels, is dedicated on the explorer's holiday. The result of a ten-year fundraising campaign by the Leif Erickson Monument Association, the thirteen-foot bronze statue is located on the capitol grounds in St. Paul. *See* October 12

October 9, 1949 John K. Daniels working on Leif Erikson statue

1979 Rose Totino patents her "Crisp Crust" frozen pizza crust, an improvement on what she called the "cardboard crust" pizzas that were available at the time. The Northeast Minneapolis entrepreneur had sold Totino's Finer Foods to Pillsbury in November of 1975 and had become a vice president in the company. By 1992 Totino's would control twenty percent of the frozen pizza market.

OCTOBER 10

1862 The Augustana Synod of the Lutheran Church gives Eric Norelius permission to open an academy. First established in Red Wing, then moved to East Union, the college that would become Gustavus Adolphus permanently located in St. Peter in 1876.

1917 The St. Paul Public Library opens its new building at Fourth and Washington Streets, with Dr. W. Dawson Johnston serving as librarian.

1918 A forest fire begins on the railroad line between Duluth and Hibbing and burns for the next three days, reaching Duluth on the thirteenth. Thirty-eight communities, including the cities of Cloquet, Carlton, and Moose Lake, and the towns of Adolph, Brookston, Munger, Grand Lake, Pike Lake, and Twig, are burned and 435 people are killed. After the blaze, forest salvagers cut 1.6 million tons of lumber. In response to a series of lawsuits, the Minnesota Supreme Court rules that the railroads, and by extension the U.S. Railroad Administration, a federal agency that controlled the railroads during the war, are responsible for damages based on poor forestry practices. The Railroad Administration eventually compensates claims at a rate of fifty percent, the final payments being made in 1935.

1949 A destructive windstorm sweeps through Minnesota, causing $10 million in losses to the corn crop and over $1 million in property damage in St. Paul alone. Amazingly, no deaths are reported.

OCTOBER 11

1887 President Grover Cleveland is in St. Paul for the second day of a three-day visit to the state. Former governors Henry H. Sibley, Alexander Ramsey, and William R. Marshall accompany him in his travels around the area.

1954 The state historical society recognizes ethnographer Frances Densmore for "distinguished service in the field of Minnesota History." Densmore, a Red Wing native, was one of the first ethnologists to specialize in the study of American Indian music and culture and is perhaps best known for her field recordings of Ojibwe songs.

OCTOBER 12

1892 The first car of iron ore travels from Mountain Iron to Duluth and assays at 65 percent iron. Minnesota would lead the country in iron ore production for many years, and iron, in the form of taconite, is still a major export.

1931 With a parade and elaborate ceremonies, a bronze statue of Christopher Columbus is dedicated on the state capitol grounds. Sculpted by St. Paul native Carlo Brioschi, the statue was sponsored by the Minnesota State Federation of Italian American Clubs. *See* October 9

1945 Columbus Day becomes a state holiday.

1997 Marcelina Anaya Vasquez, founder in 1970 of the Migrant Tutorial program, dies. Working in St. Paul's west side, Vasquez trained bilingual tutors to assist migrant children with their English reading and writing skills. The St. Paul school district had taken over her successful program in 1978.

OCTOBER 13

1857 The state constitution is ratified by popular vote. In the accompanying gubernatorial election, Henry H. Sibley beats Alexander Ramsey by a slim margin of 240 votes out of 35,340 cast.

1893 Celebrating Minnesota Day at the World's Fair in Chicago, twenty thousand of the state's residents view exhibits of the state's resources and hear the First Minnesota Regiment's band.

1919 Author Kathleen Winsor is born in Olivia. Her novel *Forever Amber,* published in 1944, would be banned in Boston because of its sexual content. With that publicity, it naturally became a best seller.

1990 The Target Center arena opens in Minneapolis.

OCTOBER 14

1853 St. Paul begins the slow process of numbering buildings with 20 Robert Street, which was home to Cathcart, Kern & Co.'s Crystal Palace, a dry-goods store.

1946 After 126 years of service to the nation, Fort Snelling is closed as a military post and placed under the Veterans' Administration's control.

OCTOBER 15

1800 Spain transfers to France the Louisiana Territory, part of which would eventually become western Minnesota. France sells the territory to the United States three years later.

1857 Daily mail service between Prairie du Chien and St. Anthony begins.

1880 A blizzard marks the beginning of the "winter of the deep snow" and kills at least six individuals in

Pipestone and Cotton-wood Counties. During that winter, the *Pipestone County Star* is printed on brown wrapping paper for eight weeks while the snow blocks supply trains.

October 15, 1880 Snow blockade, 1880–81

1884 James Thompson, St. Paul's first black resi-dent, dies in Nebraska. Thompson had the dis-tinction of being the only slave sold in Minnesota. He was brought to Fort Snelling as the servant of an army officer in 1827, where he proved himself gifted in languages, quickly learning Dakota. Bought and freed by Methodist mis-sionary Alfred Brunson, Thompson then served as an interpreter at the Kaposia mission and eventually set-tled in St. Paul, where he donated the land and much of the material for the city's first Methodist church (now the site of the St. Paul Hotel). In his time, he was also famous for defeating Edward Phelan in a fight over a pig that Phelan had stolen from him.

1891 Concordia College opens in Moorhead with a class of twelve students. At first a high school, Concor-dia would begin to offer college-level courses in 1907.

1971 In the first such case in the United States, the Minnesota Supreme Court rules that the state's prohibi-tion of same-sex marriages is constitutional. The case involves two men, Richard J. Baker and James M. Mc-Connell, who had requested a marriage license from the Hennepin County clerk of court. When the clerk denied them the license, Baker and McConnell sued, eventually taking the case to the state's highest court.

OCTOBER 16

1898 Future Supreme Court Justice William O. Douglas is born in Maine (Minn.). Briefly a resident of this state, Douglas would move further west while he was an infant as his family sought a climate more accommodating to his nearly crippling polio.

1921 The Marx Brothers play the Hennepin Orpheum Theatre in Minneapolis.

1924 Minnesota's first pheasant season begins in Hennepin and Carver Counties. The ring-necked pheasant had been introduced to the state from China in 1905, and it would eventually become Minnesota's most important upland game bird.

1930 A bookstore owned by the Communist Party and located on Third Avenue in South Minneapolis is bombed. A mob then loots the store, burning its books in a bonfire on the street.

October 16, 1930 Henning Holm, manager of a communist bookstore, holding a sign left by people who raided his store

1987 The state celebrates Henry H. Wade Day, honoring the inventor of enriched taconite, a product that has kept the iron range and its ports operating for many years.

1989 David Brom is sentenced to fifty-two years in prison for murdering his Olmsted County family with an ax. Judge Ancy Morse orders the eighteen-year-old Brom to serve three consecutive life sentences to ensure that he is never released.

OCTOBER 17

1825 William R. Marshall is born near Columbia, Missouri. He would move to Minnesota, own a hardware store in St. Paul, found the *St. Paul Press* in 1861, and serve as a general in the Civil War. As the fifth governor of the state, he would advocate extending the right to vote to African American men, and this law would be passed in 1868, two years before the fifteenth amendment extends suffrage nationwide. He died on January 8, 1896.

1924 The Phyllis Wheatley Settlement House (now the Phyllis Wheatley Community Center), named for the eighteenth-century slave-poet, opens in north Minneapolis. The oldest African American agency in the Twin Cities, the center first serves as a place where young African Americans meet for recreation and skill development and later provides a home-away-from-home for civic leaders, educators, entertainers, and students. Today the center calls itself "the cornerstone of the community" and offers integrated programs to address the needs of local families.

1975 Rochester declares an air pollution alert and earns the dubious distinction of having the highest carbon monoxide levels recorded in the state. This and other alerts in the state during the early 1970s were caused by stagnant weather systems that did not blow away industrial and automobile emissions.

OCTOBER 18

1848 Land in central Minnesota is set aside for the Menominee. The tribe decides not to move from their holdings in Wisconsin, and they cede the proposed reservation to the state on May 5, 1854.

1881 At St. Paul's Episcopal Church in Duluth, an organizational meeting is held to establish a new hospital in the city. Named for today's feast of St. Luke, the hospital is set up in an old blacksmith's shop, and the first patient is admitted on November 18.

1888 The Agriculture School of the University of Minnesota's St. Paul campus, which was known as University Farm, opens with forty-seven students and W. W. Pendergast as principal.

OCTOBER 19

1894 Otto Wonnigheit and Charles Irmisch are hanged for murder in the Federal Courts Building (now the Landmark Center) in St. Paul.

1912 The statue of Governor John A. Johnson, sculpted by Andrew O'Connor, is unveiled on the capitol grounds. *See* July 28

OCTOBER 20

1818 The northern boundary of the United States is set at the forty-ninth parallel of latitude, extending from the Lake of the Woods to the Rocky Mountains. *See* August 9

1849 The Minnesota Historical Society is incorporated by an act of the territorial legislature, and Alexander Ramsey is elected the society's first president. Minnesota is lucky to have begun preserving its history so early.

1896 Daily mail delivery begins in Cannon City.

1937 The brothel of St. Paul's most famous madam, Nina Clifford, is demolished after fifty years of business at 147 Washington Street.

1995 The movie *Mallrats* opens. Filmed at the Eden Prairie mall and directed by independent film sensation Kevin Smith, the movie flops in theaters but develops a cult following.

OCTOBER 21

1839 The U.S. War Department orders Edward Janes, Wisconsin territorial marshal, to expel the Selkirk squatters from Fort Snelling military reservation. The fort's commander had complained of the settlers selling whiskey to the soldiers. *See* May 6

1850 Swedish settlement in Minnesota begins when Carl A. Fernström, Oscar Roos, and August Sandahl build a log cabin on Hay Lake in Washington County.

1967 The Minnesota North Stars professional hockey team plays its first home game, beating the California Seals 3–1.

OCTOBER 22

1836 "General" James Dickson and a group of filibusters arrive at Fond du Lac. They plan to form an army of métis (mixed-bloods) in the Red River area, march to California and capture it from Mexico, and establish an Indian kingdom ruled by Dickson. The group travels as far as Pembina before being broken up by employees of the Hudson's Bay Company.

1989 Jacob Wetterling, an eleven-year-old from St. Joseph, is kidnapped while riding his bike. His parents launch a search for him, and Jacob's photograph appears on posters from coast to coast, but he has not been found. In 1990, Jerry and Patty Wetterling would establish a nonprofit foundation to focus national attention on missing children and their families.

OCTOBER 23

1905 Actress Ethel Barrymore appears in the play *Sunday,* which runs through October 25 in St. Paul.

1920 Sinclair Lewis's novel *Main Street* is published. In 1930, the Sauk Centre native would be awarded the Nobel Prize in Literature. *See* December 10

1934 Minnesota residents Jeannette and Jean Piccard ascend in a hydrogen balloon to a record 57,579 feet. Jeanette would make a total of six trips into the stratosphere and would later serve as a consultant to NASA. *See also* July 29

October 23, 1920

OCTOBER 24

1871 The railroad reaches Breckenridge in the Red River valley.

1988 Duluth mayor John Fedo goes on trial, charged with accepting a bribe and misusing city money. He would be acquitted.

OCTOBER 25

1892 James H. Burrell becomes the first African American member of the St. Paul police force.

1924 Charles Evans Hughes, secretary of state and future Supreme Court justice, gives a speech in which he praises President Calvin Coolidge, blasts third-party politics, and condemns corrupt politicians, in front of a crowd of 10,000 in St. Paul.

October 25, 1892

1941 Novelist Anne Tyler is born in Minneapolis. She would publish many popular books, including *The Accidental Tourist* and *Breathing Lessons,* for which she would be awarded a Pulitzer Prize in 1989.

1987 In the seventh game of the World Series, the Twins beat the St. Louis Cardinals with a score of 4–2, winning the series 4–3.

1991 Meng Kruy Ung, founder of the first Cambodian refugee center in Minnesota, dies. Born in Prey Veng, Cambodia, Ung immigrated to the United States in 1984 and later established the Refugee and Immigrant Resource Center in Farmington. In 1993 the center would merge with the Khmer Association of Minnesota to form the United Cambodian Association of Minnesota, offering cultural, legal, and employment services to refugees and immigrants.

OCTOBER 26

1950 Edward Calvin Kendall and Philip Showalter Hench, Mayo Clinic doctors, and Tadeus Reichstein, a Swiss doctor, are awarded the Nobel Prize in Medicine for their development of cortisone.

1960 Calvin Griffith decides to move his Washington Senators to Minnesota, where the team is renamed the Twins.

OCTOBER 27

1829 Christopher C. Andrews is born in New Hampshire. A pioneer advocate of the application of European forestry principles to American conditions and a persistent sponsor of the preservation of forests for posterity, he would serve as the state's first chief fire warden and as the commissioner of forestry from 1905 to 1911.

1849 The territorial legislature creates the original nine counties of Minnesota. Benton County is named for Thomas Hart Benton, senator from Missouri who promoted western expansion; Dakota is for the Indian tribe; Itasca for the headwaters of the Mississippi River; Ramsey for the new territory's governor (*see* April 22); Wabasha for a series of Dakota leaders; and Washington for our nation's first president. Three of the original counties no longer appear on a Minnesota map: Wahnahta County, near Lake Traverse, was named for Chief Wanotan of the Yankton Lakota; Pembina County included much of what would become North and South Dakota; and Mahkahta County was north of present-day Crow Wing County.

1937 The Morris Fruit Company building in Minneapolis collapses, killing two employees. On November 1, a jury of experts learns that the building had shown signs of rotting and overloading on its third floor and had not been rebuilt after a 1933 fire. Finding no criminal negligence, however, the jury simply calls for stricter enforcement of the building code.

1991 Jack Morris pitches a ten-inning shutout as the Minnesota Twins beat the Atlanta Braves 1–0 in the seventh game of an exciting World Series.

OCTOBER 28

1834 Henry H. Sibley arrives in St. Peter's (Mendota), completing a journey on horseback from Prairie du Chien.

1919 Congress passes the Volstead Act, setting in motion the prohibition of liquor sales nationwide. Andrew J. Volstead, congressman from Minnesota, had introduced the bill.

1949 President Harry S. Truman appoints Eugenie Moore Anderson of Red Wing as ambassador to Denmark, making her the United States' first woman ambassador.

October 28, 1949

1990 Popular candidate Jon Grunseth withdraws from the gubernatorial race. Grunseth had been affected by incumbent Rudy Perpich's mudslinging campaign, but his candidacy was ultimately destroyed by accusations of sexual impropriety. Grunseth's withdrawal opens the door for Arne H. Carlson, state auditor, to run on the Republican ticket. Public disgust with the entire campaign helps Carlson win, and he proves to be a popular governor.

OCTOBER 29

1775 Jean Baptiste Faribault is born in Quebec. The fur trader and pioneer would live in Iowa, Wisconsin, and Minnesota as these territories became states. In Minnesota he would reside in Little Rapids, Pike Island, and Mendota. He died in 1860. The Minnesota county honors his name, while the city commemorates his son, Alexander.

1866 The Uppertown Olympics beat the Lowertown Saxons in St. Paul to become the city's first baseball champions.

1947 Charles Babcock, the father of the Minnesota highway system, is honored with a monument dedicated in Elk River. He had served as commissioner of highways beginning in 1917, planning the state's trunk highway system and seeing three-fourths of it completed before leaving office in 1932.

1971 Actress Winona Ryder is born in Winona.

OCTOBER 30

1848 Henry H. Sibley is chosen to represent the as-yet unrecognized Minnesota Territory in the U.S. Congress. He travels to Washington, D.C., and persuades the committee on elections to allow him to sit with Congress. The territory would be formally created on March 3, 1849.

1924 In a rare instance of a tong war in Minnesota, Wong Si Wing, a laundryman, is shot in Minneapolis. Tongs, or merchant organizations, were initially formed to protect members from encroachment by rival Chinese businessmen but now are usually social groups.

OCTOBER 31

1872 Augsburg College is dedicated in Minneapolis.

1903 The Minnesota-Michigan football game ends in a 6–6 tie. Declaring a "moral victory" over the favored Michigan team, the Gophers claim for their trophy a water jug accidentally left behind by the Michigan trainer. The Little Brown Jug becomes a symbol of the two teams' rivalry from this day forward.

1920 Anoka begins earning its reputation as the Halloween Capital of the World by holding its first planned celebration of the holiday. Traditional events include a parade, football game, and 5K Grey Ghost Run.

1991 The "Halloween Blizzard" begins. A record snowfall of 24 to 36 inches blankets the area from Duluth to the Twin Cities, the state's largest recorded snowfall in a single storm.

October 31, 1903 University of Minnesota trainer with the Little Brown Jug, 1940

NOVEMBER 1

1841 Father Lucien Galtier dedicates his log church to "St. Paul, the apostle of nations." This name is deemed superior to "Pig's Eye," the community's previous moniker, and St. Paul is incorporated as a town on this date in 1849. The log structure later serves as the first school of the Sisters of St. Joseph, and in 1856 its logs are dismantled, numbered, and hauled up the hill to the St. Joseph's Academy construction site. Unfortunately, the plan to rebuild the chapel as a historic site had not been communicated to the workmen, who use the logs to warm themselves and their coffee.

November 1, 1841

1849 The legislature establishes funding for the territory's public schools. By decree of the Northwest Ordinance, one section in each township had been set aside to support a school, and in Minnesota these lands are not sold for short-term cash but are rented out to provide a steady and long-term cash flow. Martin McLeod authored the bill, which Territorial Governor Alexander Ramsey would consider his administration's most important piece of legislation.

1976 The first issue of the *Circle* newsletter is published by the Minneapolis American Indian Center.

Containing stories about the lives and values of American Indians in the metro area, the newsletter would become a newspaper in March 1980 with a grant from the Dayton Hudson Foundation.

NOVEMBER 2

1869 Measuring one-third of a township, tiny Manomin County is abolished and transferred to Anoka County. Known as Mamomin Township until 1879, the territory is now the town of Fridley.

1948 Hubert H. Humphrey wins Minnesota's race for U.S. Senate. During three consecutive terms he supports a medicare bill, a nuclear test ban treaty, and the Civil Rights Act of 1964.

1993 Sharon Sayles Belton is elected mayor of Minneapolis, the first African American and the first female to hold the office. Having previously worked for the State Department of Corrections and as assistant director of the Minnesota Program for Victims of Sexual Assault, she would tout a family-centered platform and administer numerous successful community programs, including the annual youth-oriented event, "Dancin' in the Streets."

NOVEMBER 3

1831 The one and only Ignatius Donnelly is born in Philadelphia. He would arrive in Minnesota in 1857 and build a mansion at Nininger, near Hastings. He would serve as first lieutenant governor of the state and as representative in the legislature and Congress. An author on various topics, Donnelly would oppose business monopolies in the weekly paper *Anti-Monopolist;* attest that Francis Bacon wrote Shakespeare's plays in *The Great Cryptogram;* advance the then-outlandish theory that a giant comet had once struck the earth in

Ragnarok: The Age of Fire and Gravel; and argue for the existence of Plato's fabled island in *Atlantis: The Antediluvian World.*

1895 A fire begins in a flour mill and destroys the town of Walcott, in Rice County. Walcott had prospered for nearly fifty years, but the community decides not to rebuild.

1908 Bronislav "Bronko" Nagurski is born in Ontario. In 1929 he would be named All-American as both defense tackle and offensive fullback for the Gophers, the only player to be named All-American for two positions in the same year. He would later play for the Chicago Bears football team and perform as a professional wrestler. After his retirement from sports he would operate a service station in his hometown, International Falls.

1959 The Wilson & Company packinghouse strike begins in Albert Lea. Lasting 109 days, it receives national attention.

1989 The Minnesota Timberwolves basketball team plays its first game, losing to the Seattle Supersonics, 106–94.

1992 Lawyer Alan Page is elected associate justice of the state supreme court, the first African American to so serve. Normally judges are appointed by the governor, but unusual circumstances led to a direct election. Voters undoubtedly recalled Page's career with the Minnesota Vikings and his election to the Pro Football Hall of Fame, as well as his work as assistant attorney general.

1998 Former professional wrestler Jesse "The Body" Ventura wins the gubernatorial election. The Democratic-Farmer-Labor and Republican candidates split much of the vote, and Reform Party candidate Ventura, who had been mayor of Brooklyn Park and host of a radio talk show on KSTP in the Twin Cities, takes the prize. Ventura would later switch his affiliation to the Independence Party of Minnesota, and his administration would focus on education and tax reform. Although it is too soon to evaluate his accomplishments, it is safe to say that, for color, even Rudy Perpich pales in comparison. *See* August 22

NOVEMBER 4

1850 Fort Gaines is renamed Fort Ripley in honor of Eleazar Ripley, a general in the War of 1812. The fort would be abandoned in 1878, but the National Guard's Camp Ripley preserves the name.

1864 The steamboat *John Rumsey* explodes near the lower levee in St. Paul, killing seven of the crew. Explosions, usually caused by excessive steam pressure, were a common occurrence on Mississippi riverboats.

1994 President Bill Clinton visits Duluth to stump for DFL candidates.

1997 Through a ballot initiative led by Progressive Minnesota, voters limit the amount of money city officials can spend on professional sports facilities. This spending cap defeats a proposal for a new taxpayer-funded stadium for the Twins.

NOVEMBER 5

1862 The military commission headed by Henry H. Sibley completes its trial of Dakota Indians accused of participating in the U.S.–Dakota War earlier that year. Of the 392 prisoners, 307 are sentenced to death and sixteen to prison. President Abraham Lincoln would commute many of these sentences. *See* December 26

1875 Suffrage is extended to women in elections pertaining to schools. Women would not earn the right to vote in every election until 1919. *See* August 26

1903 The Minneapolis Symphony Orchestra, conducted by Emil Oberhoffer, presents its first concert. The orchestra would replicate the concert in 1927, with Henri Verbrugghen conducting, and in 1993, as the Minnesota Orchestra, directed by Stanislaw Skrowaczewski.

November 5, 1903
Emil Oberhoffer, 1921

1905 Minneapolis saloons close their doors for "dry Sunday," and no liquor is available for purchase within the city limits.

1975 As hundreds gather in Mankato to commemorate the Dakota who were executed there (*see* December 26), eagles gather in the sky above them. Many interpret this as a sign of healing between the Dakota and the people of the United States.

1991 Choua Lee is elected to the St. Paul City School Board, the first Hmong person elected to a public position in the United States. After serving one term she declines reelection.

NOVEMBER 6

1854 Thirty-one individuals form the Pioneer Hook and Ladder Company, St. Paul's first volunteer fire-fighting force.

1860 On the same day that Minnesota votes for Lincoln, a horserace in Freeborn County determines the county seat. Albert Lea and Itasca had both been vying for the honor, and corruption and vote buying ran rampant. Adding to the excitement, an Albert Lea racehorse, Old Tom, had been put up to run a race against Itasca's best. The businessmen of Itasca had secretly bought an Iowa racehorse named Fly, the plan being to encourage Albert Lea's folks to bet on Old Tom, win their money, and then buy votes for Itasca. The best-laid plans often go awry: Old Tom won the race, and Itasca lost its money and the county seat.

1874 St. Olaf College is incorporated, growing out of the Reverend Julius Muus's preparatory school in Holden. Classes begin on November 6, 1875.

1887 The Virginia Street Church (Swedenborgian), designed by architect Cass Gilbert, is dedicated in St. Paul.

NOVEMBER 7

1885 The steamer *Algoma* wrecks on Isle Royale, killing nearly fifty passengers.

1889 Northfield illuminates its streets by installing sixty-seven electric lights.

1905 Horace Austin, sixth governor of the state, dies in Minneapolis. He was born on October 15, 1831, in Canterbury, Connecticut. After serving as judge in Minnesota's sixth district, in 1869 Austin would win the governor's seat over Democrat George L. Otis. As governor, Austin would establish a state board of health, divide the state into three Congressional districts, and initiate a geological and natural history survey supervised by the state university.

NOVEMBER 8

1898 The Kensington rune stone is discovered on Olof Ohman's farm, near Alexandria. The stone tells of a group of Vikings who traveled to Minnesota in 1362, but its authenticity has long been the subject of debate.

1890 The Grand Opera House in Minneapolis hosts the first American performance of the English translation of Donizetti's opera, *Anne Boleyn*.

November 8, 1898

1926 The old Mendota bridge to Fort Snelling opens and is dedicated to the men of the 151st Field Artillery who had been killed in World War I.

1932 Minnesota citizens are allowed to vote for all nine of the state's congressional seats because the legislature had failed to reapportion the districts following the census of 1930.

NOVEMBER 9

1862 In the aftermath of the U.S.–Dakota War a mob attacks a group of Dakota captives in New Ulm. The troops guarding the captives manage to restore order. Five days later, in Henderson, settlers attack Dakota captives being led to Fort Snelling. One infant is killed before soldiers disperse the crowd.

1891 George A. Hormel launches his packinghouse in Austin, operating out of an old creamery.

1913 Day two of the three-day Great Storm of 1913, which kills 251 people on the Great Lakes (forty-four on Lake Superior) and sinks seventeen boats.

NOVEMBER 10

1851 The Sisters of St. Joseph of Carondelet open a girls school in St. Paul, enrolling fourteen pupils and holding classes in the former Chapel of St. Paul. Originally named St. Mary's, their school would eventually be known as St. Joseph's Academy.

1855 Henry W. Longfellow publishes *The Song of Hiawatha*. Although the poet never visited Minnesota, his poem depicts locations such as Minnehaha Falls and inspired some of the state's place names, including Bena, Nushka, Osseo, Ponemah, and Wabasso.

1871 Cretin High School opens in St. Paul. Named for Joseph Cretin, the first bishop of the diocese of St. Paul, the school would merge with Derham Hall high school in 1987.

1880 Captain R. H. L. Jewett receives from the government a shipment of young carp with which to stock Rice County's lakes. A government commission had been formed in response to European immigrants' demands for the fish.

1933 Workers at the Hormel meat packing plant in Austin stage the first sit-down strike in American labor history, occupying the factory to prevent non-strikers from operating the equipment. The strike is settled on December 8 after hearings by the Industrial Commission of Minnesota.

November 10, 1855 *Hiawatha and Minnehaha* by Jacob Fjelde in Minnehaha Park, Minneapolis

1975 The ore boat *Edmund Fitzgerald* sinks in Lake Superior, and twenty-nine crewmembers drown.

1976 Governor Wendell R. Anderson announces that he will fill newly elected Vice President Walter F. Mondale's U.S. Senate seat. He resigns as governor and is replaced by Lieutenant Governor Rudy Perpich, who then appoints Anderson to complete Mondale's term. The move ends Anderson's political career and makes Perpich's: Anderson would not earn reelection to the Senate in 1978, but Perpich would serve out Anderson's term and be elected governor in 1982.

NOVEMBER 11

1856 Thirteen New Ulm residents establish the state's first chapter of *Turnverein*. The *Turnverein* motto is "a sound mind in a sound body," and members sponsor social, educational, and physical events.

1859 The Athenaeum, a structure dedicated to educational lectures and social events for Germans, opens in St. Paul.

1865 Little Six and Medicine Bottle, leaders in the U.S.–Dakota War of 1862, are executed at Fort Snelling. In December of 1863 they had been captured in Canada by Major Edwin A. C. Hatch, who had no authority to retain them, and returned to the United States for trial.

1919 The American Legion, a veterans organization, holds its first convention, in Minneapolis. The convention begins on November 10 and ends on November 12.

1940 The Armistice Day Blizzard strikes, trapping hunters at lakes and drivers on roads. Forty-nine people die when temperatures suddenly drop from the sixties to below zero. Pilot Max Conrad of Winona earns hero honors for taking his Piper Cub up into fifty-mile-per-hour winds to drop supplies and lead rescuers to trapped hunters.

November 11, 1940 Cars abandoned on Excelsior Boulevard, Minneapolis (*St. Paul Pioneer Press*)

NOVEMBER 12

1882 Five craft unions and two Knights of Labor Assemblies form the St. Paul Trades and Labor Assembly, the first centralized labor organization in the state.

1889 DeWitt Wallace is born in St. Paul. Wallace would found *Reader's Digest* in 1922, and his family's fortune has benefited many educational and performing arts associations.

1892 Walter "Pudge" Heffelfinger becomes the first professional football player in history. The Minneapolis native signs to play with the Allegheny Athletic Association and is paid $500 for his role in the 4–0 victory over the Pittsburgh Athletic Club.

1908 Harry A. Blackmun is born in Nashville, Illinois. He would spend his early years in St. Paul and return to the area after earning a degree from Harvard Law School. President Richard Nixon would appoint him to the U.S. Supreme Court on April 14, 1970. Blackmun will be remembered for authoring the controversial 1973 decision in *Roe v. Wade,* which made abortion legal in the United States, and for retracting his support for the death penalty in 1994 by writing "I shall no longer tinker with the machinery of death." He died March 4, 1999.

1977 Steve Carter's *Eden* is the first documented performance at the Penumbra Theatre in St. Paul. Founded in 1976 by Lou Bellamy, the nationally acclaimed theater won a Jujamcyn Award in 1999 and is known for producing all of the works of Pulitzer Prize–winning playwright August Wilson.

NOVEMBER 13

1833 Charles M. Loring is born in Portland, Maine. As Minneapolis park commissioner from 1883 to 1890, he would be a principal player in the development of the city's system of parks and public grounds. Central Park would be renamed Loring Park in his honor. *See* April 28

1891 Floyd B. Olson is born in Minneapolis. He would be the first Farmer-Labor governor, serving from 1931 until his death on August 22, 1936. He is remembered for implementing New Deal policies and for his skilled negotiating during the 1933 Hormel strike in Austin and the 1934 teamsters' strike in Minneapolis.

1970 Police arrest Ronald Reed, a twenty-year-old suspect in an Omaha bank robbery, on charges of conspiracy to kidnap Governor Harold LeVander and St. Paul city councilwoman Rosalie Butler and hold them hostage for exchange with black political prisoners. Police connect Reed to the Black Panther Party, but Emory Douglass, the Black Panther's national minister of culture, denies Reed's membership in the party. Reed, an ROTC member at the University of Minnesota, is held in Ramsey County jail on a $150,000 bond, the highest in the state's history.

NOVEMBER 14

1766 Englishman Jonathan Carver enters the cave that would one day bear his name. Carver writes in his diary: "came to the great stone cave called by the Naudowessies

[Dakota] the House of Spirits. This cave is doubtless a greater curiosity than my short stay and want of convenience allowed me to sufficiently explore." The St. Paul cave would be partially filled in by debris and its entrance obscured, rediscovered in 1913, covered again, and once again discovered in 1977.

1860 Telegraph service reaches Minneapolis.

1908 Harrison Salisbury is born in Minneapolis. A reporter and author, he would be especially noted for his writing on the Soviet Union, and in 1955 he would win the Pulitzer Prize for international correspondence.

1917 Mike O'Dowd, "The Cyclone of St. Paul," defeats Al McCoy to win boxing's middleweight title, which he holds until 1920.

1996 Author Meridel Le Sueur dies in Hudson, Wisconsin. Born in Murray, Iowa, on February 22, 1900, Le Sueur moved with her family to Minnesota when she was twelve. A reporter and the author of novels and short stories, she was blacklisted for being a member of the Communist Party. Her work was rediscovered and heralded by feminists in the 1970s.

NOVEMBER 15

1851 Montezuma is founded by Orrin Smith, a steamboat captain. The town is more recognizable by its present name, Winona.

1866 Pilgrim Baptist Church is formally organized. The African American congregation, granted mission status by the First Baptist Church of St. Paul, would meet at various residences for a number of years before constructing a church at Thirteenth and Cedar Streets in St. Paul. Robert Hickman would be ordained eleven years later and would become the congregation's official pastor.

1880 A fire at the St. Peter State Hospital (now the St. Peter Regional Treatment Center), a mental asylum, kills between ten and fifteen inmates. The first mental institution in the state, the asylum had opened on December 6, 1866.

NOVEMBER 16

1854 The preparatory (or high school) department of what is now Hamline University opens for business in Red Wing. Named for Leonidas L. Hamline, a Methodist bishop, the school suspends operations in 1869 and reopens in St. Paul in 1880, but its original founding date makes it the oldest college in the state.

1881 Faribault hangs its first street signs.

1883 The steamer *Manistee* sinks in Lake Superior. It had left Duluth on November 10, but a gale had driven it into port at Bayfield. Captain John McKay tries to force passage on this night, and twenty-three of the sailors aboard are never seen again. A lifeboat carrying three survivors washes ashore a few days later.

1939 U.S. Supreme Court Justice Pierce Butler dies in Washington, D.C. Born near Northfield, Minnesota, on March 17, 1866, Butler was a conservative judge who opposed many of President Franklin D. Roosevelt's New Deal programs. Butler was the final justice to pass the bar exam after studying with an attorney rather than attending a law school. He served as lawyer for Ramsey County and as regent for the University of Minnesota before President Warren G. Harding appointed him to the high court in 1922.

NOVEMBER 17

1863 Winfield Scott Hammond is born in Southborough, Massachusetts. Prior to becoming the state's eighteenth governor, he would function in various educational capacities: as high school principal in Mankato, superintendent of schools in Madelia, and president of the school board of St. James. He died on December 30, 1915, the second governor to die while in office.

1992 Jackpot Junction Casino, the first Indian casino in Minnesota, celebrates its eighth anniversary (November 16–18). Originally a bingo parlor, by 1988 it had become a fully operational casino.

NOVEMBER 18

1938 The University of Minnesota's Green Hall, named in honor of forester Samuel B. Green, is dedicated.

1985 The Liberian freighter *Socrates* runs aground on Minnesota Point in Duluth. Excursion buses carry tourists to view the stranded ship, which is later freed by tugs.

1993 The Frederick R. Weisman Art Museum at the University of Minnesota opens. Sculptor and architect Frank O. Gehry won an award from *Progressive Architecture* magazine in 1991 for his design of the building.

NOVEMBER 19

1855 Minnesota's first German-language newspaper, the *Minnesota Deutsche Zeitung,* is published in St. Paul by editors Friedrich Orthwein and Albert Wolff. It is the second non-English newspaper in Minnesota, the first being *Dakota Tawaxitu Kin* (Dakota Friend), published in English and Dakota by missionary Gideon H. Pond from 1850 to 1852.

1855 The singing Hutchinson family of New Hampshire founds the town of Hutchinson in McLeod County. From 1841 until the close of the Civil War, the Hutchinsons toured the United States giving concerts of popular and patriotic songs.

1902 Anoka's Monte Carlo casino is robbed by two masked men. An article in the *Anoka Herald* reports that "the whole thing was carried out with good humor," although it was likely not humorous for the attendant who is shot twice by the robbers when he tries to escape.

1945 Super Value Groceries receives Minnesota's first shipment of air freighted vegetables. The cargo includes tomatoes, asparagus, figs, and avocados, and a special basket is given to Minneapolis mayor Hubert H. Humphrey and Governor Edward J. Thye.

November 19, 1945 Pilot R. J. Raines presents gift baskets to Hubert H. Humphrey and Edward J. Thye

1971 Radioactive cooling water from the Monticello Nuclear Power Plant overflows its tank and eventually reaches the Mississippi River.

NOVEMBER 20

1855 The Mississippi River freezes over for the season, concluding a busy year during which 553 boats and 30,000 people traveled to St. Paul.

1967 The Nicollet Mall, a pedestrian walkway closed to traffic except buses, opens in downtown Minneapolis.

1969 Indians of All Tribes (IAT), a group of activists including Adam Nordwall, a Minnesota Ojibwe, occupies Alcatraz Island in San Francisco. IAT intends to force negotiation with the federal government and to assert the need for Indian self-determination. Members of the group remain on the island until forcibly removed in 1971, bringing national attention to Indian issues.

1979 Artificial blood is used in the United States for the first time when Dr. Robert Anderson of the University Hospital injects Fluosol, a blood substitute developed in Japan, into a Jehovah's Witness individual who had refused a regular blood transfusion on religious grounds.

NOVEMBER 21

1849 The St. Anthony Library Association is formed. A subscription library, it allows dues-paying members to borrow books and is a precursor to the free public library, which would be authorized by an 1879 law permitting tax levies to support libraries.

1902 The steamer *Bannockburn* and its twenty-member crew is seen for the last time as it sets forth from Duluth, later disappearing somewhere on Lake Superior.

1924 The steamer *Merton E. Farr* strikes and heavily damages the Duluth-Superior Bridge.

NOVEMBER 22

1838 The first wedding recorded within Minneapolis city limits binds Samuel W. Pond with Cordelia Eggleston.

1870 Gas light arrives in Minneapolis.

1879 Farmington suffers a major fire.

1950 To thwart the talents of the Minneapolis Lakers' George Mikan, the Fort Wayne Pistons basketball team plays a slow-down game that results in a 19–18 victory for the Pistons. Their tactic also results in the 24-second shot clock, implemented a few seasons later.

1995 A merger of giant railroad companies creates the Burlington Northern Santa Fe Railway. The Burlington Northern had long been a major railroad in Minnesota, itself the result of mergers between the Great Northern

Railroad, the Northern Pacific Railway, and the Chicago, Burlington and Quincy Railroad.

1996 The movie *Jingle All the Way* opens. Produced by and starring Arnold Schwarzenegger, the film takes place in Minneapolis, but scenes were shot all around the Twin Cities metro area, including locations in downtown St. Paul, in Eden Prairie, on Harriet Island, and on the Hennepin Avenue Bridge.

NOVEMBER 23

1910 Pennington County is created. It commemorates Edmund Pennington, president of the Minneapolis, St. Paul and Sault Ste. Marie (Soo) Railroad.

NOVEMBER 24

1859 Architect Cass Gilbert is born in Ohio. Gilbert's family would move to St. Paul in 1868, and he would later begin his career there. Among his most recognizable buildings are the Minnesota State Capitol, the U.S. Supreme Court Building, and Manhattan's Woolworth Building.

1864 Governor Stephen Miller declares a Thanksgiving holiday, in accordance with President Abraham Lincoln's recommendation that the last Thursday in November be used for this purpose. Minnesota had celebrated Thanksgiving Day before, usually in December. *See* December 26

NOVEMBER 25

1817 Catherine Bissell is born. She and her husband, Edmund F. Ely, would run mission schools at Fond du Lac, Pokegama, La Pointe, and other locations. She died in California in 1880.

1863 The Second Minnesota and the rest of General George H. Thomas's Army of the Cumberland charge up Missionary Ridge near Chattanooga and defeat the Confederates holding the ridge.

1903 Olive Fremstad makes her debut with New York's Metropolitan opera, singing the role of Sieglinde in Wagner's *Die Walkure*. Born in Scandinavia, she had been adopted by a St. Peter couple. A true diva, Fremstad would be legendary for her vocal powers as well as her temperament. She died in New York in 1951.

1946 In the first organized teachers' strike in the nation, 1,165 St. Paul schoolteachers walk out. The strike lasts until December 27 and receives national attention, as it demonstrates that teachers are ready to use strikes as a method to alleviate school funding problems and intolerable working conditions.

NOVEMBER 26

1849 The first election for county offices is held.

1869 As photographer Charles Zimmerman of St. Paul tries to capture frozen Minnehaha Falls, he is struck by an icicle weighing several hundred pounds. He sustains severe bruises about the head, neck, and shoulders, but none of his bones are broken.

1922 Cartoonist Charles M. Schulz, creator of "Peanuts," is born in Minneapolis.

NOVEMBER 27

1900 Cushman K. Davis dies while serving his third term in the Senate. Davis was born in Henderson, New York, on June 16, 1838. His speeches against railroad interests and in favor of Grangers led to his election as Minnesota's seventh governor in 1873. He joined the

ACCIDENT UNDER THE FALLS OF MINNEHAHA, MINN.

November 26, 1869 *Accident Under the Falls*

Senate in 1887, where he supported Civil War pensions and the annexation of Hawaii and opposed the Chinese Exclusion Act of 1892. He also authored books on the law, Shakespeare, and Napoleon Bonaparte.

1930 St. Paul's Frank B. Kellogg wins the Nobel Peace Prize. Kellogg had served as secretary of state during the Coolidge administration and as a judge on the Permanent Court of International Justice in The Hague.

NOVEMBER 28

1850 Aaron Goodrich, Minnesota Territory's first supreme court justice, is accused of adultery. An effort to impeach him fails, but President Millard Fillmore exercises his executive power to remove Goodrich from office in 1851.

1882 Indian trader and town founder Alexander Faribault dies. In 1835 Faribault set up a post in what would become his namesake town, and in 1853 he built its first frame house, which is still standing. *See* May 22

1905 The freighter *Mataafa* wrecks near the lighthouse in Duluth harbor during a storm that sank eighteen ships on the Great Lakes in a twenty-four-hour period. The crew suffers terribly from the cold winds of the storm, and nine freeze to death. The *Mataafa* is rebuilt and continues to sail until 1966.

1922 Lake of the Woods County is established.

NOVEMBER 29

1816 Henry M. Rice is born in Waitsfield, Vermont. At twenty-three he would become a sutler at Fort Snelling, running a concessionary store that sold sundry items to the soldiers. Rice would also enter the political arena, encouraging Congress to define the state's present boundaries and serving as one of Minnesota's first two senators. He died in 1894. *See* February 8

1884 Anna Ramsey dies. Admired as the governor's "helpmeet," she led efforts to create homeless shelters and support other charities.

2000 Pioneering journalist Marvel (Jackson) Cooke dies in New York. Born in Mankato in 1903, Cooke moved to Harlem in 1926 and worked for the NAACP's *Crisis* magazine, the *Amsterdam News*, and the *People's Voice*. In

1950 she joined the staff of the New York *Daily Compass,* the first African American woman to work full-time for a major white-owned American newspaper.

NOVEMBER 30

1843 Martha G. Ripley is born in Lowell, Vermont. A crusader for public health measures, Dr. Ripley would establish Minneapolis's Maternity Hospital in 1886. A memorial to her was dedicated in the state capitol in 1939.

1912 Gordon Parks is born in Fort Scott, Kansas. He would move to St. Paul as a teenager and eventually develop a career as a photographer, writer, filmmaker, composer, and musician. He would work for the Farm Services Administration, become a war photographer in 1943, and be the first African American on *Life* magazine's staff. His movies include *The Learning Tree,* based on his autobiography.

1960 Novelist Ernest Hemingway is admitted to St. Mary's Hospital in Rochester, where he undergoes shock treatment for depression. A few days later, he commits suicide in Idaho.

November 30, 1912

DECEMBER 1

1855 At the Washington Navy Yard, Susan L. Mann christens the steam frigate *Minnesota* with a bottle of Minnesota water. On April 6 of the previous year, Congress had authorized construction of this ship and, co-incidentally, the frigate *Merrimac,* which, rebuilt as a Confederate ironclad and renamed the *Virginia,* would attack the *Minnesota* during the Civil War.

1856 The first issue of Ignatius Donnelly's newspaper, the *Emigrant Aid Journal,* is published in Philadelphia. This publication encourages recent immigrants to move to Nininger, a town Donnelly had founded on the Mississippi River downstream from St. Paul. Although 1,000 people live there at its peak, the town would eventually fail. Incidentally, the editor of the *Emigrant Aid Journal* is A. W. MacDonald, who would later edit *Scientific American.*

1860 The state's first book-quality paper, manufactured at the Cutter and Secombe paper mill in St. Anthony, is used in *The Minnesota Farmer and Gardener,* an agricultural magazine.

1941 Against a background of war in Europe and bitter pro- and anti-union activity in the Twin Cities, eighteen members of the Socialist Workers Party are found guilty in Minneapolis on a count of conspiring to undermine the loyalty of U.S. military forces and of publishing material advocating the overthrow of the government. Vincent R. Dunne, a leader in Teamsters Local 544, and the other defendants are, however, found not guilty on a count of seditious conspiracy to overthrow the government by force. Five more defendants, also party members, are acquitted on both counts.

1982 Clement Haupers dies in St. Paul, in the same Ramsey Hill house in which he was born in 1900. Known for developing the Minnesota State Fair art show into a major exhibition of local work, he also led the Works Progress Administration's Federal Art Project in Minnesota. Throughout his career, Haupers insisted that artists should support themselves without government grants. In this vein, when asked to give art students a lecture on how to survive financially, Haupers's response was "Sure, that'll be $150."

December 1, 1982 Clement Haupers in front of *Along the Mississippi*, 1973

DECEMBER 2

1857 The first state legislature convenes, five months before Minnesota is admitted to the Union. Despite its questionable legality, the session passes over ninety laws and elects Henry M. Rice and James M. Shields as U.S. senators. The pair travel to Washington, D.C., and wait for statehood to become official so that their terms can begin.

1858 The term "Land of Lakes" is first applied to Minnesota in St. Anthony Falls' paper, the *Falls Evening News*.

1884 Faribault's waterworks pass their operations test, and the system is accepted December 31.

DECEMBER 3

1842 Flour magnate Charles A. Pillsbury is born in New Hampshire. Moving to Minneapolis in 1869, he would learn the flour-milling business and help introduce roller mills that could crush Minnesota's spring wheat into high-grade bread flour. Upon his death in 1899, the Pillsbury-Washburn Flour Mills Company would be the largest in the world.

DECEMBER 4

1855 During Alexander Ramsey's term as mayor, the city council establishes St. Paul's first professional fire department, which succeeds a volunteer hook and ladder company and inherits its equipment, including an engine, ladders, ropes, hooks, and axes, as well as a church bell donated by the Reverend Edward D. Neill.

1860 The local telegraph office opens in St. Anthony (now southeast Minneapolis), following the St. Paul and Minneapolis offices in linking Minnesota cities to the rest of the world by means of electric wire strung on poles.

1928 A car bomb kills "Dapper Dan" Hogan, owner of St. Paul's notorious Green Lantern speakeasy and long-time boss of the city's underworld.

DECEMBER 5

1853 Henry M. Rice easily replaces Henry H. Sibley, who chose not to run for re-election, as Minnesota Territory's delegate to Congress. Sibley had won the office by a narrow margin in a previous election following a heated campaign involving fur-trade interests, with "fur" symbolized by Sibley and "anti-fur" by Alexander M. Mitchell, the candidate supported by Rice.

1873 Lincoln County, named for the Civil War president, is created, having been established by the legislature on March 6 and approved by vote of the people in November. Three previous attempts to rename or carve out a county in honor of Lincoln had failed to garner the requisite popular vote.

1950 A snowstorm lasting until December 8 drops thirty-five inches on Duluth and twenty-five on the Twin Cities.

DECEMBER 6

1815 Abolitionist, feminist, and newspaper publisher Jane Grey Swisshelm is born near Pittsburgh, Pennsylvania. She would move to Minnesota in 1857 and establish the *St. Cloud Visiter* and, later, the *St. Cloud Democrat* (*see* March 24). During the Civil War she would move to Washington, D.C., and become a nurse. She died in 1884.

DECEMBER 7

1863 Richard W. Sears is born in Stewartville, Minnesota. While a railroad freight agent in Redwood Falls, he would buy an unclaimed shipment of watches and sell them through the mail at bargain prices. From this mail-order idea would develop the A. C. Roebuck and Company, housed on the seventh floor of the Globe Building in Minneapolis. Renamed Sears, Roebuck and Co., the business would eventually be headquartered in Chicago.

1864 The Eighth Minnesota Regiment helps defend Murfreesboro, Tennessee, from a Confederate attack, suffering ninety casualties. Murfreesboro had been the scene of the Third Minnesota's humiliating surrender two and one-half years earlier. *See* July 13

1941 Outside of Pearl Harbor, the destroyer *Ward,* its crew primarily reservists from St. Paul, attacks and sinks a Japanese midget submarine, the first shots fired on the date of infamy. Inside the harbor, Minneapolis-born Captain Franklin van Valkenburgh is killed on the bridge of his ship, the USS *Arizona.* He would be awarded the Medal of Honor by Congress.

1963 T. Eugene Thompson, a lawyer who helped to draft Minnesota's 1963 revised criminal code, begins serving a life sentence in the Minnesota State Prison for hiring a man to kill his wife, Carol.

DECEMBER 8

1863 The First National Bank of St. Paul is organized, the first Minnesota bank chartered under the national banking act of 1863. Derived from a private bank owned by Parker Paine, it would eventually lose its name through a series of mergers, although there is still a First National Bank Building in St. Paul.

1886 In a fight over the possession of Traverse County records, citizens of Browns Valley (the old county seat) brawl in the streets of their town with farmers from Wheaton (the new seat) who arrive early in the morning to claim the records. The outnumbered "invaders" flee with only one load, which is later returned to Browns Valley. All the records are eventually moved to Wheaton without further battle.

DECEMBER 9

1890 The University Avenue streetcar line from Minneapolis to St. Paul begins operation.

1935 Tabloid editor Walter W. Liggett is killed by machine-gun fire at his Minneapolis home. A crusading reporter, Liggett had ties with right- and left-wingers, was accused of blackmail, and was an opponent of Governor Floyd B. Olson. Gangster "Kid Cann" (Isadore Blumenfeld) was tried for the crime but found not guilty.

DECEMBER 10

1878 The Northwestern Telephone Exchange Company of Minneapolis is organized, with fifty-three subscribers. The exchange begins operating in February 1879, and a line is strung to St. Paul in April 1879.

1930 Sauk Centre's Sinclair Lewis receives the Nobel Prize in Literature, the first American so honored. His popular titles include *Main Street, Arrowsmith, Elmer Gantry,* and *Babbitt.*

1966 James Arness, a Minneapolis native famous for his role as marshal Matt Dillon in the western series *Gunsmoke,* appears on the cover of *TV Guide.*

DECEMBER 11

1876 Ada Louise Comstock is born in Moorhead. She would become the first dean of women at the University of Minnesota and then, beginning in 1912, serve as dean of Smith College in Northampton, Massachusetts. Although she in effect ran the school from 1917 to 1918, she would not be given the title of "acting president" because of her gender. She would become the first president of the American Association of University Women in 1921 and serve as president of Radcliffe College from 1923 to 1943.

1895 After a sensational trial, Harry T. Hayward is hanged in the Minneapolis jail for the murder of Katherine Ging, owner of a fashionable dressmaking establishment. He had arranged for her to be killed so that he could collect her life insurance money.

December 11, 1956

1956 The dwellings in Swede Hollow, a St. Paul immigrant neighborhood, are burned after the city health department declares them contaminated.

1970 Norman E. Borlaug, University of Minnesota alumnus and crop researcher, receives the Nobel Peace Prize for his research in hybridizing wheat to increase crop yields. Borlaug is known as the father of the green revolution.

1999 St. Paul native Paul Molitor announces his retirement from baseball, having spent his final three seasons with the Minnesota Twins. His career hits numbered over 3,000, most of them from his years with the Milwaukee Brewers.

1999 After sixteen month of often bitter protest, four oak trees sacred to the Mendota Mdewakanton Dakota Community are cut down to make way for the rerouting of Highway 55 in Minneapolis.

DECEMBER 12

1928 The newly finished Foshay Tower, which would be Minneapolis's tallest building for nearly fifty years, is strung with lights and lit up like a Christmas tree.

DECEMBER 13

1882 The Northwestern Telephone exchange begins operating in Faribault, with forty customers.

1994 Demolition begins on the Metropolitan Sports Center in Bloomington, former home of the North Stars professional hockey team and venue for entertainment events. The first bombing attempt, with a detonator button pressed by Michael Franson, is largely unsuccessful, with much of the building still standing ten minutes after the scheduled implosion. Eventually, the structure is brought down with bulldozers and other heavy equipment.

DECEMBER 14

1798 Fur trader Alexis Bailly is born in St. Joseph, Canada. He would precede Henry H. Sibley as an agent for the American Fur Company in Mendota. In addition to his work with the fur trade, Bailly would be one of the first wheat growers in Minnesota and a member of the territorial legislature. He died in 1861. *See* September 15

DECEMBER 15

1856 A lyceum is organized in St. Paul. Lyceums were cultural centers that sponsored lectures, classes, and other activities.

1864 Four Minnesota regiments help destroy the Confederate army of General John Bell Hood outside Nashville, Tennessee. Over the course of this two-day battle, the Minnesota losses—302 killed, wounded, or missing—are the greatest the state suffers in any Civil War engagement.

1887 The first issue of the *Northfield Independent* appears, the newspaper's editor declaring that "It comes in its own independent way, without first having asked leave to be, but intends to justify its being by filling a vacant journalistic place in this city and surrounding country. . . . It will labor that the homes it is permitted to enter may be brighter and purer for its coming, their burdens lightened, if possible, their industries enobled [*sic*]."

1892 J. Paul Getty is born in Minneapolis. An entrepreneur, he would become a billionaire in the oil business, and he would bequeath much of his fortune to the Getty Trust, a philanthropic organization that supports the visual arts.

DECEMBER 16

1814 Horace W. S. Cleveland is born in Lancaster, Massachusetts. A visionary landscape architect, he would design many parks and boulevards in the Twin Cities, including Como Park, St. Anthony Park, Minnehaha Park, Summit Avenue, and the drives along the Mississippi River.

1884 Machinist William H. Fruen of Minneapolis is issued the first U.S. patent for an automatic liquid-dispensing vending machine, which discharges a uniform amount of liquid from a reservoir when a coin is placed in a slot. An enthusiastic fisherman, Fruen had settled earlier in the year at the western edge of the city and begun excavating near his home for the construction of a fishpond in which to keep his catch fresh for eating. The discovery of a pure spring in a glen led Fruen to sell jugs, and then coolers, of fresh water and found the Glenwood Springs (now Glenwood Inglewood Water) Company.

1889 The Minneapolis Public Library opens, with Herbert Putnam as librarian. Under an agreement with the Minneapolis Athenaeum, the public library board provides a building and staff to lend the Athenaeum's books, thereby making them available to the citizens of Minneapolis.

DECEMBER 17

1839 Newton H. Winchell is born in New York. As Minnesota's state geologist, Winchell would publish twenty-four reports on the state's geology and paleontology. His discoveries include the movement of St. Anthony Falls from its origins near Fort Snelling to its present location, an event requiring an estimated 8,000 years. He died in 1914.

1915 The Mesaba Transportation Company of Hibbing is incorporated. Owners Andrew G. Anderson and Carl Eric Wickman transport passengers and freight from Hibbing to destinations in Alice and Grand Rapids. A subsidiary company, the Mesaba Motor Company, is incorporated on October 23, 1919, to build, repair, and sell buses. Through various mergers, these companies would eventually become Greyhound Lines, headquartered in Chicago.

1942 The Elizabeth Kenny Institute for the treatment of infantile paralysis is dedicated in Minneapolis. Sister Kenny, an Australian nurse, came to the United States to promote her ideas about treating polio using physical therapy and hot packs rather than the traditional method of complete immobilization. Her work with a patient, Henry Haverstock, Jr., in his

December 17, 1942

Minneapolis home brought her techniques increasing attention. Kenny would be the first woman other than a first lady to be declared the "Most Admired Woman" in a Gallup poll, and Congress would grant her free access to the United States without a passport, a rare honor. She died in Australia on November 30, 1952.

1966 Doctors Richard C. Lillehei and William Kelly of the University of Minnesota hospitals perform the world's first successful kidney and pancreas transplant.

DECEMBER 18

1985 Mary Lund is the first woman to receive a Jarvik-7 artificial heart, in Minneapolis. The device keeps her alive for about a month, until a real heart is transplanted.

1988 The Pillsbury Company announces that it has accepted a $5.7 billion buy-out offer from the British food and liquor conglomerate Grand Metropolitan PLC.

DECEMBER 19

1836 Maria Louise Sanford is born in Saybrook, Connecticut. An extraordinary and popular teacher, Sanford would be appointed to the department of rhetoric at the University of Minnesota in 1880. After her retirement in 1909, she would remain active, speaking on educational and patriotic topics. She died in 1920. A statue of her, sculpted by Evelyn Raymond, represents the state in Statuary Hall in Washington, D.C.

December 19, 1836 Maria Sanford statue in Washington, D.C.

1906 Koochiching County is established, named with the Cree word for Rainy Lake.

1957 West St. Paul sociology teacher Glen Holmquist, accused of slapping a male student at a high-school dance, is cleared of an assault charge by a municipal court. Holmquist's attorney says that his client's action was justified as an attempt to maintain order, and that there should be more discipline "instead of the wishy-washy policy parents are advocating today."

1957 Governor Orville L. Freeman appoints L. Howard Bennett to a municipal judgeship in Minneapolis, making him the first African American judge appointed in Minnesota.

DECEMBER 20

1847 St. Croix County, Wisconsin Territory, is given a parcel of land in Stillwater for a county courthouse. Finished in 1849, the building is the first courthouse in what is now Minnesota.

1863 The American House burns in St. Paul. A landmark in early photographs and paintings of the area, the hotel stood at Third and Exchange Streets.

1902 Clearwater County is established, named for Clearwater Lake and River.

1902 A fierce fire discovered shortly after 2:00 A.M. at the School for the Feeble-Minded in Faribault badly damages the main building and causes the safe evacuation of more than three hundred people who had been sleeping in the structure. Unable to get their ladder wagon to the school, local firemen drag a hose through the building and up four flights of stairs to the attic and bring the flames under control.

DECEMBER 21

1885 The Nushka Toboggan Club is formed. To promote the St. Paul Winter Carnival, the club sponsors toboggan slides on Crocus Hill, snowshoe hikes to Merriam Park, and parties on Washington's birthday. *Nushka* means "Look!" in Ojibwe.

1998 Television's original Betty Crocker, Adelaide Hawley Cumming, dies in Seattle. Cumming starred in the *Betty Crocker Show* beginning in 1949 and remained General Mills' advertising icon until 1964, after which she taught English as a second language in Seattle.

December 21, 1885 The Nushka Toboggan Club at the 1886 St. Paul Winter Carnival

DECEMBER 22

1858 The Reverend Edward D. Neill officiates at the dedication of the first House of Hope Presbyterian Church building, a chapel that stood on Walnut Street between Oak and Pleasant Streets in St. Paul. The congregation would move in 1869 to a church at Fifth and Exchange Streets and then in 1914 to its present home on Summit Avenue.

DECEMBER 23

1832 Hans Mattson is born in Sweden. A pioneer of Swedish settlement in Minnesota, he would establish the Vasa colony in Goodhue County in 1853. He would serve as colonel of the Third Minnesota Regiment during the Civil War and as U.S. consul general in India from 1881 to 1883. In 1877 he would found the Swedish newspaper *Minnesota Stats Tidning* (Minnesota State Times).

1846 A bill is introduced in Congress to create a territory called "Minasota." Although the bill fails, this is the first legislative use of the name.

1926 Robert Bly is born in Madison. A poet, translator, editor, and activist in the men's movement, he would write numerous books, including the best-selling nonfiction work on men and myth, *Iron John: A Book About Men.*

DECEMBER 24

1869 The Church of the Good Samaritan (Episcopal) in Sauk Centre holds its first service, the wedding of Miss Nellie A. Barrows and Captain Edward Oakford. The church's stained-glass windows had been donated by a friend of Bishop Henry B. Whipple and brought in by oxcart. The west wall of the church would collapse in 1999, destroying two of the original windows. The wall would be rebuilt and the windows replaced by a set from the recently closed Grace Church in Royalton.

1889 Electric streetcars begin running in Minneapolis.

1892 The Hotel Hallock in Kittson County burns. Boasting deluxe accommodations and catering to hunters, the hotel had running water, a barbershop, and kennels for patrons' dogs. Owner Charles Hallock, publisher of *Field and Stream,* helped publicize Minnesota as a hunter's paradise.

December 24, 1892 New York hunting party in front of the Hotel Hallock, 1889

1896 Red Lake County is established, named for the Red Lake River, which flows through it.

DECEMBER 25

1842 The first U.S. flag in St. Paul is raised on a pole in front of Richard Mortimer's house. Born in England, Mortimer had served successively in both the British and American armies and been a commissary and quartermaster sergeant at Fort Snelling before settling in upper St. Paul. The flag flies briefly and then is cut down by "some wicked scamp" from the lower—and rival—part of town.

1866 George Liscomb and Alexander Campbell, fur traders from Mankato, are lynched in New Ulm after they kill a citizen in a bar fight. The following day, 300 angry residents of Mankato, along with a company of militia, march to New Ulm to investigate the lynching. Liscomb and Campbell's mutilated bodies are found stuffed under the ice of the Minnesota River. Although an investigation names many members of the lynch mob, no indictments are ever made.

1874 On Christmas morning, firemen at St. Paul's No. 3 engine house on the corner of Leech and Ramsey Streets brawl with each other in "a very disgraceful fight" that leaves two seriously injured, several badly bruised, and five arrested on a charge of assault with intent to do great bodily harm. The fight is apparently caused by an "unpleasant feeling" between the principal parties, an insulting remark about a piece of equipment not working properly, and a cigar stump thrown at one of the men.

1913 Minneapolis's first public Christmas tree is lit in Gateway Park.

1943 Citizens of Minneapolis are shocked when the body of the year's ninth murder victim is found. There had been only one murder the previous year.

DECEMBER 26

1850 Territorial Governor Alexander Ramsey declares the state's first Thanksgiving Day, citing good crops; no hurricanes, droughts, or diseases; and friendly relations between Indians and settlers as worthy reasons to give thanks. *See* November 24

December 25, 1913

1862 Thirty-eight Dakota men, convicted of crimes committed during the U.S.–Dakota War, are hanged by the federal government in Mankato, the largest mass execution in American history.

1990 Sister Mary Giovanni Gourhan, founder in 1963 of Guadalupe Area Project alternative school, dies. A native of West St. Paul, Gourhan ran an unorthodox school, teaching the basics plus Mexican history and effective living and meditation techniques. The school continues her mission today.

DECEMBER 27

1846 David M. Clough is born in Lyme, New Hampshire. He would settle in Isanti County and serve as governor from 1895 to 1899. During his tenure, Minnesota would raise four army regiments for service in the Spanish-American War and begin construction of the present Minnesota State Capitol. He died in 1924.

1858 Charles J. Rinehart, accused of murdering carpenter John B. Bodell, is lynched in Lexington. His case had not yet been brought to trial.

1906 Mahnomen County is formed. *Mahnomen* is an Ojibwe word for "wild rice."

1957 Governor Orville L. Freeman announces that Minnesota will crack down on "drinking drivers," urging sheriffs in the state to resist local pressures to reduce drunk driving charges to charges of careless driving.

DECEMBER 28

1846 The state of Iowa is admitted to the Union. Iowa Territory had extended north into what would become western Minnesota, and this area is without a formal government until Minnesota Territory is created in 1849.

1909 W. E. "Pussyfoot" Johnson, who had the authority to enforce federal liquor laws on Indian reservations, leads a raid on the saloons of Park Rapids, which were illegally serving residents of White Earth Reservation, considered wards of the state and protected by an 1855 treaty. Johnson and a trainload of U.S. marshals gather every bottle they can find and demolish them on Main Street.

DECEMBER 29

1854 The first legal execution in Ramsey County, Minnesota Territory, takes place when Yu-Ha-Zee (or Zu-ya-se), a Dakota man convicted of murdering Bridget Keanor, an immigrant woman, is hanged on a gallows on St. Anthony Hill (now Cathedral Hill) in St. Paul.

1891 The Minnesota Library Association is organized in St. Paul. Professor William W. Folwell, the librarian of the University of Minnesota, is elected president of this first state library association, and other members of "that useful profession" fill the offices of vice president (Helen J. McCaine of the St. Paul Public Library) and secretary and treasurer (J. Fletcher Williams of the Minnesota Historical Society). Early concerns at meetings of the organization include education for librarianship, work with children, traveling libraries, and public access to bookshelves.

DECEMBER 30

1884 Fur trader Alexander Baker receives his patent on a land claim near International Falls, where he is the first settler.

1948 Minneapolis Symphony Orchestra conductor Dimitri Mitropoulous announces that he has taken a position with the New York Philharmonic Orchestra. Antal Dorati is hired to replace him.

1977 Legendary sports broadcaster Halsey Hall dies in his Minneapolis home at age seventy-nine. Known for his cigar-smoking, whiskey-drinking style, Hall was broadcaster of Twins games for many years and the first to use the phrase "holy cow" during a broadcast. He also coined the adjective "golden" to describe the University of Minnesota's sports teams.

December 30, 1977
Halsey Hall broadcasting
on WCCO Radio

DECEMBER 31

1894 Roseau County, named for the lake and river in its territory, is established by order of Governor Knute Nelson.

1957 University of Minnesota president James L. Morrill announces that the university will expand westward across the Washington Avenue Bridge into a "blighted area" of Minneapolis. A key part of the plan is a new two-deck bridge.

Women cleaning a Shrine Circus elephant, 1925

NOTES

A key to sources can be found in the bibliography following these pages.

JANUARY

1 *1840* OFS; *1850* MTC; *1869* SPD; *1878* RCHS; *1893* MA; *1969* BJ; **2** *1883* FD; *1890* GOV; *1917* LH; **3** *1848* MTC, S; *1905* S; *1916* BJ; *1940* MT; **4** *1854* S, MTC; *1874* S; *1920* BIO; **5** *1805* S, WJ; *1892* S; *1928* BJ; **6** *1976* LH; *1996* ST; **7** *1816* GOV; *1850* MP; *1857* CW; *1873* PM, LH, MDM; *1917* MAHS; *1972* BJ; **8** *1851* DM; *1920* NC; *1924* SPPP (Jan. 1, 1925); *1934* SPPP; *1971* MM (Oct. 1992); *1991* MST; **9** *1840* MTC; *1977* SN; **10** *1925* S; *1975* HD, SPPP; *1976* LH; **11** *1883* SPPP; *1907* S; *1909* S; **12** *1816* GOV, S; *1840* WJ; *1876* S; *1888* MDM; *1913* MHSP; **13** *1944* S; *1978* BJ, BIO; *1982* MST; **14** *1846* MTC, S; *1850* MTC; *1938* MSM; *1976* SC; *1993* MST; *1993* DNT (Dec. 26, 1993); **15** *1829* BG; *1849* MTC; *1851* S; **16** *1874* S; *1958* WD; **17** *1934* S; **18** *1849* S; *1887* S; *1892* S; **19** *1836* LH, MTC, S; *1862* MST (Mar. 22, 1993); *1928* PPPD; *1935* BJ; **20** *1896* S, MJ; *1961* BG; *1969* PMF; *1981* BJ; **21** *1844* S; **22** *1819* S; *1857* S; *1962* SPPP; *1967* BJ; **23** *1855* S, MTC; *1865* MG; *1929* PM; *1976* WC; *1986* SPPPD; *1986* SPPPD; **24** *1848* MTC; *1881* BG, RCH (spring 1966); **25** *1867* SPP; *1886* MT, MJ; *1915* MJ; *1983* DNT (Jan. 1, 2000), MST (Mar. 25, 1999); **26** *1836* S; *1861* BJ; *1924* SPPP (Dec. 28, 1924), MJ (Dec. 27, 1924); *1942* HL; *1949* KJ; **27** *1871* S, DNT (Jan. 1, 2000); *1960* DNT (Jan. 1, 2000); **28** *1890* LH; *1891* S; **29** *1900* CW; *1906* CW; **30** *1867* S; *1958* SPPP (Feb. 9, 1958), MS; *1992* SPPP; **31** *1780* FM St. Paul History, S, WJ; *1883* S

FEBRUARY

1 *1840* S; *1886* S; *1887* MH (winter 1973); *1933* GOV, BT; **2** *1842* GM, GOV; *1846* S; *1910* S; *1996* HD; **3** *1809* S; *1931* S; *1979* MBC, MT; **4** *1803* S; *1893* GA, PH; *1952* LH; **5** *1924* SPPP (Jan. 1, 1925), CCE; **6** *1862* S; *1967* FDP Accordionaires; **7** *1851* S; *1867* MAB; *1922* S; *1976* MS; **8** *1831* S; *1905* FMD; *1916* S; *1933* MT; **9** *1820* S, MH (fall 1974); *1895* HB; *1899* BJ, MDM; **10** *1763* S; *1806* S; *1971* MT; **11** *1811* WJ; *1888* S; *1891* S; **12** *1895* S; *1939* S, DNT; *1988* DNT; *2000* SPPP (October 2 and December 9, 2000); **13** *1857* S; *1906* S, TW; *1909* BJ; *1918* BJ;

1933 MWP; *1976* SPPP; **14** *1833* S, SPPP (Jan. 1, 1925); *1850*
OFS, S; *1852* S; **15** *1822* PC, S, CW; *1870* S, RL; **16** *1855* S; *1860*
S; *1864* S; **17** *1815* HJT; *1881* S; *1921* MST, COR, SPD (Feb. 15,
1968); *1972* GA; **18** *1868* S; *1870* S; *1931* GOV, S; *1953* MLM;
19 *1840* GOV; *1851* S; *1902* PH; **20** *1811* S, GOV; *1855* S; *1862*
S; *1992* MST; **21** *1855* S; **22** *1855* S; *1861* S; **23** *1854* S; *1854* S;
1856 S; *1892* MJ, SPPP; *1983* MST; **24** *1858* S; *1925* LW;
25 *1856* S; *1860* S; *1879* S; **26** *1853* S; *1857* S; *1857* LH, S; *1883*
S; *1985* MST; **27** *1843* S; *1857* S; **28** *1866* S; *1872* S; *1891* LH;
29 *1844* S; *1868* S

MARCH

1 *1856* S, LH; *1856* S, LH; *1881* S, MST (May 25, 1992); *1899* S;
1921 DNT (Jan. 1, 2000); *1994* MST; **2** *1859* LH; *1878* S; *1922*
MJ, SPPP; *1949* MAHS, AF; *1974* MST; **3** *1849* MTC, S; *1853* S;
1855 S; *1855* S; *1990* BJ, MST; **4** *1854* S; *1892* HJD; *1911* S, MJ;
1941 BJ; *1942* MTF; **5** *1814* S, WJ; *1852* S; *1853* S; *1853* S, PC; **6**
1852 S; *1857* S; *1862* WH; *1868* S; *1871* S; *2000* DNT; **7** *1882* S;
1913 MJ; **8** *1858* S; *1892* MDM; *1920* S; **9** *1848* S; *1858* S, BT;
1874 S; **10** *1804* S; *1858* BIO; *1983* SPPP; **11** *1862* MR; *1863* KC;
1893 BJ; **12** *1872* SPD; *1877* BJ; **13** *1858* S; **14** *1841* S; *1919* BJ;
1924 S; **15** *1927* DNT (Jan. 1, 2000); *1941* MDM; **16** *1876* KV;

1882 S; *1912* GOV; **17** *1851*
BG; **18** *1858* S; *1858* S; *1891* BJ,
DNT (Jan. 1, 2000); **19** *1849* S;
1867 S, KR; *1880* BG; *1992*
MST; **20** *1858* S; *1920* LH; *1992*
SPPP; **21** *1864* BT; *1913* MJ;
22 *1882* BJ, PM; *1908* BJ; *1958*
BJ; *1993* MST; **23** *1823* GOV;

March 10, 1983

1860 MH (winter 1997–98), TW; *1971* BJ, SPPP; **24** *1858* S;
1999 SPPP; **25** *1854* S, GOV; *1886* PR; *1888* SBG; *1963* MLM;
26 *1804* S; *1857* S; **27** *1819* OFS, S, WJ; *1905* S; *1912* S; **28**
1992 MST; **29** *1823* S; *1855* S; *1916* BJ; *1928* MJ; *1980* SPD;
1998 SPPP; **30** *1844* S; *1917* LH; *1924* SPPP, MJ; *1930* MHSP,
COR; *1992* MST, GOV, BT; **31** *1810* S; *1847* OFS; *1918* FDP
Celebrities; *1934* BJ, S

APRIL

1 *1880* S; *1923* SPPP (Mar. 27, 1938); *1924* SPPP (Jan. 1, 1925);
2 *1849* S; *1982* MST; **3** *1859* TW; *1920* S; *1970* FA; **4** *1888* BG;
1893 BJ, S; *1914* BIO; **5** *1830* S; *1852* S; *1876* LH; *1904* BIO;
1929 MDM; *1937* S, SPPP; **6** *1808* S; *1851* S; *1956* MHSP; *1982*
MBC; **7** *1846* S; *1866* S; *1924* SPPP; **8** *1897* MJ; *1905* S; *1911* BJ;

1953 MT; **9** *1789* S; *1839* BG; *1849* SPPP (Oct. 30, 1949), S; *2000*
MST; **10** *1855* S; *1895* SPD; **11** *1680* S; **12** *1923* FM St. Paul
History; *1937* BIO; *1976* SPD; **13** *1849* S; *1907* GOV; *1967* MST;
1993 SPPP; **14** *1805* GA; *1861* S; *1870* S; *1894* MA; *1901* PM;
1977 MAA; **15** *1892* S; *1912* FM St. Paul History; *1916* LH; *1944*
MLM; **16** *1901* PM; *1917* HJD; *1927* S; *1991* MCT; **17** *1856* BJ;
1895 S, JHM; *1965* SPPP; *1990* GA; *1997* IPA; *2000* ST; **18** *1807*
S; *1820* MDM; *1888* MJ; **19** *1858* AN; *1865* FM St. Paul History;
1866 S; *1902* S; *1945* S; **20** *1836* S; *1891* S; *1899* KJ; *1921* NB
(May 12, 1923); *1949* BJ, DNT (Jan. 1, 2000); **21** *1883* BIO;
1891 AP; *1899* S; *1940* MT; *1961* MBC; **22** *1818* S; *1903* GOV,
BG; *1911* TW; **23** *1857* S, GOV, OFC; *1881* S; *1897* KJ; *1992*
SPPP; **24** *1846* OFS; *1914* MAHS, MB; *1956* MBC; **25** *1892* BJ;
1924 SPPP (Jan. 1, 1925); **26** *1840* S; *1877* S; *1896* GOV; *1924*
SPPP (Jan. 1, 1925); *1972* MT; **27** *1915* S; *1948* S, MST (May
25, 1992); *1967* MHSP; **28** *1849* S; *1871* GA; *1882* MHSP, MST
(Apr. 23, 1981); *1916* S; **29** *1816* S, OFS; *1858* S; **30** *1803* S;
1853 S; *1901* FM St. Paul History; *1961* MBC; *1967* MDM

MAY

1 *1840* S; *1873* S; *1896* S; *1926* DNT (Jan. 1, 2000); *1933* MGH;
1976 LH, GG (Oct. 1993); **2** *1670* S; *1878* S, LH; *1903* S; *1976*
MBC; *1986* SPPPD; *1992* MST (May 2, 1993); **3** *1865* PM, TW;
1959 DNT (Jan. 1, 2000); *1989* SPPPD; **4** *1863* BJ, S; *1888* S; *1925*
S, MJ; *1975* MBC; *1984* MBC; **5** *1820* OFS, S; *1880* CW; *1884*
TJ; *1973* HJD; *1974* IHB; **6** *1834* S, OFS; *1840* OFS; *1865* S, LH;
1896 BJ; *1965* MDM; **7** *1800* S; *1850* WJ; *1900* CW, FJ; **8** *1881*
S; *1910* S; *1924* SPPP (Dec. 28, 1924); *1968* MBC; **9** *1887* CW;
1918 BJ, GOV; *1921* BJ; *2001* SPPP; **10** *1823* OFS, S; *1827* S;
1902 MBC, SPPP; *1941* MHSP; *1993* ST; *2000* DNT, ST; **11** *1844*
GOV, CT; *1858* S, MST (May 25, 1992); *1869* LH; **12** *1806* S;
13 *1824* OFS; *1858* S, SPPP (Mar. 27, 1938); *1956* MT; **14** *1852*
S, PM; *1988* COR; **15** *1896* S, MBC; **16** *1850* S; *1898* S; *1938* S,
BJ; **17** *1837* S; **18** *1905* BG, SPPP; *1931* SPDN; **19** *1857* S; *1860*
RW; *1968* SPD; **20** *1882* PC; *1902* AP; *1927* S; **21** *1839* S, BG,
WJ; *1882* S; *1934* MHSP; *1961* MBC; *1972* LH; **22** *1888* S; *1945*
MH (Sept. 1957); **23** *1857* S; *1879* MAHS; *1884* MHSP; *1908* S;
24 *1841* S; *1858* WJ, S, GOV; *1941* BJ, DNT (Jan. 1, 2000);
25 *1850* S; *1859* S; *1867* MST (May 25, 1992); *1877* LH; *1926*
SPPP; *1997* MST; **26** *1780* KV; *1861* S; *1900* S; **27** *1858* OFS;
1858 S; *1902* AN; *1930* KJ; **28** *1827* OFS; *1859* DJ; *1866* S; *1896*
S; *1903* FM St. Paul; *1936* BJ, S; **29** *1848* S; *1896* GOV; *1897* FM
St. Paul History; *1916* MA; *1919* KJ; *1935* S; **30** *1871* S; *1899* S;
31 *1819* S; *1853* S

JUNE

1 *1849* WGC, GOV, S; *1859* SPPP (Mar. 27, 1938); *1927* LH;
1979 SPPP; 2 *1838* BG, WJ; *1924* AN; 3 *1836* S; *1839* BG; *1859*
AI; *1916* DNT (Jan. 1, 2000); *1990* MST; *1999* DNT; 4 *1869* S;
1993 MST; *2000* MST; 5 *1806* CWF; *1873* S; *1885* MH (winter
1973); 6 *1736* CEV; *1849* S; *1877* S; *1889* COR; *1910* S; *1945*
DNT; 7 *1838* BG; *1892* S, KJ; *1902* S; *1921* S; *1958* BJ; *1987* MST
(May 25, 1992); 8 *1848* OFS; *1854* S, BG; *1880* S; *1898* PM; *1910*
BJ; *1927* BJ; 9 *1871* S, DNT (Jan. 1, 2000); *1892* CW; *1894* S;
1921 S; *1979* GA; 10 *1864* MST (Mar. 22, 1993); *1902* PC; *1922*
BJ, DNT (Jan. 1, 2000); 11 *1835* OFS, S; *1849* S, WGC; *1858* S;
1877 MST (May 25, 1992); *1899* FM St. Paul History; *1945* JN;
12 *1838* S; *1873* S; *1905* S; *1914* MHSP; 13 *1820* S; *1838* S; *1886*
MHSP; *1968* MDM; 14 *1671* S; *1868* S; *1918* LH; *1959* RCHS;
1981 MDM; 15 *1838* S; *1851* S; *1892* MDM; *1909* FM St. Paul
History; *1920* S, MST (May 25, 1992); *1933* S, BJ; *1939* SC;
16 *1854* LH; *1863* S; *1931* S; *1945* S; *1955* GA; *1999* SPPP;
17 *1673* S; *1889* AP; *1890* S; *1909* GOV; *1913* BJ; 18 *1847* S;
1855 S; *1892* S; *1893* MDM; *1934* HJD; *1939* MDM, S; 19 *1816*
BGS; *1852* S; *1873* S; 20 *1823* S; *1887* LH; *1970* GR; 21 *1839*
AN, BT; *1867* S; *1899* BG; *1925* LH; *1973* DNT (Jan. 1, 2000);
22 *1806* PC; *1861* S; *1919* S; 23 *1870* GOV; *1911* DNT; *1927* S;
1975 DNT (Jan. 1, 2000); 24 *1924* SPPP (Dec. 28, 1924); *1948*
MST (May 25, 1992); *1996* SPPP; 25 *1849* BG; *1977* DNT (Jan.
1, 2000); 26 *1834* OFS; *1851* S; *1948* S; *1953* MT; *1959* DNT;
1993 MST; 27 *1928* GOV; *1975* LH; *1977* HS; 28 *1818* FWW;
1849 BG; *1862* RCHS, S; *1880* LH, PM; 29 *1837* S; *1854* S; *1863*
S; *1905* TJ; *1916* DNT (Jan. 1, 2000); *1922* ZD; 30 *1853* GA;
1888 S, DNT (Jan. 1, 2000); *1992* MST (July 1, 2000)

JULY

1 *1922* MS; *1931* S; *1974* RC; 2 *1679* S; *1863* LH, MR; *1882* ME;
3 *1839* S; *1863* S; *1863* FM St. Paul History; *1917* S; *1941* MSHS
(Oct. 1941); 4 *1836* PM, S; *1859* BG; *1862* PM; *1868* S; *1875* S,
LH; *1896* S; *1999* DNT; 5 *1876* ME; *1928* S; 6 *1849* BG; *1883* S;
1889 S; *1974* PK; 7 *1849* WGC, S; *1862* S; *1871* DJ; 8 *1775* S;
1887 BG; *1889* RT; *1939* S; 9 *1823* S, OFS; *1832* OFS; *1835* S;
1902 AP; *1932* MHSP; *1975* OCJ; 10 *1823* S; *1930* MHSP; 11
1999 DNT; 12 *1829* OFS; *1869* S; 13 *1787* S, AN; *1832* BJ; *1862*
MST (Mar. 22, 1993); *1881* CW; *1890* MDM, PM, S; *1977* DNT
(Feb.-Mar. 1978); 14 *1864* BG, MST (Mar. 22, 1993); *1901* PM;
1903 SAI; *1924* SPPP (Dec. 22, 1924); *1948* TJC; *1991* BJ; 15
1856 S; *1872* SPD; *1881* MDM; *1917* MB; *1929* SPD; *1951* BIO;

16 *1817* RCHS, S, BG; *1858* S; *1862*
CW, PC, COR; *1992* MST; **17** *1817* AN;
1854 S; **18** *1840* S; *1847* BG, S; *1908*
SPD; *1913* GOV; *1918* MT (Nov. 11,
1956), BJ; *1962* BJ; **19** *1815* OFS; *1850*
S; *1858* S, OFS; *1967* MST; *1982* BJ,
DNT (Jan. 1, 2000); *1987* BJ; **20** *1837* S,
OFS, WJ; *1858* S; *1907* MH (fall 1967);
1934 S; *1940* S; **21** *1820* S; *1820* S; *1856*
S; *1879* GOV; **22** *1850* S; **23** *1838* S;

July 2, 1863

1851 AN; *1872* PM, S; *1924* SPPP (Dec. 28, 1924); *1943* LH;
24 *1786* S; *1998* MST (July 10, 1998); **25** *1847* S; *1917* LH; *1990*
MST (May 26, 1992); **26** *1820* OFS; *1892* FM St. Paul History;
1895 DAB; *1896* FM St. Paul History; *1937* LH; **27** *1898* S, MST
(May 25, 1992); *1972* MST; **28** *1861* GOV; **29** *1827* GOV, S;
1856 S; *1887* BG; *1927* BJ; *1974* BJ; **30** *1805* OFS, BG; *1835* S;
1884 S; **31** *1859* TW; *1866* USA; *1873* BG; *1910* BJ; *1928* S

AUGUST

1 *1820* S; *1849* S; *1870* S; *1989* DNT (Jan. 1, 2000); **2** *1847* S;
1873 CEV; *1874* FD; *1928* VD; *1956* DNT (Jan. 1, 2000), MT;
3 *1794* S; **4** *1854* S; *1857* S, WJ; *1892* FM St. Paul History; *1916*
SPPP; **5** *1851* S, AN; *1945* BJ; *1957* MBC; **6** *1886* MH (winter
1973); *1945* DNT (Jan. 1, 2000); *1969* MDM; **7** *1898* MHSP;
1915 S; *1942* BJ, DNT (Jan. 1, 2000); **8** *1849* S; *1857* MBC, S;
9 *1820* S, OFS; *1823* S; *1842* S; **10** *1853* LH; *1887* S; *1909* DNT
(January 11, 1984); **11** *1900* ME; *1906* S; *1992* MST; **12** *1940* S;
1981 RP; *1983* WF; *1984* MBC; **13** *1849* S; *1893* CG; **14** *1830*
OFS; *1848* S; **15** *1933* BJ; **16** *1909* BJ; *1964* MT; **17** *1862* S; *1946*
MDM; **18** *1929* S; *1993* MST; **19** *1862* WJ; *1863* LH, S; *1957* KJ;
20 *1892* FM St. Paul History; *1904* S, BG; *1928* LH, S; **21** *1833*
S; *1860* S, BJ; *1883* MDM, S; *1893* PM; *1965* SPPP; *1995* SPPP;
22 *1888* LH; *1912* BGU; *1999* MST; **23** *1852* S; *1862* S; *1899* S;
24 *1819* S, FWW, BT; *1839* S; **25** *1827* S; *1901* BJ; *1917* LH;
1937 S, LH; **26** *1731* S; *1848* S; *1919* LH; *2000* MST; **27** *1979*
SJ; **28** *1857* S; *1883* GOV; *1977* LC; **29** *1857* PS; *1857* CE; *1860*
S, RW; **30** *1812* S; *1813* S; *1924* SPPP (Dec. 28, 1924); *1968*
SPPP; **31** *1823* S; *1929* S

SEPTEMBER

1 *1851* S; *1857* S; *1894* LH, S; *1918* S, MHSP; *1941* S; **2** *1844* S;
1862 S; *1868* S; *1873* LH; *1924* FS; *1952* KJ; **3** *1783* S; *1849* S,
WGC, COR; *1860* S; *1883* MHSP; **4** *1839* S; *1882* AC; *1884* S;

1908 LH, S; *1939* S; **5** *1882* S; *1893* MH (fall 1968); *1917* MST
(May 25, 1992); **6** *1877* S; *1889* FWW; *1952* RP; **7** *1876* S; *1885*
S; *1885* S; *1996* MST; **8** *1884* MDM; *1906* S; *1975* LH; *1991*
MST; **9** *1849* OFS; *1861* WJ; *1863* MH (Dec. 1934); *1884* MT;
1903 CT, DAB; *1933* MST; **10** *1820* WJ, OFS; *1863* COR; *1934*
TJ; *1988* MST; **11** *1835* S; *1888* S; *1896* AN; *1900* KR; *1971* MT;
12 *1881* S; *1883* GOV; *1883* S; **13** *1900* CW; *1930* DNT (Jan. 1,
2000); *1956* KJ; **14** *1871* S; *1996* D (July-Aug. 1999); **15** *1801*
AN; *1834* OFS; *1862* S; *1869* S; **16** *1885* S; *1928* LH; *1995* MST;
17 *1727* S; *1885* S; *1887* MK; *1907* BJ; *1961* BJ; **18** *1844* OFS;
1923 GOV; **19** *1857* LH, S; *1865* S, PM; *1926* DNT (Jan. 1, 2000);
1930 MHSP; *1970* BJ; **20** *1863* MST (Mar. 22, 1993); *1891* SB;
1939 S; **21** *1805* WJ; *1836* S; **22** *1895* LH, DAB; *1968* MBC;
23 *1805* OFS, BG, S; *1857* S; *1862* S; *1897* S; **24** *1848* S; *1867*
MBC; *1886* S; *1924* SPPP (Dec. 28, 1924); *1934* GOV; *1963* DNT;
25 *1867* S; *1896* SPPP; *1937* BJ; **26** *1862* S; *1992* SPPP; **27** *1862*
S, LH; *1888* S, BIO; *1894* HM; *1996* SPPP; **28** *1839* BG, WJ;
1908 MAHS; *1935* MST (Sept. 12, 1997); *1955* MBC; **29** *1837*
KC; *1964* BG; *1983* MST; **30** *1841* OFS; *1854* KC; *1876* LH;
1887 S; *1892* S; *1924* SPPP (Dec. 28, 1924); *1981* MBC

OCTOBER

1 *1700* S, PM; *1847* S; *1908* KJ; *1929* KD; *1946* MAB; *1992* MST;
2 *1843* S; *1863* S, KC; *1900* FM St. Paul History; *1900* SPD; *1950*
BJ; *1968* NPS; **3** *1887* S; *1951* TJ; *1977* BJ, 162; *1997* DNT (Jan.
1, 2000); **4** *1869* S, USA; **5** *1898* S, BJ, PM; **6** *1860* FWW; *1972*
LH; **7** *1794* S; *1910* MDM, S; *1935* LH, SBG; **8** *1858* LH; *1910*
BJ, 162; *1956* MT; **9** *1846* BG; *1876* LH; *1933* S; *1949* SPPP;
1979 MHI; **10** *1862* S; *1917* LH, S; *1918* S, MDM, DNT (Jan. 1,
2000); *1949* MDM; **11** *1887* SPG; *1954* LH; **12** *1892* S; *1931*
SPD; *1945* S; *1997* MST; **13** *1857* S; *1893* S; *1919* BIO; *1990* BJ;

14 *1853* S; *1946* S;
15 *1800* S; *1857* S; *1880*
S, MDM; *1884* BG; *1891*
S; *1971* MST (May 25,
1992); **16** *1898* BJ; *1921*
S; *1924* S; *1930* MHSP;
1987 MST; *1989* MST
(May 25, 1992); **17** *1825*
GOV, S; *1924* PW; *1975*
LH; **18** *1848* AN; *1881* S;
1888 S; **19** *1894* BG; *1912*

October 31, 1920

S; **20** *1818* OFS, S; *1849* S; *1896* CW; *1937* BG; *1995* MST;
21 *1839* WJ, OFS; *1850* S; *1967* BJ; **22** *1836* S; *1989* MST

(May 25, 1992); **23** *1905* MHSP; *1920* S; *1934* BJ; **24** *1871* UW; *1988* DNT (Jan. 1, 2000); **25** *1892* LH; *1924* SPPP (Dec. 28, 1924); *1941* BJ; *1987* BJ; *1991* MST; **26** *1950* RP; *1960* MBC; **27** *1829* S; *1849* UW; *1937* MHSP; *1991* BJ; **28** *1834* WJ; *1919* BJ; *1949* MHSP; *1990* MST (May 25, 1992); **29** *1775* S; *1866* MBC; *1947* LH; *1971* BJ; **30** *1848* WJ, S; *1924* SPPP (Dec. 28, 1924); **31** *1872* S; *1903* S, BJ; *1920* S; *1991* MDM

NOVEMBER

1 *1841* S, SPPP (Mar. 27, 1938 and Nov. 2, 1947); *1849* S; *1976* CI; **2** *1869* S; *1948* BIO; *1993* SBG; **3** *1831* S; *1895* S; *1908* DNT (Jan. 1, 2000); *1959* ET; *1989* BJ; *1992* SPPP; *1998* DNT (Jan. 1, 2000); **4** *1850* S; *1864* S; *1994* DNT (Jan. 1, 2000); *1997* MST; **5** *1862* FWW; *1875* S; *1903* MST (June 7, 1993); *1905* MT; *1975* LH; *1991* SPPP; **6** *1854* S; *1860* PM; *1874* S; *1887* SPPP; **7** *1885* DNT (Jan. 1, 2000); *1889* CW; *1905* GOV, S; **8** *1898* BJ, PM; *1890* MT; *1926* S; *1932* WB; **9** *1862* SDP; *1891* S; *1913* LH; **10** *1851* S; *1855* S; *1871* S; *1880* FR; *1933* AD; *1975* DNT (Jan. 1, 2000); *1976* MST (May 25, 1992); **11** *1856* S; *1859* BG; *1865* S; *1919* KJ; *1940* BJ, MDM, WR; **12** *1882* S; *1889* BJ; *1892* BJ; *1908* BIO; *1977* PT; **13** *1833* S; *1891* GOV, S; *1970* MT; **14** *1766* S; *1860* SPPP (Aug. 28, 1960), FM; *1908* SH; *1917* BJ; *1996* SPPP; **15** *1851* BJ; *1866* HJD; *1880* SPPP; **16** *1854* S; *1881* CW; *1883* TM; *1939* BIO; **17** *1863* GOV, S; *1992* PCM; **18** *1938* S; *1985* DNT (Jan. 1, 2000); *1993* FW; **19** *1855* BG, S, HG; *1855* S, HG; *1902* MST (May 25, 1992); *1945* MHSP; *1971* BJ; **20** *1855* S; *1967* MT; *1969* SPD; *1979* KJ; **21** *1849* S; *1902* S; *1924* SPPP; **22** *1838* MH (Sept. 1934); *1870* S; *1879* S; *1950* BJ; *1995* DNT (Jan. 1, 2000); *1996* MST; **23** *1910* S; **24** *1859* GG (Dec. 5, 1993); *1864* S; **25** *1817* S; *1863* MST (Mar. 22, 1993); *1903* SS; *1946* SPPP; **26** *1849* S; *1869* MJ; *1922* BJ; **27** *1900* GOV, S; *1930* S; **28** *1850* BG; *1882* PC; *1905* MST (May 25, 1992), S, DNT (Jan. 1, 2000); *1922* S; **29** *1816* S; *1884* BG; *2000* MST; **30** *1843* S; *1912* EW; *1960* MJR

DECEMBER

1 *1855* PM, S; *1856* PM; *1860* S; *1941* S, MT; *1982* BG, SPD; **2** *1857* S; *1858* S; *1884* CW; **3** *1842* S; **4** *1855* RW; *1860* SPPP (Aug. 28, 1960); *1928* BG; **5** *1853* BT; *1873* S; *1950* MDM; **6** *1815* S; **7** *1863* S; *1864* MST (Mar. 22, 1993); *1941* RCH (winter 1991), BJ; *1963* DJ; **8** *1863* S; *1886* S, WG; **9** *1890* S; *1935* S, WM, MPJ; **10** *1878* S; *1930* MST (May 25, 1992); *1966* TV; **11** *1876* BJ; *1895* S; *1956* MHSP; *1970* MT; *1999* MST; *1999* MST; **12** *1928* MHSP; **13** *1882* CW; *1994* MST; **14** *1798* S;

15 *1856* S; *1864* MST (Mar. 22, 1993); *1887* NI; *1892* BJ;
16 *1814* S; *1884* KJ; *1889* S; 17 *1839* S; *1915* S; *1942* HCH;
1966 UM; 18 *1985* BJ; *1988* MST; 19 *1836* S; *1906* S; *1957* MS;
1957 MS; 20 *1847* S; *1863* BG; *1902* S; *1902* FJ; 21 *1885* S;

December 11, 1970

1998 MST; 22 *1858* BG; 23 *1832* S;
1846 S, FWW; *1926* BJ; 24 *1869* HI;
1889 S; *1892* S; *1896* S; 25 *1842* WJ;
1866 PM; *1874* BG; *1913* MHSP;
1943 MST (May 25, 1992); 26 *1850*
BG, S; *1862* S; *1990* SPPP; 27 *1846*
GOV, S, BT; *1858* TW; *1906* S; *1957*
MT; 28 *1846* S; *1909* PM; 29 *1854*
WGC, WJ; *1891* SPPP, S; 30 *1884* S;
1948 MT; *1977* MST (May 25, 1992);
31 *1894* S; *1957* SPPP (Feb. 9, 1958)

BIBLIOGRAPHY

MHS refers to the Minnesota Historical Society.

AF *Air Force Magazine,* March 1999. AC American Crane corporate history online, available: www.american-crane.com. AN
The Anishinabeg: Walking the Good Road (calendar). Minneapolis:
Minneapolis Public Schools, Department of Indian Education,
1991. AP *The Appeal* (St. Paul). AI Atwater, Isaac, ed. *History of
the City of Minneapolis, Minnesota.* New York: Munsell, 1893.
AD *Austin Daily Herald.*

BGU Beito, Gretchen Urnes. *Coya Come Home: A Congress-
woman's Journey.* Los Angeles: Pomegranate Press, Ltd., 1990.
BIO *Biography Resource Center* (subscription database). Gale
Group, 1999. BJ Blashfield, Jean F. *Awesome Almanac Minnesota.*
Fontana, Wisc.: B&B Publishing, 1993. BT Blegen, Theodore C.
Minnesota: A History of the State. Minneapolis: University of
Minnesota Press, 1975. BG Brueggemann, Gary John. *Fort Road/
West 7th History Calendar.* St. Paul: COMPAS/Intersection, 1982.
BGS Bryce, George. *'Seven Oaks': An Account of the Affair at
Seven Oaks . . . .* Winnipeg, Manitoba: Manitoba Free Press, 1892.

CE Carlstedt, Ellworth T. "Minnesota and the Panic of 1857."
Paper, University of Minnesota, 1933. CG Carruth, Gorton.
Encyclopedia of American Facts and Dates. Cambridge: Harper &
Row, 1987. CEV Chapin, Earl V. *The Angle of Incidents: The
Story of Warroad and the Northwest Angle.* Warroad, Minn.:
Warroad Historical Society, 1970. CT Christianson, Theodore.
*Minnesota: The Land of Sky-Tinted Waters: A History of the State
and Its People.* Chicago: American Historical Society, 1935. CI
The Circle. Minneapolis: Minneapolis Regional Native Ameri-
can Center, 1980–. CCE Clark, Clifford E., Jr., ed. *Minnesota
in a Century of Change: The State and Its People Since 1900.*
St. Paul: MHS Press, 1989. COR Correspondence, in the pos-
session of the author. CW Curtiss-Wedge, Franklin. "Incidents
and Events, 1857–1910," from History of Rice and Steele
Counties, Minnesota. Chicago: H. C. Cooper, Jr., 1910. CWF
Curtiss-Wedge, Franklin. *History of Wright County.* Chicago:
H. C. Cooper, 1915.

DAB *Dictionary of American Biography.* New York: Scribner's,
1964. DM Diedrich, Mark. *The Chiefs Hole-in-the-Day of the*

Mississippi Chippewa. Minneapolis: Coyote Books, 1986.
D *The Duluthian.* Duluth: Duluth Chamber of Commerce.
DNT *Duluth News Tribune.* **DJ** Dunn, James Taylor. *The St. Croix: Midwest Border River.* St. Paul: MHS Press, 1979.

EW *Encyclopedia of World Biography.* Farmington Hills, Mich.: Gale Group, 1997. **ET** *The Evening Tribune* (Albert Lea, Minn.).

FS *Fairmont Daily Sentinel.* **FD** *The Faribault Democrat.* **FJ** *The Faribault Journal.* **FR** *The Faribault Republican.* **FDP** Files arranged by topic in the Duluth Public Library. **FM** Files arranged by topic in the MHS Library. **FA** First Avenue website, available: www.first-avenue.com. **FWW** Folwell, William Watts. *A History of Minnesota* (4 vols.). St. Paul: MHS, 1969. **FMD** Foster, Mary Dillon, comp. *Who's Who among Minnesota Women.* St. Paul: M. D. Foster, 1924. **FW** *The Frederick R. Weisman Art Museum at the University of Minnesota* (pamphlet). Minneapolis: The Museum, 1993.

March 2, 1922

GM Gieske, Millard L. and Steven J. Keillor, *Norwegian Yankee: Knute Nelson and the Failure of American Politics.* Northfield, Minn.: Norwegian-American Historical Association, 1995. **GOV** *Governors of Minnesota, 1849–1991* (pamphlet). St. Paul: MHS Library. **GG** *The Grand Gazette.* St. Paul: Roger E. Swardson, 1973–. **GA** Greiner, A. E. *The Minnesota History Calendar 1993: Historic Events for Every Day of the Year.* St. Paul: S. K. Press, 1992. **GR** *Guinness Record Breakers.* New York: Mint Publishers, 1997.

HG Hage, George S. *Newspapers on the Minnesota Frontier, 1849–1860.* St. Paul: MHS, 1967. **HM** Harris, Moira F. *The Paws of Refreshment: The Story of Hamm's Beer Advertising.* St. Paul: Pogo Press, 1990. **HJT** Heidler, Jeanne T. and David S. Heidler, ed. *Encyclopedia of the War of 1812.* Santa Barbara: ABC-Clio, 1997. **HS** Hendry, Sharon D. *Glensheen's Daughter: The Marjorie Congdon Story.* Bloomington, Minn.: Cable Publishing Inc., 1998. **HCH** *Hennepin County History* 37:1 (spring 1978). **HI** Hildebrand, Ivy Louise. *Sauk Centre: The Story of a Frontier Town.* Sauk Centre, Minn.: Sauk Centre Area Historical Society, 1993. **HD** "Historical Data Retrieval and Climate Summaries" section of Minnesota Climatology Working Group online, available: climate.umn.edu/climatology.htm. **HB** "The History of Basketball at Hamline University: 'Birthplace of Intercollegiate Basketball,'" Hamline University web site, available: web.hamline.edu/alumni/cla/paa/huttontourney.html. **HJD** Holmquist, June Drenning, ed. *They Chose Minnesota: A Survey of the State's Ethnic Groups.* St. Paul: MHS Press, 1981. **HL** *Hutchinson Leader.*

IHB In the Heart of the Beast website, available: www.hobt.org. **IPA** *1998 Information Please Almanac.* Boston: Houghton-Mifflin Co., 1998.

JHM Jacobsen, Hazel M. *The Spiral Bridge of Hastings: Its Beginning and End.* Hastings, Minn.: Hastings Bicentennial Commission, 1976. **JN** Johnson, Nellie Stone. *Nellie Stone Johnson: The Life of an Activist* (as told to David Brauer). St. Paul: Ruminator Books, 2000.

KJ Kane, Joseph Nathan. *Famous First Facts: A Record of First Happenings, Discoveries, and Inventions in American History.* New York: H. W. Wilson, 1981. **KC** Kappler, Charles J., ed. *Indian Affairs: Laws and Treaties.* Washington, D.C.: GPO, 1904. **KR** Keen, Richard A. *Minnesota Weather.* Helena, Mont.: American and World Geographic Publishing, 1992. **KD** Kolacky Days information online, available: montgomerymn.org. **KV** Kunz, Virginia Brainard. *St. Paul: The First 150 Years.* St. Paul: St. Paul Foundation, 1991.

LH *Labor History Calendar, 1977.* In the possession of the author. **LC** *Lake City Graphic.* **LW** Lass, William E. *Minnesota's Boundary with Canada: Its Evolution since 1783.* St. Paul: MHS Press, 1980.

MPJ Maccabee, Paul. *John Dillinger Slept Here: A Crooks' Tour of Crime and Corruption in St. Paul, 1920–1936.* St. Paul: MHS Press, 1995. **MG** Malen, Gordon M. *"Firstory": Biography of a Bank Attuned to Tomorrow: First Bank Minneapolis.* Minneapolis: First National Bank of Minneapolis, 1982. **MK** Marling, Karal Ann. *Blue Ribbon: A Social and Pictorial History of the Minnesota State Fair.* St. Paul: MHS Press, 1990. **MA** Martin, Albro. *James J. Hill and the Opening of the Northwest.* St. Paul: MHS Press, 1991. **MGH** Mayer, George H. *The Political Career of Floyd B. Olson.* St. Paul: MHS Press, 1987. **MJR** Mellow, James R. *Hemingway: A Life Without Consequences.* Boston: Houghton-Mifflin, 1992. **MAHS** Melrose Area Historical Society, *1990 Melrose Area Historical Calendar.* Melrose, Minn.: The Society, 1989. **MB** *The Melrose Beacon.* **MTF** Messner, Tammy Faye. *Tammy: Telling It*

My Way. New York: Villard, 1996. **ME** Meyer, Ellen Wilson. *Happenings Around Wayzata: The First Hundred Years, 1853–1953.* Excelsior, Minn.: Tonka Print Company, 1980. **MJ** *Minneapolis Journal.* **MSM** *Minneapolis Spokesman.* **MS** *Minneapolis Star.* **MST** (Minneapolis) *Star Tribune.* **MT** *Minneapolis Tribune.* **MAA** *Minnesota Asian American Project Newsletter* 1.1 (June 1977). **MBC** *1985 Minnesota Baseball History Calendar.* Stillwater, Minn.: Brick Alley Books Press, 1984. **MCT** Minnesota Chippewa Tribe. *Speaking of Ourselves.* Cass Lake, Minn.: The Tribe, 1977–. **MTC** Minnesota Historical Society. *Official Calendar of the Minnesota Territorial Centennial: One Hundred Years of Progress, 1849–1949.* St. Paul: MHS, 1948. **MDM** Minnesota Historical Society, Division of Library and Archives, "Major Disasters in Minnesota" (information sheet). St. Paul: The Division, 2001. **MAB** Minnesota Historical Society, Metronet, and the Minnesota Center for the Book. *Minnesota Author Biographies Project* online, available: people.mnhs.org/authors/index.cfm. **MHSP** Minnesota Historical Society Photograph Collection online, available: www.mnhs.org/library/search/vrdb/bsearch.html. **MH** *Minnesota History.* St. Paul: MHS, 1925–. **MHI** *The Minnesota History Interpreter.* St. Paul: MHS, 1974–. **MSHS** *Minnesota Horticulturist.* St. Paul: Minnesota State Horticultural Society. **MLM** *Minnesota Legislative Manual.* St. Paul: State of Minnesota. **MM** *Minnesota Monthly.* Collegeville, Minn.: Minnesota Public Radio, 1976–. **MP** *The Minnesota Pioneer* (St. Paul). **MWP** *Minnesota Women's Press.* St. Paul: Minnesota Women's Press, Inc., 1985–. **MR** Moe, Richard. *The Last Full Measure: The Life and Death of the First Minnesota Volunteers.* New York: Henry Holt, 1993.

NPS National Park Service. "Wild and Scenic Rivers" online, available: www.nps.gov/rivers/index.html. **NC** Nelson, E. Clifford, ed. *Lutherans in North America.* Philadelphia: Fortress Press, 1975. **NE** Nelson, Edward P. and Barbara Sommer, eds. *It Was a Good Deal: The Civilian Conservation Corps in Minnesota.* Duluth: St. Louis County Historical Society, 1987. **NI** *Northfield Independent.* **NB** *The Northwestern Bulletin.* St. Paul and Minneapolis: Bulletin Publishing Company, 1922–24.

OCJ "Old 201, Casey Jones and the Union Depot" (pamphlet). In the possession of the author. **OFS** *Old Fort Snelling.* St. Paul: MHS.

PK Pankake, Marcia and Garrison Keillor, eds. *A Prairie Home Commonplace Book: Twenty-five Years on the Air with Garrison Keillor.* St. Paul: HighBridge Company, 1999. **PS** Patchin, Sydney Allen. "The Development of Banking in Minnesota." Master's

Thesis, University of Minnesota, 1919. **PT** Penumbra Theatre Company (Jennifer Blackmer, contacted June 2001). **PW** Phyllis Wheatley Settlement House. *Ten Years a Neighbor: Phyllis Wheatley Settlement House, 1924–1934.* Minneapolis: The House, 1934. **PC** *Pictorial Calendar of Early Faribault.* In the possession of the author. **PCM** *Players Choice Magazine* (Morton, Minn.) 2:10 (October 1992). **PII** Poatgieter, A. Hermina and James Taylor Dunn, eds. *Gopher Reader: Minnesota's Story in Words and Pictures: Selections from the Gopher Historian.* St. Paul: MHS and Minnesota Statehood Centennial Commission, 1966. **PM** Potter, Merle. *101 Best Stories of Minnesota.* Minneapolis: Harrison and Smith, Co., 1931. **PMF** *The Presidential Medal of Freedom: Winners and their Achievements.* Washington, D.C.: CQ Press, 1996.

September 9, 1861

PR *The Progress.* White Earth, Minn.: Gus H. Beaulieu, 1886–89.

RCHS Ramsey County Historical Society. *Life on the Mississippi.* **RCH** *Ramsey County History.* **RC** The Raptor Center website, available: www.raptor.cvm.umn.edu. **RL** Renz, Louis T. *The History of the Northern Pacific Railroad.* Fairfield, Wash.: Ye Galleon Press, 1980. **RP** *Rochester Post-Bulletin.* **RT** Ross, Thomas E. and Tyrel G. Moore, eds. *A Cultural Geography of North American Indians.* Boulder, Col.: Westview Press, 1987. **RW** Ryland, William James. *Alexander Ramsey: A Study of a Frontier Politician and the Transition of Minnesota from a Territory to a State.* Philadelphia: Harris and Partridge Co., 1941.

SS Sadie, Stanley, ed. *New Grove Dictionary of Opera.* New York: MacMillan, 1992. **SPDN** *St. Paul Daily News.* **SPD** *St. Paul Dispatch.* **SPG** *The St. Paul Globe.* **SPP** *St. Paul Pioneer.* **SPPP** *St. Paul Pioneer Press.* **SPPPD** *St. Paul Pioneer Press Dispatch.* **SH** Salisbury, Harrison E. *A Journey for our Times: A Memoir.* New York: Harper and Row, 1983. **SC** *The Sauk Centre Herald.* **SB** Schells' Brewing Company online, available: schellsbrewery.com. **SDP** Schultz, Duane P. *Over the Earth I Come: The Great Sioux Uprising of 1862,* New York: St. Martin's, 1992. **SAI** Smith, Allen H. and Ira L. Smith. *Low and Inside: A Book of Baseball Anecdotes, Oddities, and Curiosities.* Halcottsville, NY: Breakaway Books, 2000. **SJ** Spencer, John, ed. *UFO Encyclopedia.* New York: Avon

Books, 1991. **SN** *The Sporting News Pro Football Guide* 1998. St. Louis: The Sporting News, 1998. **SBG** Stuhler, Barbara and Gretchen Kreuter. *Women of Minnesota: Selected Biographical Essays.* Rev. ed. St. Paul: MHS Press, 1998. **S** Swanson, Roy. *The Minnesota Book of Days.* St. Paul: Perkins-Tracy Print Co., 1949.

TJC Thompson, Jane C. ed. *Wit and Wisdom of Hubert H. Humphrey.* Minneapolis: Partners Press, 1984. **TM** Thompson, Mark L. *Graveyard of the Lakes.* Detroit: Wayne State University Press, 2000. **TJ** Thorn, John, et. al. *Total Baseball: The Official Encyclopedia of Major League Baseball.* 6th ed. New York: Total Sports, 1999. **TW** Trenerry, Walter N. *Murder in Minnesota: A Collection of True Cases.* St. Paul: MHS, 1962. **TV** TV Guide.

USA U.S. Army Corp of Engineers, St. Paul District. *Crosscurrents: Special 125th Anniversary Edition, 1886–1991.* St. Paul: The District, 1991. **UM** University of Minnesota, Twin Cities, homepage, available: umn.edu/twincities. **UW** Upham, Warren. *Minnesota Place Names: A Geographical Encyclopedia.* 3rd ed. St. Paul: MHS Press, 2001.

VD *Virginia Daily Enterprise.*

WGC Warner, George E. and Charles M. Foote. *History of Ramsey County and the City of St. Paul.* Minneapolis: North Star Publishing Co., 1881. **WF** WeFest online, available: wefest.com. **WC** *West Central Daily Tribune* (Willmar, Minn.). **WG** *The Wheaton Gazette.* **WH** Whipple, Henry Benjamin. *Lights and Shadows of a Long Episcopate.* New York: Macmillan Co., 1899. **WB** White, Bruce M., et. al. *Minnesota Votes: Election Returns by County for Presidents, Senators, Congressmen, and Governors, 1857–1977.* St. Paul: MHS, 1977. **WJ** Williams, J. Fletcher. *History of the City of St. Paul to 1875.* St. Paul: MHS Press, 1983. **WD** *Winona Daily News.* **WR** *Winona Republican and Herald.* **WM** Woodbury, Marda Liggett. *Stopping the Presses: The Murder of Walter W. Liggett.* Minneapolis: University of Minnesota Press, 1998.

ZD Zabecki, David T., ed. *World War II in Europe: An Encyclopedia.* New York: Garland Publishing, 1998.

INDEX BY SUBJECT

Hockey player, 1900

Winter in Sleepy Eye, 1909

"June is Dairy Month" statue, 1939

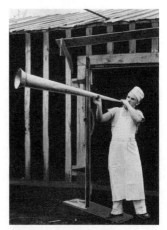

Nett Lake Lumber Camp, 1957

Fur trader Alexis Bailly

Fairmont, Jul. 5

Falls Evening News (newspaper), Dec. 2

Faribault, Alexander, trader and pioneer, Feb. 16, May 22, Jun. 22, Sep. 21, Nov. 28

Faribault, Jean Baptiste, trader and pioneer, Feb. 20, Aug. 9, Oct. 29

Faribault, Pelagie, landowner, Aug. 9

Faribault, Jan. 7, Feb. 16, May 5, Jun. 10, Jul. 13, Nov. 16, Dec. 2, 20

Faribault County, Feb. 20

Faribault gas works, lightning strikes, May 5

Farm and Labor Party, Aug. 22

Farmer-Labor Party, Apr. 15, Jul. 1, Aug. 22, Sep. 22

Farmers' Holiday, May 1

farming. *See* agriculture

Farmington, Nov. 22

F.B.I. *See* Federal Bureau of Investigation

Featherstonhaugh, George, explorer, Sep. 11

Federal Bureau of Investigation, Mar. 31

Fedo, John, mayor, Oct. 24

Fences (play), Jun. 7

Fermstad, Olive, opera singer, Nov. 25

Fernström, Carl A., settler, Oct. 21

Field, Ira S., founding father, Jun. 9

Field and Stream (magazine), Dec. 24

Field of Dreams (film), Jun. 29

Fillmore, Millard, president, Mar. 3, Jun. 8, Nov. 28

Fillmore County, Mar. 3

Finney, William K., police

chief, Jul. 16

fire engines, horse-drawn, Jul. 23

fires, Jan. 3, 20, 25, 29, Mar. 1, Apr. 14, 27, May 9, 16, 23, Jul. 4, Aug. 4, 13, 14, Nov. 3, 15, 22, Dec. 20, 24. *See also* forest fires

First Avenue, music club, Apr. 3

First Baptist Church (St. Paul), Apr. 6, Nov. 15

First Minnesota Regiment, Mar. 11, Apr. 14, 17, Jun. 22, Jul. 2

First National Bank and Trust Co. of Minneapolis, Jan. 23

First National Bank of Minneapolis, Jan. 23

First National Bank of St. Paul, Dec. 8

First Presbyterian Church (Minneapolis), Jun. 11

First Presbyterian Church (St. Paul), Aug. 9

fish and fishing, Apr. 15, May 20, Nov. 10

Fisk, James L., miner, Jul. 7

Fitzgerald, F. Scott, author, Sep. 27

Fjelde, Jacob, sculptor, Apr. 10

Flandrau, Charles E., judge, Aug. 23, Sep. 9

Flat Mouth, leader, Jul. 20

Flight Transportation Corporation (Eden Prairie), Jan. 23

Flint Furniture factory, May 9

floods, Apr. 7, 17, Jun. 3, Aug. 4

Folgero, Capt. Gerhard, Jun. 23

Folwell, William W., university president, Jan. 31, Feb. 14, 18, Dec. 29

football (sport), Jun. 11, Sep. 19, Oct. 31, Nov. 3, 12. *See also* specific players and teams

Buffalo, 1910

"Miss Minne Sota," 1907

A Minnesota State Automobile Association vehicle mired in mud, 1927

Lumberjack, near Cass Lake, 1915

Dr. Martha G. Ripley

Henry H. Sibley

Minna Sillman and cow, 1902

Children and rooster, 1900

INDEX BY YEAR

Women leaning against haystack, Burnsville, 1943

Field of oats near Morris, 1910

Winter Carnival, 1916

JOIN THE MINNESOTA HISTORICAL SOCIETY TODAY! IT'S THE BEST DEAL IN HISTORY!

The Minnesota Historical Society is the nation's premier state historical society. Founded in 1849, the Society collects, preserves, and tells the story of Minnesota's past through innovative museum exhibits, extensive collections and libraries, educational programs, historic sites, and book and magazine publishing. Membership support is vital to the Society's ability to serve its ever-broadening and increasingly diverse public with programs and services that are educational, engaging, and entertaining.

What are the benefits of membership?

Members enjoy:
- a subscription to the quarterly magazine *Minnesota History;*
- *Member News* newsletter and events calendar;
- Unlimited free admission to the Society's 25 historic sites;
- Discounts on purchases from MHS Press, and on other purchases and services in our museum stores, Café Minnesota, Library, and much more;
- Reciprocal benefits at more than 70 historical organizations and museums in over 40 states through Time Travelers;
- Satisfaction of knowing your membership helps support the Society's programs.

Membership fees/categories:
- $55 Household (2 adults and children under 18 in same household)
- $50 Senior Household (age 65+ for 2 adults)
- $45 Individual (1 adult)
- $40 Senior Individual (age 65+ for 1 adult)
- $100 Associate
- $250 Contributing
- $500 Sustaining
- $1,000 North Star Circle

Join by phone or email. To order by phone, call 651/296-0332 (TTY 651/282-6073) or e-mail membership@mnhs.org. Benefits extend one year from date of joining.

To learn more about Minnesota history, visit us on the World Wide Web at http://www.mnhs.org, where you can explore *This Day in Minnesota History* and a wealth of other resources, and you can contribute to the story of the state by proposing additional entries for *The Minnesota Book of Days.*

The Minnesota Book of Days was designed and set in type by
Percolator, Minneapolis, who used Stone Serif, designed
by Sumner Stone in 1987, for the text type. This book was
printed by Transcontinental Printing, Peterborough, Ontario.

Publicity for state centennial, 1958